PHILIP HOFF

PHILIP HOFF

HOW RED TURNED BLUE IN THE GREEN MOUNTAIN STATE

SAMUEL B. HAND, ANTHONY MARRO, AND STEPHEN C. TERRY

Castleton
A VERMONT STATE COLLEGE

PUBLISHED BY UNIVERSITY PRESS OF NEW ENGLAND
HANOVER AND LONDON

Castleton State College
In association with University Press of New England
One Court Street, Lebanon NH 03766
www.upne.com
© 2011 Castleton State College
All rights reserved
Manufactured in the United States of America
Designed by Kaelin Chappell Broaddus
Typeset in Janson Text LT Std by Kaelin Chappell Broaddus

University Press of New England is a member of the Green Press Initiative.
The paper used in this book meets their minimum requirement for recycled paper.

For permission to reproduce any of the material in this book, contact
Permissions, University Press of New England, One Court Street,
Suite 250, Lebanon NH 03766; or visit www.upne.com

Library of Congress Cataloging-in-Publication Data

Philip Hoff : how red turned blue in the Green Mountain State /
Samuel B. Hand, Anthony Marro, and Stephen C. Terry.
p. cm.
Includes index.
ISBN 978-1-61168-207-6 (cloth : alk. paper) — ISBN 978-1-61168-032-4 (ebook)
1. Hoff, Philip H. (Philip Henderson), 1924–
2. Governors—Vermont—Biography. 3. Vermont—Biography.
I. Hand, Samuel B., 1931– II. Marro, Anthony. III. Terry, Stephen C.

F55.22.H64P55 2011
974.3′043092—dc23
[B]

2011037722

5 4 3 2 1

The authors dedicate this book to Steve Terry's late wife, Sally West Johnson. Sally was a very gifted editor and writer, who unerringly could make any sentence tighter and crisper. Her work in 1991 took what had been a long newspaper series about the Hoff years and shaped it into what eventually became the structure for this book. Sally's great skill was to bring clarity and structure to any newspaper story or magazine article. Also, for many years Sally was a mentor to many aspiring journalists. To Steve, Sally was a loving companion, newspaper colleague, wife, and mother of their son, Will. She died before this book was published, but we know she would be pleased that it is done, because without her it would not have been.

Samuel B. Hand also dedicates this book to his wife, Harriet; and Anthony Marro dedicates it to his wife, Jacqueline Cleary Marro, and his daughter, Alexandria Cleary Marro.

CONTENTS

Illustrations follow page   82

PREFACE

NOTE TO READERS

This book began with a series of newspaper articles by Stephen Terry about the years that Philip H. Hoff served as governor of Vermont. The series appeared in the *Rutland Herald* late in 1968, at a time when Hoff was getting ready to step down after three two-year terms that had seen more dramatic and far-reaching change in Vermont government than any six-year period before then. In fact, not only had the legislative, judicial, and executive branches all changed in important ways, but the very character of the state—its demography, its economy, and its political and social structure—had been transformed. Terry, who was a reporter at the Vermont Press Bureau, had covered state government during much of this time.

In 1991, realizing that no book about Hoff's governorship had yet been written, Samuel B. Hand, a professor of history at the University of Vermont (UVM), and Sally Johnson, a longtime editor at the *Herald*, *Vermont Magazine*, and elsewhere (and also Terry's wife), edited down the Terry series into a monograph. It was privately published and made available free of charge to people interested in Vermont history and politics.

Hand was involved in other projects at the time, including writing *The Star That Set: The Vermont Republican Party, 1854–1974*, which was published in 2002, and his work as a coeditor of *The Vermont Encyclopedia*, published in 2003. He and Terry (who had served in the '70s as a legislative aide to U.S. Senator George D. Aiken) also compiled and coedited *The Essential Aiken*, published in 2004, which was a collection of Aiken writings and speeches, with commentary by the two. In 2005 they decided to set about doing this book, with the 1968 *Herald* series as a starting point.

It is often said that journalism is a "first rough draft of history," and that's what the original newspaper series was. Journalism often involves anonymous sources, secondhand hearsay, and descriptions of things as they are seen in the short run, not necessarily as they turn out to be. At its best, journalism is the most accurate, complete, and balanced account of things that can be done at a given moment, often under deadline pressure. Hand and Terry set out not only to expand and broaden the 1968 newspaper series, but also to transform it into serious history by adding the benefit of hindsight, perspective, and context afforded by the passage of three decades. This involved not only many additional interviews and much additional reporting, but extensive use of the oral histories in the libraries of the University of Vermont and also the Hoff papers there. The oral history interviews given by Hoff himself and by Richard Mallary were particularly helpful, as were the papers of Hoff aide Benjamin Collins, which also are at UVM. Anthony Marro, a former student of Hand's at UVM and a former colleague of Terry's at the Vermont Press Bureau, joined the project in the summer of 2009 to both edit the manuscript and to expand it with additional research and interviews. Marro's "Major Paper" for his 1968 master's degree from the Graduate School of Journalism at Columbia had focused on the changes that had taken place in Vermont during the Hoff years, and some of that material—which included interviews with Hoff, Lieutenant Governor John J. Daley, House Speaker Richard Mallary, and legislators John O'Brien, Emory Hebard, Sanborn Partridge, Reid Lefevre, Fred Westphal, George W. F. Cook, Stoyan Christowe, and others—also was incorporated into the manuscript.

Hoff made himself available for many interviews over the years, and his wife, Joan, was helpful in interviews of her own. The late William F. Kearns Jr., Hoff's commissioner of administration, granted extensive interviews—both in person and by phone—and read and gave detailed and candid critiques of each of the chapters. Although a Hoff partisan and an insider, his reviews of the chapters tended to be not only detached but often brutally frank, as he himself tended to be during all his years of public service. Philip Savory was very helpful in reconstructing the details of Hoff's first gubernatorial campaign. Marro and Terry went back into their files to retrieve their firsthand reports on his last campaign for governor. The late Paul Guare, who headed many different planning operations in the Hoff years, seems to have saved every piece of paper that ever crossed his desk; the access to this material that his widow, Claire, provided the authors was enormously helpful. The interviews and insights provided by T. Garry Buckley, a former state senator, lieutenant governor, and founder of the Vermont Independent Party; Elbert G. Moulton, Hoff's commissioner of development and later the Republican state chairman; and Charles (Chuck) Fishman, who headed Hoff's campaign for the U.S. Senate, also were valuable. Important information and insights were provided by Samuel Miller—who in 1959 became the Vermont Democratic Party's first full-time executive secretary—both in interviews and in his master's thesis (which remains in the archives at UVM) on the changing nature of the Vermont Democratic Party. Arthur Ristau, who as a reporter for the Associated Press covered Hoff and who later worked for him as a key aide, also was helpful in several important areas. Much material about Hoff's years at Williams College and in the navy was obtained from a lengthy oral history interview that Hoff gave to Williams College when he served on the board of trustees there. The report that former governor and then federal judge Ernest W. Gibson Jr. and his committee of inquiry issued on the racist incident that became known as the "Irasburg affair" was an important source of information about an embarrassing and highly unpleasant episode in Vermont history.

Stephen Wrinn's *Civil Rights in the Whitest State* (University Press of America, 1998) also was an important source of information on race relations in Vermont, as were Richard Cassidy's "Civil and Human Rights," in *Vermont State Government since 1965* (University of Vermont, 1999); John Stackelburg's 1972 UVM master's thesis, "The Irasburg Affair: A Case Study of Racial and Ideological Conflict in Vermont"; Hugh Moffett's 1969 Life magazine article "The Case That Had the Gossips Buzzing in Vermont"; and *The University of Vermont: The First Two Hundred Years* (University Press of New England, 1991), edited by Robert V. Daniels.

Other valuable sources on changes in Vermont government and politics and the state itself included *The Vermont Encyclopedia* (University Press of New England, 2003); Joe Sherman's *Fast Lane on a Dirt Road: Vermont Transformed, 1945–1990* (Countryman Press, 1991); Madeleine Kunin's *Living a Political Life* (Alfred A. Knopf, 1994); William Doyle's *The Vermont Political Tradition and Those Who Helped Make It* (Northlight Studio Press, 1984); Chris Graff's *Dateline Vermont* (Thistle Hill Press, 2006); and *Deane C. Davis: An Autobiography* (New England Press, 1991), by Davis and Nancy Price Graff. Also helpful were the Edward Janeway Papers at UVM and Alison Brady's 2007 Middlebury College student paper on the impact of bulk tanks on Vermont dairy farms, "White Gold in the Green Mountains: The Evolution of Vermont's Dairy Industry."

The authors are grateful to all who helped with this project, and in particular to David Wolk, the president of Castleton State College, for his great encouragement and support.

PHILIP HOFF

INTRODUCTION

As the only state to have supported every Republican presidential candidate since the founding of the party in 1854, Vermont in 1962 could still claim to be the star that had never set in the Republican firmament. Not only had it backed every nominee from John C. Frémont to Richard M. Nixon, but it consistently had elected large Republican majorities to its state legislature and hadn't had a Democratic governor since 1853. In 1912, along with Utah, Vermont had been one of only two states to support the incumbent Republican president, William Howard Taft, in his losing campaign against Woodrow Wilson and Theodore Roosevelt. Despite occasional political insurgencies, it had refused to support such popular national movements as Woodrow Wilson's "New Freedom," Franklin Roosevelt's "New Deal," and Harry Truman's "Fair Deal," cementing its reputation as a scrupulously conservative state.

That reputation was deserved, although there were instances when Vermonters would do things to confound it. The most spectacular deviation had been the 1946 Republican gubernatorial primary, in which Ernest Gibson Jr. had defeated the conservative incumbent governor, Mortimer Proctor, in a major upset. The Gibson name was well known and well respected in Vermont. His father had been a U.S. representative and U.S. senator, a leader of the state's Progressive movement, and a Vermont National Guard officer who had helped protect towns on the Mexican border from raids by Pancho Villa and then had served overseas in World War I. The younger Gibson himself had served briefly in the U.S. Senate, having been appointed to complete his father's term when the elder Gibson had died, and then had earned war hero status as a colonel with the Forty-third Infantry Division in the Pacific in World War II, receiving a Silver Star, a Legion of Merit, and a Purple Heart.

But the Proctors were even better known, far wealthier, had deeper roots in Vermont government, and in fact had largely dominated Vermont politics since 1876. Mortimer was the fourth member of the family to serve as governor, the first being Redfield Proctor Sr., who had commanded the Fifteenth Vermont Regiment at Gettysburg (the Fifteenth had been assigned to guard supply wagons and suffered no casualties in the fighting, or in fact in its entire nine-months' service) and then had come back to Vermont to accumulate great wealth from the marble business and to create a strong political organization built largely around Civil War veterans. He had served as governor, as Benjamin Harrison's secretary of war, and then as a U.S. senator, sometimes disparaged as the "Tombstone Senator" because of the contracts his Vermont Marble Company had obtained to provide headstones for military cemeteries. The "Proctor wing" was the more conservative wing of the Vermont Republican Party, closely allied with the state's business and banking interests. But Gibson, who along with his friend and mentor U.S. Senator George Aiken represented a more liberal faction, had attracted the support of many Democrats, organized labor, and recently demobilized World War II veterans. Mortimer Proctor himself was a war veteran, having served with the artillery in France in World War I. But that was in the past and largely forgotten, while many of the World War II veterans identified with Gibson, whose combat record had been documented by a photograph showing him being bandaged by a medic after receiving a slight but bloody head wound. The picture had been considered newsworthy and had been widely reproduced nationally, including in *Life* magazine, because there weren't many former senators suffering head wounds in war zones.

Handsome and articulate, with a crop of wavy gray hair, Gibson had campaigned aggressively against what he called "the rule of reaction." He caused Mortimer Proctor to be the first sitting Vermont governor in modern times to lose a primary contest, and then presided over a reform administration that funneled so much money into education, welfare, health care, and highway-building programs that one historian, Richard Judd, later labeled it as Vermont's own New Deal.

An earlier, less noted, instance of Vermont's straying from the conservative path had been in 1935 when Aiken, as lieutenant governor, had kept the legislature in session so that it could approve Vermont's participation in Social Security, becoming the first state in the nation to do so. But that acceptance of a major New Deal program didn't prevent Vermont from quickly reverting to form, joining with Maine as one of only two states to vote against Franklin Roosevelt in the 1936 presidential election and thus retaining its status as a lonely Republican eminence.

The man who helped cause the Republican star to set, Philip Henderson Hoff, burst upon the nation's political scene in November 1962 when he became the first Democrat to be elected Vermont's governor in 109 years. The victory by a Vermont Democrat was considered so extraordinary that it became not only national but international news. This book will examine Hoff's activist administration, his impact on the state and its government, and his role in the creation of a new Vermont liberal tradition. But it is important to underscore at the start that his victory was stunning to many because Vermont's abhorrence of Democrats had been so long and so deep-rooted that it had pre-dated even the founding of the Republican Party. In 1832, when Andrew Jackson had sought reelection as the first modern Democratic presidential candidate, Vermont had been the only state to instead cast its electoral votes for the Anti-Masonic candidate, William Wirt. While small numbers of Democrats had been elected to the state legislature, none since John Robinson of Bennington—who had served a single year as governor, from October 1853 to October 1854—had attained higher state office, and few had seriously tried. Vermont Democrats had been discredited in the second half of the nineteenth century by their party's association with slavery and rebellion (both of which most Vermonters had fiercely opposed) and had been marginalized in the first half of the twentieth century by the state's rural, Protestant, and largely Yankee population that was distrustful of the Democrats' ties to an urban, Catholic, and immigrant constituency. It further hurt Democrats that for many years Vermont's principal farm occupations, dairying and wool production, relied heavily on tariff protections, as did the marble industries. For all three of these important economic sectors, Democratic free-trade policies were anathema.

The Vermont Democratic Party had limped into the mid-twentieth century weak, ridiculed, and mistrusted, and yet in some respects seemingly content to have it that way. For many years it had functioned as little more than a nominal organization, interested mainly in the federal patronage that became available when the Democrats were in power in Washington. In 1945, a Vermont newspaper editor writing in the *American Mercury* described the state's Democratic Party as "a tightly organized, rather cliquish affair, closely managed by five or six men at the top." The author, *Rutland Herald* editor Robert Mitchell, went on to note, "The same candidates run repeatedly in election after election, and newcomers have difficulty breaking into this exclusive coterie of losers. As a result, young Democrats feel that the leadership is more interested in maintaining its control of the organization than in conducting a winning campaign against the Republicans."

Andrew Nuquist, a former chair of the Political Science Department at the University of Vermont, liked to tell his classes about the 1946 election in which Berthold Coburn, a farmer from the tiny mountain town of Chelsea, had been nominated by the Democrats to run against Gibson. Coburn had been virtually unknown outside Orange County before his nomination, and did little to make himself better known during the campaign. Shortly before the election, two of Nuquist's friends became involved in an argument over just who the Democratic candidate was, and decided to settle the matter by phoning Frank H. Duffy of Rutland, the genial, patronage-dispensing Democratic national committeeman. There was a long pause on the telephone, and then Duffy replied, "Oh, some fellow from up north." He paused again and then added, "But we don't concede his defeat."

At the same time, while it wasn't close to being a two-party state, Vermont was a state with two opposing and very different Republican factions, and there were forces for change within the Republican Party itself. For decades the party had been split into what were popularly referred to as the Proctor and anti-Proctor factions. The Proctors were closely tied to business interests, particularly the marble and granite industries, the banks, the insurance companies, and the electric power utilities. The anti-Proctor wing appealed more to small farmers (who distrusted the bankers), labor (George Aiken had been quicker than Duffy to seek and obtain the support of Vermont's few organized-labor groups), and some of the more-progressive Republicans, who in a different time and different place might have been Democrats. Even at its strongest, the "Proctor dynasty" couldn't always impose its will. It had failed often in its attempts to subdue rivals and capture political posts for family members and Vermont Marble Company presidents. And while it for the most part was staunchly conservative, one of the Proctor governors, Fletcher Proctor—the son of Redfield senior and the father of Mortimer—had been a progressive who had brought improvements to the management of state government during his 1906–1908 term and who had rejected the stern fiscal conservatism of his father by declaring that Vermont had "a higher duty than to [just] live cheaply."

After World War II the anti-Proctor wing increasingly became known as the Aiken-Gibson wing because of the leadership of Senator Aiken and Governor Gibson, who themselves often referred to the Proctor faction as the "Old Guard." Because the Aiken-Gibson wing was more liberal than the Proctors, it received significant support from Democrats, who often voted in Vermont's open primaries against the more conservative of the Republican candidates.

The political realities of the time made it more practical for politically ambitious people with progressive leanings to try to achieve their goals by ascending the Republican ladder as opponents of the Proctor wing rather than by challenging the party as Democrats. And for lawyer-politicians there was an economic reality as well. Many of them believed that identification with the Democratic Party could hurt them financially in a state where the heads of most law firms were Republicans and much legal work was generated by Republican businessmen.

During the 1950s, however, the political climate had begun to change. While the state continued to provide Republican presidential candidates with the largest percentage vote in the nation, its gubernatorial races began reflecting the emergence of a more vitalized Democratic Party. There were many reasons, but a significant one was a new Democratic leadership that set out to take advantage of Republican factionalism, a move that was given impetus—although perhaps inadvertently—by Harry Truman.

When Truman entered the White House, the Democratic national committeeman for Vermont was Frank Duffy, a Rutland real estate dealer who had been put into the job many years before with the help of Franklin Roosevelt, a longtime personal friend. Duffy became the dispenser of much federal patronage during the New Deal (his son ended up as Rutland's postmaster, which was a major patronage plum), but his special relationship with Roosevelt didn't carry over to Truman. In November 1949, Truman bypassed Duffy and the state party by appointing Gibson, who was still Vermont's sitting Republican governor, as the state's only federal judge, a post that carried considerable court patronage with it. Truman had become friendly with Gibson when they served together in the U.S. Senate, and the two had often met for drinks after the daily sessions ended. Drew Pearson, the newspaper columnist, said that the two men had "a bourbon affinity" for each other. After Truman became president and after Gibson, with the help of Aiken, had arranged a transfer for himself from the South Pacific to a post with Army Intelligence at the Pentagon, Gibson had been summoned often to the White House for personal and somewhat back-channel briefings for Truman. Whether the appointment was a case of friendship crossing party lines or of Truman wanting to send a message that he expected Vermont Democrats to earn their patronage, the decision sent shock waves through the organization, which had come to see federal patronage as its raison d'être.

Duffy died in 1950, and in 1952 the Democrats nominated as their candidate for governor Robert W. Larrow, thirty-six years old, a bright and articulate Burlington attorney who had considerable energy and drive despite his Sydney Greenstreet–size girth. The convention was held at Montpelier's Pavilion Hotel, but Bill Kearns, who at the time was reporting on state government for the *Burlington Free Press* and the *Rutland Herald,* said that he "didn't even cover it because there was so little interest in the damned thing."

"The Democrats used to drag a few people to Montpelier every other year, call it a 'convention,' and twist somebody's arm to put their name on the ballot," Kearns said. "But when [Larrow] got it, he warned them that he was going to campaign; he said he was going to go out and find out what the hell was going on in the state. And he did it. He had no organization and no help from the party. But he got the party moving all by himself." Larrow lost to incumbent governor Lee Emerson, a colorless country lawyer who had been handpicked by the Proctors to try to undo the Gibson reforms, as almost everyone in the state had expected he would.* But Larrow received nearly 40 percent of the popular vote, which was more than any Democratic candidate had received in a century. The 60,051 votes he got were nearly 40,000 more than the Democratic candidate had gotten in 1950, and it caused party leaders to realize that maybe they in fact could win elections.

Truman's appointment of Gibson to the bench had two important consequences. The first was that it helped transform Democrats from an organization focused mainly on patronage into one interested in winning elections. The second was that because no one took Gibson's place as a leader of the liberal faction (Aiken was still influential but in faraway Washington), the Republican leadership in the '50s began moving toward a more conservative and narrower base, making progressive Republicans more willing to support like-minded Democrats.

It also was significant that Vermont's economic and demographic base was changing. Its rural landscape was shrinking with the decline of the dairy industry, and by 1962 the development of the interstate highway system was helping to bring skiers, tourists, second-home buyers,

---

*Although low-keyed and colorless in most respects, Emerson was quick to embrace some of the harsh anti-Communist rhetoric of the time, supporting a bill that would have denied a place on the ballot for any party "directly or indirectly associated with Communist, Fascist, or any other un-American principle," and pressuring the University of Vermont trustees into firing a teacher who had refused to disclose former Communist associates from his time on the Brooklyn College faculty. His campaign to force his GOP primary rival, Peter Bove, from his job with the State Liquor Commission also gave him a reputation for vindictiveness that he never managed to shake.

new industries (like IBM), and new residents into the state. The transformation was rapid and fairly dramatic, causing traditional political folkways to erode. And Democratic strategists had begun planning ways of taking advantage of these twentieth-century changes with a nineteenth-century ploy that had been used with stunning but short-lived success in 1890. It was known as a "still hunt."

A "still hunt," politically speaking, had nothing to do with standing still and everything to do with silence and stalking. Dictionaries define "still hunt" as a pursuit for game in a steady manner by stalking or by ambush; it involves hunting in so slow, deliberate, and quiet a fashion that the prey doesn't get warning that the hunter is closing in for a kill. During the late nineteenth century, when most Vermont males were hunters who understood what a still hunt entailed, Vermont Democrats adapted the still hunt to political campaigning. It was used only in nonpresidential years, when the Republican voter turnout usually declined significantly while the Democratic turnout remained pretty much the same. The strategy was for Democrats to target areas of opportunity caused by a combination of Republican factionalism and off-year lethargy. In 1890, Democrats had quietly set about contesting an unusually large number of House seats. It was done without fanfare because the object was to lull Republicans and keep them away from the polls. The result of what became known as the "Great Democratic Still Hunt of 1890" was that the Democrats won sixty-two House seats, which by Vermont standards was a spectacular triumph. But it also was one not easily repeated. Seemingly exhausted from the 1890 still hunt, Democrats promptly reverted to a token opposition, more intent on patronage than governing. The Republicans won back twenty-two of those seats in 1892, and it would be 1964 before the Democrats would again claim as many seats in the House.

By 1958, however, the great fluctuation in Republican voter turnout between presidential-year and off-year elections had become apparent even to Democratic leaders who may not have been able to define a still hunt or remember that early strategy, but who knew that something like it could bring in even bigger game. In this case, the favorable conditions included not only the expected drop in Republican voters in an off-year election but also an unpopular Republican congressional candidate, Harold Arthur, and a national recession whose impact negated a countrywide campaign for Republicans by Vice President Richard M. Nixon. Arthur, who had been Gibson's lieutenant governor while sharing almost none of his progressive ideals, had served briefly as governor after Gibson went on the bench. But instead of then running for election to a full term as governor, he instead ran for Congress. He lost to Winston Prouty in the congressional primary of 1950, and then lost to Consuelo Northrup Bailey in the primary for lieutenant governor in 1952. A former grand master of the Vermont Grange (he sometimes was derided as "The Lone Granger" and sometimes depicted in the Vermont press as a bit of a buffoon), Arthur had won the congressional nomination against five other Republican candidates with just 30 percent of the vote, and even the devoutly Republican *Burlington Free Press* allowed that "on the basis of ability" almost any of his primary opponents "would have been a better choice." The voters agreed.

Nixon declared the results of those national elections a disaster, saying "the defeat was massive and November 4, 1958, was one of the most depressing election nights I have ever known." The Vermont results were particularly humiliating, because this most Republican of all states not only had elected a Democratic congressman (William Meyer, a forester from the tiny town of Rupert, so little known that when he showed up in Burlington for a Democratic celebration dinner, Larrow said, nobody recognized him) but barely managed to elect a Republican governor, by just 719 votes. The governor's race had pitted Republican Robert Stafford of Rutland against Democrat Bernard Leddy of Burlington, who was said by friends to have considered his defeat a narrow escape, since he would have had to abandon a lucrative law practice for a $12,000-a-year governorship that he didn't particularly want. Leddy had been selected through an authentic draft and had campaigned for only a month. At first he hesitated to ask for a recount—friends insisted it was for fear he would win—but he finally asked for one because he felt he owed it to the party.

While the congressional victory owed a great deal to the unpopularity of Arthur, unpopular Republican candidates had never been denied election in the past. And that, along with the narrowness of the Stafford win, showed—as had the Larrow campaign six years before—that the Republican star was beginning to set, and that Democrats had opportunities for gains in off-year elections. Crucial to Meyer's victory was a decline of more than 22,000 votes in the Republican turnout from the presidential election year of 1956, while the Democratic off-year vote declined by fewer than 4,000.

In the 1960 presidential election year the Republicans enjoyed their customary sweep. Nixon carried the state by almost 30,000 votes, while Stafford—who had won by just 719 votes two years before—captured the congressional seat from Meyer by over 23,000 votes. F. Ray Keyser Jr., a

Proctor-wing Republican who had won the gubernatorial primary with less than a 30 percent plurality, was eased into office by a 21,000-vote victory over Democrat Russell Niquette. Undaunted by John F. Kennedy's presidential victory, Vermont Republicans celebrated a return to "normalcy."

Some Democrats, among them L. Samuel Miller, saw things differently. Miller had become the party's first full-time executive secretary in 1959 and was completing a political science master's thesis at the University of Vermont that was depicting the coming 1962 election as a Democratic opportunity. Born in New York City but raised in Weston, where his mother was a well-known liberal Catholic political activist, Miller realized that the realities of the state's legislative apportionment made capturing control of the legislature beyond reach. But he believed that with the right candidate and the right campaign, the governor's office was attainable. Republican voter turnout in the off-year election of 1958 had been 30,000 below what it was in 1960. An increase in Democratic voters and a similar drop-off in Republican voters in 1962 could make victory possible, particularly if the candidate could attract liberal and moderate Republicans.

Democratic chances were further enhanced during 1961 when Keyser lost control of the legislature during a long and contentious seven-month session. He found himself politically throttled by the Senate president pro tem, Asa Bloomer of Rutland, a staunch anti-Proctor Republican, while the House Speaker, although an ally, found himself unable to exercise the authority needed to push through Keyser's programs. With the House Speaker ineffective, members without formal leadership credentials began filling the leadership vacuum. These included a bipartisan coalition of eleven House members (ten of them freshmen) that had become known as the "Young Turks." Younger, more activist, more willing to accept change than most of their House colleagues, they would later surge to the top of their respective party ranks and remain prominent in Vermont politics for decades. Among them was Philip Hoff.

In 1962, Hoff was selected by party leaders to be the Democratic candidate for governor. This was a sharp break with tradition, because Hoff was neither a native Vermonter nor a Catholic. Nor did he have great political experience. He was a political fledgling and an Episcopalian, a Massachusetts native who had arrived in Vermont in 1951 after being recruited from Cornell Law School to join the Burlington law firm of Black & Wilson. He was, however, handsome and energetic, had the potential to be a charismatic candidate in the Kennedy mold, and had a vivacious wife who would prove to be an effective campaigner. After serving as chairman of the Burlington Planning Commission and running a close but unsuccessful race for the City Council from a heavily Republican ward, he had been tapped in 1960 to run for Burlington's lone seat in Vermont's 246-seat legislature, which he won.

His one term in the House included two legislative sessions, during which he earned a reputation as an articulate spokesman for liberal causes and as someone who could work with Republicans. These were crucial factors, but also contributing to his nomination was the belief—particularly on the part of Democratic state party chairman John (Jack) Spencer—that it had been Leddy's Catholicism that had cost him the election in 1958, while William Meyer, who was not a Catholic, had slipped through to victory. Spencer believed that not being a Catholic would be a big asset to Hoff, although not all senior Democrats, most of them Catholics, agreed.

The principal opposition to Hoff's selection came from Russell Niquette of Winooski, who had been the party's 1960 gubernatorial candidate. Known as "the Silver Fox" because of his full head of silver gray hair, Niquette felt his strong showing merited renomination. He had outpolled Kennedy, and while he had lost to Keyser by 20,000 votes, he nonetheless had received more votes than any previous Democrat. Spencer, Larrow, and Leddy all disagreed, fearing Niquette's negatives outweighed his positives. Not only was he Catholic, but he had been educated in Canada and still spoke with a strong French Canadian accent, the combination of which they feared could prove a drawback in the many areas where the voters were mostly Yankee and Protestant. In addition, victory would depend of attracting liberal Republican votes. Niquette in the past had worked to help the Proctors get the votes of Winooski mill workers in Republican primaries, which was not likely to gain him the support of liberal Republicans. After a meeting with Larrow and Leddy in which they threatened to mount a primary against him, Niquette agreed to withdraw.

Democratic primaries were virtually unprecedented. The only previous instance had been an unsuccessful attempt to deny Meyer—whom traditional Democrats considered too much of a maverick—renomination in 1960. But with Meyer intending to take on Aiken in 1962, Democratic leaders decided that another one was needed. Not many people thought Meyer posed a threat to Aiken, but Meyer was a spirited campaigner who might provoke the generally laconic Aiken into a more rigorous campaign that could bring out more Republican voters than the Democrats wanted. Following the spirit of their "still hunt" predecessors, the Democratic leaders organized a primary campaign against Meyer. Their candidate was W. Robert Johnson, a furniture dealer whom they touted as a true Democrat (unlike the maverick Meyer), and who admitted to not having had the time to study the issues. A self-described political neophyte, he was more likely to attack Keyser than Meyer in his public appearances, Keyser being the real target of the Democrats that year. Party literature carrying Leddy and Larrow endorsements attacked Meyer for advocating an end to the draft and the recognition of Red China—two proposals that were radical at the time but that the distinctly nonradical Richard Nixon would implement just a decade later when he was president. Johnson beat Meyer by 1,000 votes and then, just as party leaders intended, disappeared back into his furniture business and was hardly heard from again.

Philip Hoff was the only Democrat to emerge victorious from the 1962 general election, but it was a stunning victory in every respect. In addition to running as a Democrat, Hoff had been listed on the Independent Democrat line and had received the endorsement of the Vermont Independent Party. That latter party had been organized by anti-Keyser Republicans to serve as a sort of political halfway house that would allow Republicans to support Hoff without actually having to vote Democratic. Keyser drew more votes as a Republican than Hoff did as a Democrat, but the independent votes gave Hoff a 1,300-vote edge, making him Vermont's first Democratic governor since 1853, when John Robinson, while having failed to secure a popular majority, had been elected by the legislature over the Whig and Free Soil candidates. But even the independent votes would not have been enough to give Hoff the win had there not been 40,000 fewer votes in 1962 than in 1960. The drop-off rate of approximately three Republicans for every Democrat seemed to confirm the wisdom of allowing Aiken to run virtually unchallenged.

Not all Democrat strategists in 1962 may have been familiar with still hunts, and the still hunt in any case had morphed into the "Miller Rule." Sam Miller—who in fact was himself a deer hunter and knew what a still hunt was—had correctly calculated that the growing numbers of Democratic voters combined with a low Republican turnout in a nonpresidential year could result in Democratic triumph if the Democratic candidate could appeal to moderate Republicans. He had become the principal advocate of that strategy. The architects of the Great Democratic Still Hunt of 1890 would have gloried in the success of the Miller Rule in 1962.

Hoff supporters were euphoric, as was Hoff himself, showing up late that night at a victory rally in the Democratic stronghold of Winooski, his hair rumpled, his face beaming, and shouting repeatedly to the excited crowd surrounding him, "A hundred years of bondage broken!"

His election in fact did end a century of Republican domination of Vermont politics, which is what made it national news. The more important reality wasn't just that the Republican star was setting but that a major transformation was beginning. The 1962 election was both a narrow and an individual victory, but in the years to come Hoff would twice win reelection by overwhelming margins, and Vermonters also would elect Democrats as lieutenant governor, attorney general, treasurer, auditor of accounts, and secretary of state, as well as voting for Democratic president Lyndon Johnson is his campaign against Barry Goldwater. Hoff would oversee changes more sweeping and dramatic than in any comparable period in the state's history before or since—changes that would stay in place long after he had left the governor's office. He would become a more activist governor than any of his sixty-nine predecessors and have more impact on the state than even the most progressive of the modern-day Republicans, Aiken and Gibson. He would become a catalyst for change that would move Vermont's government into a much less complacent and far more aggressive role in meeting the needs of its citizens. He would transform a state in which change had come only slowly and grudgingly into one that developed a national reputation for cutting-edge initiatives in the areas of social policy and the environment. And he would become the central figure in the creation of a new and lasting Vermont liberal tradition.

CHAPTER 1

POLITICAL BAPTISM

Philip Hoff arrived in Vermont in June 1951 with his pregnant wife, Joan, his young daughter, Susan, and all their family possessions squeezed into a two-door Dodge coupe, including a washing machine that was lashed into the trunk. In terms of mileage, it wasn't a long trip. His hometown of Turners Falls, Massachusetts, was barely twenty miles south of Brattleboro. But he had come by a circuitous route that had taken him first to Williams College, then into the navy's submarine service in the Pacific during World War II, and then through Cornell Law School. He had driven east from Ithaca to Burlington, where he had been offered a job with the law firm of Black & Wilson. Boone Wilson, himself a graduate of Cornell, had contacted a faculty member about his need for another associate and then had phoned Hoff just as he was about to be interviewed for another job. It was a phone call that, in ways neither of them could have imagined at the time, would have an enormous and long-lasting impact on the state.

Vermont was still a bastion of Republicanism in 1951, and politically ambitious newcomers almost invariably joined the Republican Party. Boone Wilson, Hoff's new boss, himself was a Republican and was active in local Republican politics. Hoff's decision to identify as a Democrat was a rare exception, and it was a break with his family history as well. Many years later, when asked why he had done so, he facetiously suggested that it probably was because his parents, Olaf Hoff Jr. and Agnes Henderson Hoff, had been such rock-ribbed Republicans. His move to the Democrats may in fact have been at least partly a gesture of independence. But he also said, "I came out of World War II convinced that our country was going to go through tumultuous change . . . [and] I wasn't sure the Republican Party could deal with these changes. I wasn't sure the Democrats could either, but I thought they were the best bet."

Philip Henderson Hoff was born in Greenfield, Massachusetts, on June 29, 1924. The family home was in nearby Turners Falls, but Greenfield was where the regional hospital was located. He was the third of four

children, the younger brother of Dagny and Olaf and the older brother
of Foster. He grew up in a politically activist family. Both parents served
on the Turners Falls Republican town committee. His father also was a
member of the Republican state committee and served three terms in
the Massachusetts General Court, the state's legislature. Both parents
had graduated from Cornell University in 1913, and after his father's service as a lieutenant in World War I, they had moved to Turners Falls,
where Olaf Hoff Sr., a Norwegian-born, highly successful engineer, had
helped provide the financial backing that Olaf Hoff Jr. needed to set up a
castings factory. In addition to running a household with three sons and
a daughter, Agnes was a commentator on local radio and a newspaper
stringer for the *Greenfield Recorder Gazette*.

Turners Falls was a small blue-collar town (Hoff later would com-
pare it to Winooski in size, character, and ethnic mix), with streets of
nineteenth-century brick row houses that had been built to house the
cotton, cutlery, and paper mill workers. Located at a steep waterfall on
the Connecticut River, it had been named for Captain William Turner,
who in 1676, during King Philip's War, had led about 150 men and boys
in an attack on a sleeping Indian encampment there, killing not only the
warriors but also many women and children. Turner's men had butch-
ered the Native Americans—maybe as many as two hundred of them—
while most were still in their wigwams, the attackers themselves initially
suffering only one casualty. But the attack had alerted other nearby Indians, who came rushing to the site and managed to kill at least forty of the
attackers, including Turner himself, during what became a wildly disor-
ganized and panicky retreat.

All four of the Hoff children attended Turners Falls public schools,
where—despite the "Turners Falls Massacre," as it was called in the history books—the high school sports teams were known as the Indians.
During the Great Depression of the '30s, Olaf was forced to close his
factory and become an insurance salesman. His son said that while selling insurance provided a decent living and enabled the family to keep its
home in a fashionable part of town, his father "never really liked the job."
Yet Phil Hoff himself had fond memories of those years and said that the
high value the town placed on education was seen in the fact that it had
voted to build a new high school in the depths of the Depression and despite high unemployment.

Nearly all his teachers had been Catholic—Turners Falls was about
85 percent Catholic, mainly Irish, French Canadian, and Polish—and
Hoff found himself impressed by their openness as well as their teach-

ing skills. "They may have worried whether [as a Congregationalist] I was going to heaven or hell, but they always accepted me the way I was," he said. It was an experience that caused him to develop "lots of tolerance" on his own part, he said. And it was while he was still in school that he also developed deep feelings about the importance of treating all people as equals. One incident he remembered vividly was the taunting by his classmates of a disadvantaged young girl. The school was in the better part of the village, up on a hill, and students from the working-class parts of town had to pass through Hoff's neighborhood to get there. The young girl was from "a dirt poor family," and "her clothes were close to rags," he recalled. And some students had taken to gathering at the top of the hill near the school and taunting her as she walked past them to school every day, making fun of her poverty and her clothes. Finally, Hoff told them to stop it "or they'd have to deal with me." The young Hoff was no one the others wanted to deal with, since he was tall, muscular, and ruggedly athletic. The taunting stopped, and the girl no longer had to run the gauntlet of insults and jeers to get to school.

An able student, Hoff also was involved in a wide range of high school activities. He had a lead part in the senior play. He took part in speaking competitions. He played tennis and was a good enough football player that he was named an "honorable mention" as an end on the Massachusetts All-State football team his senior year. He had always planned on going to college, as his parents had intended, and his football coach thought he could get a football scholarship at either Williams or Amherst. At the time, Williams College told incoming students that fees for tuition, room and board, and other things would amount to between $525 and $575 a year. "My father's economic situation was not strong, so it became imperative that I have some help wherever I went," Hoff said in a 1998 interview for an oral history project at Williams. "I was a good student and I played football. I was by no means a level one athlete, but I played a decent game. And at that time both Amherst and Williams had what was known as general scholarships. They would pay your tuition. They would guarantee you a job waiting on tables, so that took care of your board. The room they gave you a break on. . . . Well, I had the same opportunity at both Amherst and Williams. I went down to Amherst to watch football practice. At that time the football coach was a fellow by the name of Lloyd Jordan, who ultimately went on to Harvard as their head coach. They called him 'sir' on the football field. Well, I had no compunction about calling a professor 'sir,' but not my coach, so I came to Williams." He enrolled in the fall of 1942.

During his freshman year, he played football and also waited on tables in the dining hall and delivered newspapers to supplement his scholarship. But it was impossible to escape the reality of World War II, and he was eager to enlist. After completing his second semester, he enrolled in the navy's V5 program at Williams. The formal name of the program was the Naval Flight Preparatory School, which kept enlistees in college for another three months of classroom work in navigation, physics, math, communications, and aircraft engines before sending them off to pilot training and, hopefully, a commission as an officer in the Naval Air Corps. Hoff's father questioned the choice, since he doubted his son's aptitude for flying. "Hell, Phil," he told him, "you don't even know how to drive a car."

Hoff nonetheless entered flight school in 1943 and learned to fly a Piper Cub. He then moved on to Steermans, the open-cockpit biplanes later used extensively by crop dusters and stunt fliers, which were the navy's primary training planes during World War II. His takeoffs were fine, but his landings were disasters waiting to happen. A problem with depth perception caused him to constantly misjudge the runways on landing. When it became clear that he wouldn't be able to land larger planes, he washed out of the program. "After I'd done some damage to three airplanes, they decided to dispense with my services," he said. He then volunteered for the submarine service as an enlisted man (though he had vision problems, he wasn't claustrophobic) and was sent first to boot camp at the Great Lakes Naval Training Station and then for submarine training at New London, Connecticut. Eventually, he was assigned to the USS *Sea Dog* (SS-401). The *Sea Dog* was a Balao-class submarine, at just over 311 feet long the largest class of submarines in the navy at the time. Powered by diesel engines, it had a surface speed of just over 20 knots and could stay submerged for forty-eight hours.

Hoff joined the *Sea Dog* late in the war. He was transported to the Philippines on an escort carrier, and since he was in effect a passenger, not a crew member, and had no work to do on the trip, he found himself going up to the deck most days, putting his back against one of the tires of an airplane and reading in the shade of the plane's wing. "I read *War and Peace* and *Crime and Punishment* on that trip," he recalled.

Hoff served as a quartermaster on the *Sea Dog*. In the army, a quartermaster is in charge of providing socks, blankets, underwear, and everything else needed to equip troops. In the navy, however, the job is completely different and involves navigation. The term dates back to the days of wooden sailing ships, when the ship's wheel was on the quarter-deck, and the master of the quarterdeck (or quartermaster) steered the ship. Even in the modern-day nuclear navy, the quartermaster's insignia remains an old-fashioned wooden ship's wheel. In the World War II navy, the quartermaster was an enlisted man who reported to the officer of the deck, providing him with all the nautical charts and information about currents, depths, and other things needed to plot a safe and swift course. He was stationed in the conning tower and in many ways was responsible for the safety of the entire crew, since any miscalculation about depth, currents, speed, or location could cause the submarine to run aground.

The *Sea Dog* was headed from Pearl Harbor toward Japan on another war patrol when the war ended, and Hoff then was sent on a mission that, as he later described it, could have been a scene in a Marx Brothers movie. There was a rumor that a Japanese submarine off Manila was looking to surrender, and a detachment from the *Sea Dog* was switched to a submarine chaser, a small and very fast boat armed with depth charges and machine guns, to seek it out. "They strapped revolvers on us than none of us knew how to use," Hoff said. "I couldn't have hit a barn door with it. None of us spoke or understood a word of Japanese." Once out of the submarine and onto the fast-moving and wildly bouncing submarine chaser, the officer in charge became violently seasick and spent most of the mission throwing up. "So we went out to get the surrender of a Japanese submarine with revolvers we didn't know how to use, with no one knowing a word of Japanese, and with a commander so sick he didn't know his own name."

They never found the Japanese submarine, and the *Sea Dog* returned to Hawaii, where it stayed several months before returning to the states, arriving at San Francisco on the morning of February 2, 1946. Hoff was in the conning tower on a 3 A.M. to 7 A.M. watch when the sub motored under the Golden Gate Bridge. All three of the Hoff boys were in the service, with Philip's older brother Olaf a navigator on a B-24 bomber and his younger brother Foster a crewman on an aircraft carrier. As the *Sea Dog* entered San Francisco Bay, Hoff spotted Foster's carrier alongside them. He sent a message for his brother to meet him the next day, a Sunday, in San Francisco. He didn't tell him *where* to meet him, but they eventually found each other at a USO club. They had a spirited reunion, spending much of the next few weeks playing golf and "eating at wonderful restaurants and hearing wonderful music," which they could do because food and entertainment were still being provided cheaply to returning veterans. The next month, Hoff was discharged as a seaman first class, with two battle stars. He shaved his navy mustache, which had surprised the sandy-haired Hoff by growing in red, and went back to school.

When Hoff had first entered Williams in 1942, it was with thoughts of becoming a doctor. By the time he returned in 1946 he had abandoned those plans, having learned that "chemistry wasn't my cup of tea." He instead majored in English literature. Having returned from the navy weighing just 145 pounds, he also abandoned football, realizing that 145 pounds was too light to play college football, even at Williams. T. Garry Buckley, subsequently a Vermont lieutenant governor and a key player in Hoff's 1962 gubernatorial election, was a student at Brown at the time who partied frequently at Williams, which was just down the road from his Bennington home. Buckley belonged to Delta Kappa Epsilon fraternity and so stopped often at the DKE house at Williams where Hoff was a member. He described Hoff during those years as an academic grind. "He was quiet and studious," he said. "He wasn't a high-flying boozer back then." Hoff in fact was a serious student, graduating cum laude.

The instructor who had the biggest impact on Hoff was a professor of English named Fred Stocking. "I'll remember the first class he taught as long as I live," Hoff said more than fifty years later, "because he stood up in front of that class (which was a pretty big lecture class) and said, 'It is my view that while you are here at Williams you ought to question every belief that you have had before you came here, including your belief in God.' Now for a country boy from Turners Falls, that was a pretty heady statement. But you know, I think that did as much for me as anything I can remember because from that point on I really did review my beliefs in everything, including my father's belief in the Republican Party. And I've been that way ever since."

In addition to studying, he renewed his acquaintance with Joan Brower, an attractive young woman he had met a few years before. Hoff had been undergoing submarine training in New London when a friend had arranged a blind date between him and Brower, who was a student at the Connecticut College for Women, also in New London, which often was referred to as "Co Co for Wo." Hoff recalled that they had had dinner at a restaurant on the beach. It was a nice night, and they decided to go for a walk along the shore, where they found a big barrel stave. Hoff told her that he would bend over and let her hit him with it if she would then bend over and let him hit her. She agreed. Hoff bent over, and she whaled him with the stave and then immediately threw it far out into the water before he could use it on her. On the way back, they passed a small road construction site blocked off by sawhorses and a red lantern. They decided to steal the lantern, which Joan hid under her coat when she returned to her dormitory room. They had "quite a few" more dates before Phil went overseas, Joan recalled, but didn't correspond with any regularity while Phil was gone. That may not have been because of lack of interest. Hoff often said later that while he was comfortable speaking in public, he had no ability to write anything at all, "not even a letter."

In the fall of 1946, Joan learned that Phil was back at Williams. A Connecticut College friend mentioned that she had been there on a weekend and had seen Phil, who had asked about her. After learning this, Joan boxed up the red lantern and sent it to him with the message "It's your turn to polish it for a while." Shortly thereafter he contacted her again, and their romance blossomed. They were engaged in the fall of 1947 and got married in August 1948, on what they both remembered as being the hottest day of the year.

By this point, Hoff had decided to go to law school, but without any intention of practicing law. He still had GI Bill benefits due him and "wasn't ready for work." He figured that law school would serve well as a general background for whatever he eventually decided to do. He applied both to Harvard and Cornell, Harvard because it was Harvard and Cornell because it was where both his parents had graduated from. He sent off his application to Harvard on a Sunday and received a letter of acceptance the following Thursday. But Ithaca had a small-town flavor that appealed to a native of Turners Falls. And there was a practical reason as well to choose Cornell. Joan's mother had a cousin who was married to the librarian at Cornell Law School, and she not only arranged for a low-cost apartment for the young couple but helped arrange for Joan to get a job as a file clerk in the office of the dean of the College of Arts and Sciences. "With an apartment and a job, Cornell was the definite choice," Hoff said. "With the GI Bill and [her] salary, we actually saved money." On Christmas Day 1949, Joan gave birth to their first daughter, Susan. That summer Phil worked for a law firm in New York City while they stayed with Joan's parents in West Englewood, New Jersey.

When Hoff returned to Cornell for his final year, infant Susan proved an extra dividend. With a child, the Hoffs were eligible for an even cheaper apartment in "Vetsburg," a married students' housing complex for veterans with children. With one child, they were assigned a two-room unit, which Joan remembered as a great place to live despite

its barrackslike austerity. The families of many of Phil's law school classmates were there, and it provided the opportunity for social gatherings
on weekends without having to line up a half-dozen babysitters. "Since
we lived in close proximity, we assigned someone to make the rounds,
checking the children every fifteen or twenty minutes," Joan recalled. "I
can't believe we did this—fortunately it worked."

By the time he came out of the war, Hoff had become a Democrat.
His parents seemed more bemused than angry about the switch. Shortly
after he graduated from Williams, Hoff overheard his father saying to a
friend, "Phil says he's a Democrat, but he'll get over that." But he didn't,
and indeed would become increasingly liberal as the years went by. In
fact, his faith in the Republican values of his parents had started eroding even while he was still in high school. During the summer between
his junior and senior years, he had worked at a Massachusetts fish hatch-
ery close to where a "New Deal" Works Progress Administration (WPA)
work gang was located. "I had always been led to believe that anybody
who really wanted to work worked and that someone who was on WPA .
. . was pretty suspect." As he got to know the WPA workers and watched
many of them leave the WPA as quickly as they could find other jobs, his
respect both for them and for the social and economic benefits of the
WPA grew. He later credited that as being the "single biggest thing in
leading me to reevaluate the [Republican] position" that his parents had
taken on a range of social and political issues. In the 1948 election, Joan
voted for Thomas Dewey, while Phil voted for Truman. Over time they
came to see things more alike, Joan converting to his Democratic Party
and Phil to her Episcopal Church.

By the time Hoff graduated from law school in June 1951, Joan was
again pregnant, which helped him decide that practicing law was the
most logical and economically feasible way to support a growing family.
His summer work for a Wall Street firm had softened his resistance to
practicing law, while at the same time dampening any ardor for living or
working in a big city. A lot of twenty-seven-year-old lawyers would have
been excited about the chance to practice law in New York, but Hoff had
mixed feelings. "I was a small-town boy. I wanted to be more a part of
the community, and I couldn't do that in New York," he said. He could
have been involved in many of the suburban communities that surrounded Manhattan, but his travel back and forth between the city and West
Englewood also had convinced him that he didn't want to deal with a
regular commute. He nonetheless was being recruited by firms both in

New York and Cleveland, and—playing the hand he was dealt—was interviewing in Cleveland when Boone Wilson tracked him down. There were two young associates in Wilson's Burlington firm. One of them (Alfred Coffrin, another Cornell Law School graduate who eventually would become a federal judge) already had been recalled into the navy for the Korean War, and Wilson was fearful that the second (Steve Richardson, yet another Cornell Law School graduate) would be as recalled into the navy well. "Boone was really desperate," Hoff recalled. In this case, Hoff's lack of depth perception and washing out of flight school worked to his advantage. Roughly 198,000 Navy Reserve members—including many pilots—were recalled during the Korean War, but there wasn't a pressing need for submarine quartermasters.

Hoff drove to Burlington and immediately decided it would be a good place to live and raise children. "After one look, I decided this was the place I really wanted to be," he said. Joan Hoff maintained that as a dutiful wife she didn't try to influence his decision, except that "every time he mentioned Cleveland I frowned, and every time he mentioned Burlington I smiled." Vermont required a six-month clerkship to qualify for the bar examination, and until he was eligible to be certified as a Vermont attorney his clerk's salary was just $25 a week, compared with the $3,600 annually he had been told he could make in New York.

There was little pay but much work. "I came in and had very little time to study for the bar exam, because Steve Richardson was called back for Korea," Hoff recalled. "Several significant cases came up and like it or not I was drawn into the fray. I remember that period very well, because for a period of a year or more, until Al Coffrin came back . . . we literally worked seven days and six nights a week. And in terms of law, it was the greatest experience I ever had, because I had to produce."

Hoff's first solo effort was to try an automobile injury suit, representing an insurance company in federal court. Since the woman's injuries weren't that severe, it seemed to be a case that he could handle himself. The judge was former Republican governor Ernest Gibson Jr., who in his short time on the bench already had developed a reputation as a plaintiff's lawyer. But Hoff felt that he nonetheless had a good chance to win, not only because he thought he had a strong case but because the attorney for the injured woman was Harold Arthur, who had been Gibson's lieutenant governor and successor, and who was a man Gibson was known to have little regard for. But no sooner had the trial started than Hoff found Gibson "all over" him, questioning him sharply and often.

The woman was awarded $5,000. That was hardly an astronomical sum even back then, but Hoff felt he had presented a case that he should have won. The next morning, while he was licking his wounds, he was summoned to Gibson's office, where the judge apologized for the way he had treated him. "I had no choice," Hoff said Gibson told him. He told Hoff that he felt the woman deserved some sort of compensation, and "If I hadn't come down hard on you that damned fool [Arthur] would never have gotten a verdict."

Hoff initially had stayed clear of partisan politics, but after Boone Wilson successfully campaigned for a Burlington alderman's seat as a Republican, he felt free to work for the Democrats. After paying his dues by working checklists, driving voters to the polls, and other kinds of political scut work, he was given an appointment to the Burlington Zoning Board. By then the Hoff family had grown to four daughters—in addition to Susan there were Dagny, Andrea, and Gretchen—and the family had moved to a comfortable home at 214 Prospect Parkway, a new development on the southern fringe of Burlington in a heavily Republican ward.

Prospect Parkway in the '50s was like thousands of other suburban and suburban-like communities springing up all over the country, the streets filled with young children, the backyards filled with smoke from barbecue grills, and the families headed by young men looking to move ahead quickly in their careers, eager to make up for the years spent in uniform. Most of the women stayed at home, managing the house and caring for children. One of Joan Hoff's first acts of political activism, in fact, was while pushing a baby carriage. There were few married women in the workplace in the '50s, and most of the women who did work outside the home were relegated to jobs as secretaries, bookkeepers, teachers, nurses, and salesclerks. This was a time when the University of Vermont (UVM, as it was called, which was located in Burlington) was still actively discouraging women from courses in business and medicine and instead trying to steer them into education, dental hygiene, and home economics. This nationwide division of labor was very much true of the Prospect Parkway neighborhood, where most of the men went off to outside work every day while most of the women spent their days cooking meals, managing the house, and taking the major responsibility for raising the children. The Hoffs played golf and tennis and skied and became increasingly involved in the community, Phil Hoff joining the Rotary Club and the Elks Club as well as a local country club and the Chamber of Commerce. In short, it was a comfortable life and an interesting one, with the promise of even better things to come.

Burlington was about as cosmopolitan a place as existed in Vermont at the time, not just because of its 35,000-plus population but also because the three colleges in the area (UVM, Trinity, and Saint Michael's) provided many cultural offerings and created a critical mass of educated and activist people involved in the social and political life of the city. But Hoff's legal work also took him into different parts of the state, including rural areas where he came to develop an appreciation for the frankness and honesty of the people he found there.

One story he liked to tell was about a trip he made into the Northeast Kingdom looking for a witness who was important to a case but who had been avoiding all attempts to contact him. Hoff had finally decided there was no choice but to get in his car and go looking for the man. After a long and unsuccessful search, he spotted a farmer plowing in a field. He got out of his car, climbed over a fence, and walked across the field to ask the farmer if he knew the man he was looking for.

"Yeah," he was told.

Could he tell him how to find him?

"Go up the road a mile and take your first right and your next left."

Hoff thanked him and headed back to his car, but then stopped, turned again, and asked, "What sort of person is he?"

"Ain't no good, never was, never will be."

And with that the farmer got back on his tractor and continued plowing.

In 1959 Hoff declined an opportunity to run for the Board of Aldermen, but in the spring of 1960 he agreed to run. By then the Hoffs were neighborhood fixtures, and Joan recently had involved herself in neighborhood activism. When they had first moved to Prospect Parkway, the residents—in order to hasten the paving of the road—had signed an agreement with the city to forgo sidewalks. But as the numbers of families with children grew tremendously, the traffic became a concern. And then on February 1, 1959, the Catholic diocese closed its decaying Cathedral High School in downtown Burlington, and the nine hundred students marched en masse to the new Rice Memorial High School (named for Bishop Joseph Rice, who had opened Cathedral High School in 1917), just a few blocks from Hoff's Prospect Parkway home.

Concerned that much more automobile traffic would be cutting through the neighborhood to get to the school, a group of neighborhood mothers protested that the increased traffic, particularly with no sidewalks, threatened their children. The protest failed to change things, but there was heavy press coverage that included a photograph of mothers blocking the road with their baby carriages. Smack in the middle of it was Joan Hoff. There were mutterings by some that the protest had more to do with anti-Catholicism than safety, and a Democratic rival of Phil's, State Senator Bob Spencer, suggested that Hoff "control the actions" of his wife.

Hoff later said that Joan's participation in the protest may in fact have contributed to his defeat, although he was quick to add that his opponent, incumbent George K. Hauck, was the best alderman in the city. He also reminded himself that he never had been successful in running for office in high school or college, and later described himself as always having been "conspicuous in defeat." As such, he appeared well prepared for a career in Vermont Democratic politics. But in any case, the defeat may have turned out for the best, because it allowed him to remain a fresh face when the opportunity arose for a more important office just a few months down the road. "I think now I would have been badly tarnished if I had won . . . because I would have been caught up in the factionalism which is the trademark of Burlington politics," Hoff later said.

An election-night gathering had assembled at the Hoff household to learn the results, but instead of becoming the sort of wake that usually marks a political defeat, it turned into a celebration of Hoff's strong showing in a heavily Republican ward. Among those present was Burlington mayor James Fitzpatrick, to whom Hoff said that he hoped someday to run for the sole Burlington seat in the Vermont House of Representatives. Fitzpatrick nodded and replied that maybe that could be arranged. The Democratic incumbent, Joseph E. Moore, already had indicated to Fitzpatrick and Bernard Leddy that he wouldn't seek reelection, and the Democratic leaders were looking for a candidate. Some months later, Moore announced that he would seek election as an assistant county judge (that is, a side judge), and Hoff was nominated as the Democratic candidate for the House seat.

Hoff's opponent was the Ward 5 alderman, Edward Keenan. Although Keenan himself was quite popular (he would be elected Burlington's mayor in 1963), Hoff clearly was favored in 1960. In fact, unlike the aldermanic race in which he had, he said, campaigned "day and night," Hoff's House campaign was virtually no campaign at all. He was deeply involved in a high-profile case involving the bankrupt Rutland Railroad, and the case took virtually every minute of his time for more than six months. The railroad was trying to undo agreements concerning work rules and wages that it earlier had agreed to, and Hoff was representing the unions in their efforts to prevent it from doing so.*

The trial ended the Friday before the Tuesday election. Hoff slept through most of Saturday, then set out on Sunday with several of his daughters to distribute campaign literature in their neighborhood. (Hoff much later recalled that he had "never campaigned a minute" until then.) He didn't even have any campaign literature of his own, so they distributed literature for John F. Kennedy's presidential campaign. They were still going door to door when a local Red Cross official drove up and told Hoff they had a desperate need for his type of blood and asked if he could go down and donate. "Of course I did, and that ended my campaign," Hoff said. "But it was a sweeping Democratic year and Burlington is essentially a Democratic city. Thus, I was elected."

In fact, there was one more day before the election, and while most assumed that Vermont would give its electoral vote to Richard Nixon, Kennedy nonetheless stopped at the Burlington airport that Monday on his way back home to Massachusetts. Chittenden County, where the airport is located, was Kennedy country, but no one anticipated the size and enthusiasm of the crowd that would come from all parts of Vermont to welcome him. It included children from local parochial schools who had been bused to the airport to greet the Irish Catholic candidate. Hoff was among the official greeters. It was the first time he had met Kennedy and seen up close the great popular appeal the candidate had. He later recounted often and with great relish how he and other candidates and party officials had to be pressed into service as crowd control to help Kennedy make his way through the excited mob of admirers and get back to his airplane. Kennedy didn't carry the state, and none of the Democratic statewide candidates came close to winning. But the visit helped invigorate the party's growing core constituency. Chittenden County gave a popular majority to Kennedy and the entire statewide Democratic ticket.

---

*The dispute struggled along until January 1963, when the railroad finally was abandoned at the request of its president, Rutland businessman William Ginsburg, with the acquiescence of Governor Keyser and the federal Interstate Commerce Commission. Ginsburg had been Democratic state party chairman, but his fight with the union and efforts to abandon the line had caused him to be replaced as party leader by Jack Spencer in May 1962. Keyser's lackadaisical efforts to save the railroad prompted even more public ire than Ginsburg's efforts to abandon it. And Hoff, because of his work on the case, became identified with the workers on a major and volatile political issue.

And in the state as whole, despite 15,000 more voters in 1960 than had voted in 1956, Nixon received 12,000 fewer votes than Eisenhower had four years earlier. Kennedy won more votes than any previous Democratic presidential candidate, and the Democratic gubernatorial candidate, Russell Niquette, also a record-setter, topped Kennedy by more than 2,500 votes.

Hoff, running only in the city of Burlington, won easily, 8,202 to 5,689. Some GOP leaders, exuberant over the statewide results and particularly over the recapturing of the state's sole congressional seat from William Meyer, heralded the results as the harbinger of a "return to normalcy." But they nonetheless had—or should have had—reasons for concern. The most ominous was the increasing size of the Democratic vote. Another less obvious one was the newly elected representative from Burlington.

When Hoff arrived in Montpelier the following January, he was one of just 50 Democrats in the 246-member House. There were 190 Republicans and 6 members who listed themselves as "Independent" but who were popularly viewed as Republicans. The average age of the House members was fifty-nine, and over half the House members—132 of the 246—were more than sixty years old. One section of the House that was populated by senior legislators in fact was known as "Sleepy Hollow" because a visitor looking down from the balcony often could find four or five heads nodding peacefully through the legislative routine. Hoff, at thirty-eight, was among just eighteen members under the age of forty, the youngest of them being Tracy Kenyon, a Republican from Shaftsbury, who was twenty-four years old when the session started and who became known as "Cornwallis" after he started showing up day after day wearing a brilliant red blazer. Hoff also was one of just nine lawyers in the House, not counting W. Clark Hutchins, who had a law degree from Columbia but who didn't practice. The House included forty-five women (twenty-seven of whom listed themselves as housewives) and ninety-seven farmers. It also included loggers, carpenters, plumbers, electricians, car salesmen, a slate worker, a funeral director, two clergymen, a janitor, a funeral director, and a poet.

The Republicans also controlled the thirty-person Senate, twenty-three to seven.

Although the Senate was reasonably well apportioned, as the state's constitution said that it had to be, the Vermont House in 1961 was one of the most malapportioned bodies in the country. As it was, 200,000 Vermonters could elect only 21 representatives, while 200,000 of their more rural brethren elected 225. A House majority could be achieved by representatives from towns that made up of just 11.5 percent of the state's population. The inequity was underscored by the fact that the state's twenty-two largest communities generated 64 percent of the state's income tax and over half the property taxes, yet made up less than 9 percent of the House membership. Hoff, who represented more than 35,000 voters, was seated next to Representative William Jay Smith, a Democrat from Pownal, who represented about 1,500 voters. Sitting close by was Ethel Eddy, a Republican of Stratton, who represented just 24. Hoff, Smith, and Eddy each had one vote.

Smith, who was a poet and a professor of English at Williams College, later wrote a piece in *Harper's* magazine in which he compared the Vermont House to the eighteenth-century British House of Lords. "Larger and richer states have long ago made some attempt to reapportion their houses; but we still allow the state to be run by our small towns," he wrote, adding that what existed in Vermont was not a rural dictatorship but a rural aristocracy. "Ours is a benevolent aristocracy: our small towns tell us they will be perfectly happy as long as their way is paid," he wrote. "They dislike state control, but as long as they control the state and the state pays most of the bills, they will be happy."

Smith wasn't the only poet in the Vermont government. At a music festival in Rutland that year, Governor Keyser recited a short poem he had written:

> These two clean sheets
> Between I lie
> Have come from unknown lands
> From unknown hands.
> And somewhere they were spun
> By the engine's silent hum.
> It feels so good to sleep—
> Thanks for a world, and two clean sheets.

Keyser's poem had no title, but some others quickly dubbed it the "Textile Tango" or "Ode for Insomnia." Smith, as the poet of the opposition, composed a shorter poem in response, called "On Being Chosen."

> These two clean sheets
> Between I lie;

> They elected me their Governor—Why?
> They elected me their Governor—Why?

The "why" was complicated. Keyser had been just thirty-three years old when he was elected governor in 1960, the youngest person ever to be elected governor of Vermont. Born in Chelsea, the son of a politically active lawyer (later a judge), he had served in the navy in World War II, had graduated from Tufts in 1949, and then from Boston University Law School in 1952. He had served in the House in 1954, 1956, and 1958, developing a reputation as a conservative Republican and a member of the Proctor wing, although by the late '50s the Proctor wing was becoming more of a memory than a reality, and the leadership of the conservative faction was passing from the Proctors and the Vermont Marble Company to Deane Davis and the National Life Insurance Company. Davis, in fact, had been a law partner of Keyser's father's. Keyser had been elected House Speaker for the 1959 and 1960 sessions and had emerged as the winner of a four-way race in the 1960 Republican primary with just 29 percent of the total vote. He had defeated Lieutenant Governor Robert Babcock by 729 votes and likely wouldn't have except for a rare and fierce Democratic primary race for probate judge in Chittenden County (Babcock's home base) that had attracted unprecedented numbers of voters into that primary and denied the liberal Babcock many of the Democratic crossover votes that he otherwise might have gotten.

Keyser was young, fit, and in fact played basketball with a local semi-pro team called the Thunder Road All-Stars. But he was also balding, reserved, and seemed older than he was. T. Garry Buckley, who had served in the legislature with him and who later would help block his reelection, said that Keyser was "the oldest young man I ever met in my life."

The state's youngest governor quickly became one of its most beleaguered. Despite a 23–7 Republican majority in the Senate and a plurality of over 150 in the House, Keyser never gained control of the legislature. Senate president pro tem Asa Bloomer, a Rutland Republican who had long been a foe of the Proctor faction, repeatedly throttled Keyser initiatives. House Speaker Leroy Lawrence, a Keyser ally from Stamford (population 600), found himself unable to manage the House. Keyser's support for abandonment of the bankrupt Rutland Railroad outraged citizens on the western side of the state. His proposal to sell Lyndon State College (he didn't think Vermont could afford to help maintain three teachers colleges, a technical college, and UVM) alienated the Northeast

Kingdom and Lyndonville's W. Arthur Simpson. His supervision of the state's largest budget elicited protests from his more conservative supporters. Representative Richard Mallary, a Republican of Fairlee, grumbled in a newspaper column that "for reasons best known to himself Governor Keyser has worked harder and longer to repeal the electric energy tax than any other single piece of legislation." Repeal of the tax, Mallary calculated, would save the power companies, "who are not notably poor," $450,000 annually.

Looking back on the situation nearly forty years later, Sanborn Partridge said he thought Keyser had been handicapped by a literal concept of the separation of powers that poisoned his relationship with legislators. Hoff thought there was an even more basic problem. "Keyser was not the worst governor in the world, but he had the habit of not listening," he said. "You can't do that in Vermont." Hoff himself vowed at the start to listen to everyone, even to the point of keeping his home phone number listed in the Burlington telephone directory all the while he was governor.

Before 1960, the legislature had met only every other year, and just for short sessions. With so many farmers in the legislature, the goal for many years was to end the sessions just before Town Meeting Day, the first Tuesday in March, which coincided with the start of the maple sugaring season. The sessions started becoming longer in the years after World War II, sometimes lasting into May. But the 1961 session dragged on for 209 days, with the press repeatedly referring to it as "the longest and costliest to date." With Lawrence unable to manage the House, freewheeling coalitions formed to fill the vacuum. The most celebrated of these was the so-called Young Turks, a group of eleven members—three Democrats and eight Republicans, and all but one of them freshmen. This extraordinary group included Democrats Hoff, Smith of Pownal, and Stanley Lazarus of Middlebury; Republicans Mallary, Franklin S. Billings Jr. of Woodstock, John Downs of St. Johnsbury, Anthony Farrell of Norwich, Ernest W. Gibson III of Brattleboro, Sanborn Partridge of Proctor, Dalton Mann of Peru (the only nonfreshman in the group, in his second term), and Byron Hathorn of Hartford.

As a group, they were younger and better educated than most of the House members, Billings having graduated from Harvard, Mallary and Farrell from Dartmouth, Downs, Gibson, and Mann from Yale, Partridge from Amherst, Hoff from Williams, Lazarus from Washington University, Hathorn from Norwich, and Smith (who spoke fluent Italian and French) from the Institut de Touraine, Columbia, the University of Florence, and Oxford, where he had been a Rhodes Scholar. A hundred and twenty-nine of the House members had no college degrees at all, and a fair number of them had never finished high school, which was not unusual for older people in Vermont at the time. Most of the Young Turks also had deep Vermont roots. Billings and Gibson were the sons of governors, and Partridge the son of a U.S. senator who also had been the president of the Vermont Marble Company. Except for Mallary and Hathorn, who were still in high school when the war ended, all had served in World War II: Downs, Gibson, and Lazarus in the army, Mann, Smith, and Hoff in the navy, Billings with the British Eighth Army's Sixth Armored Division, and Partridge and Farrell with the Army Air Forces. The combination of their education, youth, and war service made them young-men-in-a-hurry, impatient with the slow pace of the legislature, with its resistance to change, and with its domination by what Billings described as "right-wing Republicans," who because of their seniority had been given most of the important committee posts. The Young Turks had already proved themselves in the war and were tired of taking orders.

In the winter of 1961 the interstate highway system hadn't yet been completed, and travel to and from Montpelier took longer and often was more hazardous than it now is. Rather than commute back and forth daily, even members who lived fairly close to Montpelier usually chose to stay in hotels such as the charming but fusty Pavilion Hotel or in rooming houses during the week. Billings said that the group was drawn together both philosophically and socially—socially "because we were the only young people" in the legislature, meaning people still in their thirties.

What happened, in short, was that Hoff and Downs decided to form a law school–type study group whose members would study the legislation in their individual committees and report back to the group as a whole. Hoff recruited the Democrats, and Downs, who would become the senior partner in Vermont's largest law firm, recruited the Republicans. They began meeting every Monday in the living room of the boardinghouse owned by Louise Pierce on State Street, where Billings and Farrell rented rooms. Partridge said the first rule was that there would be no drinking for the first hour of the sessions. The eleven were scattered among thirteen of the seventeen House operating committees. "We traded information about the committees on which we served," Partridge said. "And we could clue each other on what was coming up" for a floor vote. Mallary said that discussion would lead to drinks and discussion, and that usually they would go out for dinner together and "sit around and talk all through the evening."

Kendall Wild, the longtime reporter and editor of the *Rutland Herald*, thinks it was Dick Levine, a reporter for the *Herald*, who first dubbed them the Young Turks, after the secret societies of university students and military cadets that had set out in the late nineteenth and early twentieth century to modernize and reform the Ottoman Empire. By the time the session ended, the term had come into common use, and the members had come to be seen as bipartisan progressives committed to change. To a large extent, the Young Turks owe their fame more to what they later became than to what they achieved in 1961. Hoff would become governor. Billings would become House Speaker and then a judge. Mallary would become House Speaker and a member of Congress. By the 1963 session, the Young Turks were wielding significant influence by heading most of the important House committees. And apart from a nasty but temporary falling out between Hoff and Mallary, they would remain lifelong friends.

Their initial join effort, however, was not promising. The Vermont Senate, with the approval of the governor, had passed a bill to eliminate the payment of the poll tax as a requirement for voting in local elections. Inexplicably, no one had introduced a similar bill in the House until the Young Turks decided to. John Downs recalled that once the debate began, six or seven of them rose to speak in favor of it. Hoff led off the debate, and the others followed. The House members listened respectfully as one Young Turk after another argued for the bill. One of the crustiest and most entrenched of the Old Guard, Republican Sam Parsons of Hubbardton, pronounced it the best presentation he had ever heard. "The legislature listened with great interest," Downs said. But when the vote was taken, "there were [just] 13 votes for our position. . . . So that was a very sobering experience, but a very good one." Not until 1964 and the ratification of the Twenty-fourth Amendment to the United States Constitution, barring the poll tax as a requirement for voting in federal elections, did Vermont follow suit.

As the session continued, the Young Turks gained in respect and success. They would never win as often as they lost, but they sent a message that some of the best and brightest of the young legislators felt that change was overdue and that they intended to push for it. Hoff recalled that they would "do things they knew they'd get clobbered on simply because they believed in the goal and felt it was important to begin achieving it."

During that first session, Hoff himself sponsored over forty bills. One day in March, after he introduced nine of the fourteen bills proposed, the Speaker suggested they name it Phil Hoff Day. Some legislators who didn't share Hoff's ideas for the future suggested he had come to Montpelier with a bill to cure almost every malady that afflicted Vermont and some that didn't. Nonetheless, sixteen of his bills were enacted into law. His biggest triumph came when, with the support of the other Young Turks, he engineered the passage of a medical aid to the aged bill that brought the benefits of the federal Kerr-Mills Act (the precursor of Medicare) to Vermonters. Keyser had opposed the bill and had tried to have it killed. But Hoff and the others drummed up so much support for it that Keyser didn't dare veto it.

That same year, Republican state representative William Mikell of South Burlington brought suit in Vermont state courts in the wake of the recently decided *Baker v. Carr* case in which the U.S. Supreme Court had extended jurisdiction over reapportionment to the judiciary. The Vermont constitution mandated that the Senate be reapportioned regularly to keep up with population shifts, but there was no constitutional mandate requiring reapportionment of the House. The Senate hadn't been reapportioned since 1941, and in July 1962, as the primary season neared, the Vermont Supreme Court ordered that the Senate be reapportioned. Keyser responded by convening a special session of the legislature. During the two-week session, the legislature—at Keyser's urging—took away a seat from Rutland County and added it to the Chittenden County delegation, thus deepening the rift between Keyser and the Rutland-based Bloomer.

By then, preparations for the 1962 elections were well under way. As early as the previous fall there had been persistent rumors that Bernard Leddy, the state's most popular Democrat, would not accept his party's gubernatorial nomination, and the word was circulating that party leaders were focusing on Hoff. Jack Spencer of Cuttingsville, the new party chairman, suggested that the party had a number of "very competent and attractive political candidates," but Hoff's name always was at the top of his own six-man list. And Hoff himself had been crisscrossing the state on a "pulse-testing" tour, sounding very much like a candidate and saying repeatedly, "Vermont has not had a governor willing to face the serious problems of government since the time of Ernest Gibson." He announced his candidacy officially on February 28.

Leddy didn't want the job. "What most people don't understand about Bernard is that he was a very retiring sort of person," Hoff said in 1978. "He was genuinely not interested in running." Russell Niquette was interested, and thought he deserved another chance after having done so well in 1960. But, for all the reasons already mentioned, party leaders had decided it was time for a progressive non-Catholic to lead the ticket. Spencer, Leddy, and Bob Larrow pressured the Catholic and French Canadian Niquette to stay out of the race.

In 1959 the Democrats had named L. Samuel Miller as their first full-time director, and he had set out to create Democratic town committee structures in places that never had them before. It was Miller who had concluded while doing graduate work in political science at UVM that the Democrats in fact could win a statewide race in an off-year election if they put up the right candidate with the right issues. The combination of Miller and Spencer brought not just energy and organizational skills to the party but also money, since Spencer was a beneficiary of the Spencer Corset Company fortune (the Spencers were a leading maker of foundation garments back when most women still wore them) and could personally bankroll many things that he wanted to do. It was Spencer who persuaded Philip Savory, then the head of the Morning Press Bureau, which covered state government for both the *Rutland Herald* and *Burlington Free Press*, to go to work for the party as a press spokesman, and put $6,000 in an escrow account for his salary, with the promise of up to $6,000 more if Hoff lost and Savory couldn't quickly find other work. He also persuaded Walter Paine of Woodstock, the wealthy publisher of the *Valley News* in West Lebanon, New Hampshire, to put up enough money to underwrite a major poll by Oliver Quayle—then one of the country's leading pollsters—which concluded it would be crucial for the Democratic candidate to campaign heavily on the east side of the mountains, something that Democrats had seldom done in the past. (In fact, it may have been Paine who also put up the money for the Savory position. Paul Guare, who later became a Hoff aide, left written notes saying his recollection was that Paine had contributed $10,000 for a publicist, but fifty years later neither Savory, Miller, nor Hoff could remember for certain.)

Hoff later said that he wasn't interested in being cannon fodder and decided to run only because he really thought he could win. "I was rather convinced that I could do more than [just] put up the good fight," he said. "And so I worked at it. I carried on the longest, hardest campaign that was carried on by anybody up until that time." In the past, there had been little or no serious campaigning before Labor Day, but Hoff spent much of the whole year traveling the state, trying to attract attention wherever he could. Much of the scheduling was handled by Hoff's law office secretary, Priscilla LaPlante. T. Wesley Grady, an Underhill businessman who was the chairman of the Chittenden County Democratic Committee, volunteered much time to the campaign, and often served as chauffeur as well. Sometimes trips were made on very short notice. Sam Miller recalled once having phoned Hoff at his Burlington home sometime shortly before 6 A.M. and telling him that he had lined up a speaking engagement for him at 9 that morning in Brattleboro—about as far away from Burlington as anyplace in the state. "I'm not a machine," Hoff told him. But he got up, got into his car, and showed up for the meeting.

It was, however, a very low-budget campaign. Aside from the money Walter Paine had put up for the Quayle poll and some minor funding that the state party did for Democrats in general, Hoff later estimated that he spent a total of $12,500 for his own campaign. Of that, about $7,500 was raised from individual donors, and near the end, organized labor kicked in $5,000. Things were so tight and available cash so limited that in the last days of the campaign Hoff made a call to James Marro of Rutland, a backer who owned the popular Fairmont Restaurant there. Marro got into his car, drove south to Bennington, then east over the mountains to Brattleboro, north through Bellows Fall and Springfield, and then back west to Rutland, stopping all along the way to pry cash and checks out of fellow Democrats. The amount wasn't great. He later remembered it being just a few thousand dollars. But it provided enough for a last-minute barrage of newspaper, radio, and television advertising that Hoff considered important.

The Democrat slate that year was a blend of old and new, with Hoff heading the ticket, Bob Larrow the candidate for attorney general, and Peter J. Hincks, an elderly and courtly Middlebury banker who had been appearing on the ticket since 1938, running for treasurer. With a WASP heading the ticket, the choice for lieutenant governor was Frederic Delany Jr., a forty-one-year-old attorney from Rutland who could appeal to the traditional Democratic constituency since he was both Irish and Catholic. He also was a combat veteran, having been a navy dive-bomber pilot in World War II and a jet fighter pilot in Korea, and was the son-in-law of the enormously popular Major General Leonard F. Wing, who first commanded Vermont's 172nd Infantry Regiment and then went on to become the only National Guard general to command a combat division in World War II.

But tragedy struck suddenly on the morning of October 6, when Delany was driving Jack Spencer from Rutland to his Cuttingsville home in a sports car convertible. At sometime around 1 A.M., on a sharp curve leading to a steel truss bridge on Route 103 just north of Clarendon, Delany's car went into a skid and collided with a station wagon. Spencer was thrown from the car and emerged bruised but not seriously injured. The brunt of the impact had been on the driver's side, and Delany, still semiconscious, was rushed to Rutland Hospital, where he was found to have many internal injuries, including fractured ribs, a torn diaphragm, lacerations of a lung, and a displacement of the heart from the left side to the right. He died eight hours after the crash, leaving a widow, a four-year-old son, and a seven-month-old daughter.

"It was very emotional, of course," Sam Miller recalled. And it seemed like a great political setback as well. "The combination of Hoff and Delany was very strong," Miller said. "You had an Irish name. You had a Protestant name. You had two war veterans. That combination had a lot of things going for it."

It was too late to put a replacement on the ballot. The Democrats now had no candidate for lieutenant governor. They had no expectation of winning other statewide races or the congressional race, and as a matter of strategy had decided to run a minimalist campaign against U.S. Senator George Aiken, hoping to keep him mostly quiet and mostly in Washington, where he would do little to help Keyser. So the focus now was entirely on Hoff, who for the last month of the campaign had to go it alone.

Vermont campaigns in the 1960s were built mainly around personal appearances, press releases, and political advertising, most of it in newspapers but some of it on billboards. With only one Vermont-based television station (WCAX in Burlington) reaching only a portion of the state, television didn't play a big role. There were no one-on-one debates between Hoff and Keyser. Savory said he can't remember Hoff and Keyser even being at the same venue at the same time at any point in the campaign. Newspapers seldom staffed events outside their immediate area, but they did give coverage to the dueling press releases issued almost daily by Phil Savory for the Hoff campaign and Barry Locke for Keyser. The main theme of the Hoff campaign was that it was time to end "a century of one-party rule." Savory picked up this theme and expanded on it regularly, cranking out releases on a range of subjects—they could be on anything from Republican failures to adequately deal with needed highways or provide more funding for education or push for legislative reapportionment—and then adding a version of the campaign theme line, such as, "Hoff charged this is the kind of irresponsible action on the part of the administration that climaxes a century of one-party rule in Vermont."

Savory was a soft-spoken man who had spent six years in Japan as a Central Intelligence Agency officer, although almost no one in Vermont knew that at the time, because the CIA in those days discouraged former officers from talking about their work. He had gone into the CIA right after graduation from Georgetown University, where he had learned to speak passable Russian. His focus in the agency was Russian operations in Asia, and he had operated under the pretense that he was a civilian analyst for the Defense Department unit in the Tokyo embassy. He had enjoyed his time in Japan, but after being rotated back to headquarters in Washington had found the CIA bureaucracy "pretty overpowering." He spotted an ad in *Editor & Publisher* for an opening for a reporter at the *Bennington Banner*, applied for the job, and got it. He went from there to the Morning Press Bureau, where he became knowledgeable about state government.

He said that he had agreed to work for Hoff because he had covered him in the legislature and thought he was very different from the usual run of Chittenden County Democrats in Montpelier. "They were a pretty pathetic bunch," he said. "People like Fred Fayette were only watching out for themselves, in my opinion. They didn't have any convictions about anything. But Hoff was very different and I was impressed by him."

Spencer had set up Savory in a small office in the Pavilion Hotel, just south of the Capitol. Hoff would spend almost every day on the road, and Savory would talk with him early by telephone, find out where he was going and what he was going to be talking about. Then he would write a news release about it and walk it over to the Capitol, where the Associated Press, United Press International, and the Morning Press Bureau all were clustered in cramped work spaces at the top of the building, just under the dome.

It was slow going at the start, and for a time it seemed as though the Hoff campaign would never shift out of low gear. Repeatedly, the Hoffs would show up for a "rally" and find only the town chairman and a handful of party faithful present. Once, in Brattleboro, which had a population of about 12,000, only four people showed up for an event at which

Hoff was scheduled to speak. "You have no idea how depressing it is to go to someone's house for a meeting and find that only one other person has showed up," Hoff later said.

But going into houses turned out to be one of the things he did best. Hoff's most effective campaign technique was modeled on John Kennedy's coffee klatch, which had been built around the premise that, as one savvy Republican put it, "there's no limit to how far a young man can go in politics these days if he's good looking, has a photogenic wife, and can down gallons of coffee without going into shock." As Hoff himself recalled it, "Jack Kennedy had started a thing called the coffee klatch. And I seized on that. And it was a natural vehicle for Vermont. And it had never been done before. And it fitted in our organizational capacity because we had no organization. But we could get somebody in town who would hold a coffee klatch. Sometimes more than one. It was a natural vehicle for me. Also another reason, I wasn't a terribly effective political speaker. . . . Sam Miller [worked] to drum up this activity, and there was just Sam, Joan, and me. That was it. If there was a factory, I would go through it. Joan would go house to house."

Sam Miller recalled that the coffee klatches were low-key but effective. "There wasn't much talk about issues," he said. "People just wanted to see him and sit with him and talk with him, especially women." A handsome and energetic campaigner, Hoff found himself being compared to John Kennedy, and did nothing to discourage the comparison. After the Cuban missile crisis of late October 1962, Kennedy was at the height of his popularity, and Hoff's efforts to identify with him bolstered his campaign. Joan Hoff also developed into an effective campaigner—so effective in fact that it was considered a big loss when she developed pneumonia and had to withdraw during the last days before the election. "Joan was an integral and very important part of that first campaign," Hoff later said. "She really made a huge difference." And at one point, even nine-year-old daughter Andrea became involved. She and her grandmother were shopping in Burlington one day when Keyser came into the store. He had no idea who Andrea or Joan Hoff's mother were. He said hello and shook their hands, only to have Andrea then stomp on his foot, saying, "That is what we do to people who are against my father."

There in fact were issues, not just coffee klatches, and increasingly sharp barbs were traded as the campaign progressed. Keyser dismissed Hoff as a "part-time freshman legislator" who had been absent on the day of voting for the reapportionment of the Senate. Hoff accused Keyser of ignoring the state's brain drain (some fifteen thousand Vermonters between the ages of twenty and forty-four had left the state in the previous ten years), and of trying to cover up the loss of a thousand manufacturing jobs on his own watch. Hoff argued that the time had come for better state planning, for House reapportionment, for more state funding of education, and for an end to caretaker governors. And he managed to lay the blame for the proposed abandonment of the Rutland Railroad on Keyser, despite the initiative's having come from former Democratic state party head William Ginsburg, the president of the line.

But Keyser also was under attack from Republicans. Asa Bloomer, whose home was in West Rutland, remained furious at him for causing the shift of a Senate seat from Rutland County to Chittenden County, and refused to support his reelection. W. Arthur Simpson and many others in the Northeast Kingdom deserted Keyser to support Hoff because of Keyser's backing of plans to privatize Lyndon College, which they feared would mean the end of the school. Hoff, in contrast, argued that "if the Northeast Kingdom is to prosper and grow, it is essential that they have a college that can act as a cultural and educational center."

And then, during the final weeks before the vote, Hoff found an issue that gave added spark to his campaign. Keyser had claimed an $853,000 budget surplus, but David Anderson, the Republican auditor of accounts, had told Phil Savory, whom he knew from back when Savory had covered him as a newspaper reporter, that it was only a "paper surplus" that had been created by a bookkeeping technique he didn't approve of and wanted to change. In short, Anderson said that Keyser was claiming a surplus while in fact there were outstanding bills that hadn't yet been submitted and thus hadn't been paid. Anderson was angry with Keyser because the governor had refused his request for more auditors on his staff, and Savory said many years later that he assumed that was why Anderson told him what he did.

The question was how to go public with Anderson's charge. While television didn't play a major role in the campaign, WCAX had a very popular Saturday night news program, called *You Can Quote Me*, that was watched by almost everyone in the state who cared about politics and was within broadcast range. "Everybody watched that program, so it was important," Savory recalled. It was hosted by Mickey Gallagher, the anchor of the Monday through Friday evening news program, and usually involved several newspaper journalists, who along with Gallagher would question a guest. Keyser was due to appear, and Hoff and Savory decided to plant the question with Ben Collins, a reporter with the *Free Press* whom both of them knew.

Keyser arrived planning to use the show to tout his successes but instead was blindsided with the question by Collins. Both Savory and Sam Miller recalled that Keyser was thrown badly off balance and never recovered. "It was obvious Keyser didn't know how to answer it," Savory said. "In effect, he was being called a liar. He was thrown off base, and instead of being able to show his stuff, he spent most of the program on the defensive." Hoff quickly began calling the surplus a "phony surplus" and "a monstrous hoax." And when other reporters asked Anderson whether Hoff or Keyser was right, Anderson said "Hoff is figuring the proper way."

In fact, Keyser had been relying on a bookkeeping method that had been used by the state for thirty-five years. The *Rutland Herald*, which gave its editorial backing to Keyser, said in an editorial that the issue raised by Hoff was "a lot phonier than the surplus" but conceded that it had generated excitement in the campaign at a time when Hoff needed it.

Keyser exploded into frantic activity. He announced he was calling in his own set of accountants to prove him right. Hoff noted that in doing so Keyser also was trying to prove his own Republican auditor wrong. Anderson, running for reelection himself, retired into a sulky silence. The Keyser accountants looked at the books, and all they could say was that each side was using a different method of reckoning. They said Keyser wasn't wrong—but they wouldn't say that the Hoff-Anderson method was wrong either.

"These accountants," Keyser press spokesman Barry Locke said dismally two days before the election, "they speak a completely different language." Keyser himself was very clear in his language, calling Anderson "that Benedict Arnold."

Savory believed it was time for a change and that Keyser wasn't seen as the sort of person to lead it. "Keyser was a pretty colorless guy," he said. "He was competent. He knew how to run things. But he wasn't an exciting guy," while Hoff was. "Vermonters . . . tend to be very pragmatic, and they concluded that [Hoff] was the sort of person needed to bring the state out of the nineteenth century."

In the end, it was splinter parties that tipped the scale, namely the Vermont Independent Party (VIP), which had been created by prominent Republicans T. Garry Buckley of Bennington and A. Luke Crispe of Brattleboro as a way of letting Republicans vote for Hoff without having to cast ballots on the Democratic line. Buckley said that he thought Keyser was a "stiff, and just because we're Republicans is no reason to return a stiff." Crispe had been a political opponent of Keyser's, having run against him in the primary in 1960. But the decision to form the VIP had less to do with politics than with horse racing, as Buckley later admitted.

Vermonters had voted in a referendum to allow pari-mutuel racing in Vermont, and Crispe, Buckley, and other associates were among the groups seeking the license to operate the planned racetrack. The point man for their effort was Gerald McLaughlin, a well-known and popular Vermont newspaperman. "We thought it should be given to a group from Vermont, not to some hustler from outside the state," Buckley said. "We told Keyser that if he didn't give it to a Vermont group—not necessarily to us, but to a group from Vermont—we'd campaign against him to make sure he didn't get re-elected."

Buckley later added, "When you make a threat like that, you have to make sure that it sticks." So when the franchise to operate the track at Pownal was given to a group from Rhode Island, Buckley and Crispe decided to form the Vermont Independent Party to oppose Keyser, with Bennington lawyer George Van Santvoord doing much of the actual legal work to create the party and gather the necessary signatures on the petitions.

Buckley didn't think highly of Keyser to begin with. "He was a perfectly nice guy and he had a wonderful wife. He wasn't dishonest. He wasn't a hypocrite," he said. "But he was a typical post–Civil War Vermont Republican—very conservative, very prim and proper—and he acted like an old man." As for Hoff, whom he had known casually back when Hoff had been at Williams, "He was a wonderful guy. He was right for the times. But we weren't altruistically supporting him. It was a negative support, against Keyser. . . . And we got Hoff the votes that caused him to win. If we hadn't done that, he would have been a perfectly nice guy also-ran, like Bob Larrow and Frank Branon."

When the ballots were counted, Keyser had 60,035 votes on the Republican line (the only line on which he was listed), while Hoff trailed with 56,196 on the Democratic line. But in addition to his Democratic vote, Hoff received over 3,200 votes from the Vermont Independent Party, and just short of 1,900 votes on an Independent Democrat line, giving him 50.6 percent of the vote—a 1,348-vote edge.

The final votes came from Winooski.

Winooski, just north of Burlington, had been a mill town until most of the mills moved away in the '50s, leaving behind 7,500 people, many of them French Canadians, and an eroding economic base. It had long been the most Democratic of cities in the most Republican of states, and for years every Democratic candidate for governor had wound up his campaign at the traditional Winooski election-eve rally, which was a boisterous evening of fire-breathing oratory and torchlight parades. Hoff had been to the election-eve rally and had promised to return on election night if he won.

As they watched the returns flow in from the rest of the state, party officials there realized that Hoff in fact was going to be elected, and decided that Winooski should have the honor of pushing him over the top. They decided to withhold their returns until the very end.

At the Hoff home on Prospect Parkway, a large crowd of supporters and well-wishers had gathered. Norman James, a reporter with radio station WDEV in Waterbury, recalled that Hoff had spent the evening checking returns against those of past years, encouraged but not entirely confident. By midnight, the more politically savvy of the crowd concluded that if Keyser's lead was less than 1,000 when everything except the Winooski vote was tabulated, Hoff would be the new governor. Meanwhile, Arthur Ristau, the Associated Press bureau chief in Montpelier, concluded that Hoff couldn't overcome the Keyser lead, and typed out a bulletin declaring Keyser the winner.

As soon as Winooski officials heard the AP bulletin being broadcast on local radio, they released their returns, showing that Hoff had outpolled Keyser by an amazing 1,768 to 188. "You've won! You've won!" James screamed as he pushed his WDEV microphone in front of Hoff.

And so, at about 1 A.M., Hoff returned to Winooski. A crowd of about three hundred townspeople and college students had rushed to the city's main street, where a single policeman was trying frantically, hopelessly, to keep them out of the road. When Hoff arrived, standing in the front of an open convertible, he immediately was surrounded by the shouting, shoving, arm-waving crowd. Those at the rear could only catch glimpses of him in the flashes of portable television lights and still-camera flashguns. His sandy hair was tumbled in disarray down over his forehead. He kept waving his arms over his head in a victory sign. Someone pushed through the crowd and managed to shove a tinfoil crown on his head. It had "King of Winooski" written on the front of it. For a moment, a sheepish grin came over Hoff's face, as though the royal ritual was too much even for Winooski. But he quickly slipped back into the spirit of things, and when a reporter managed to get a microphone near him, he grabbed it and shouted with mock gusto, "A hundred years of bondage broken! A hundred years of bondage broken!"

CHAPTER 2

"THE ONLY DEMOCRAT IN MY ADMINISTRATION"

Almost immediately after the election, Phil and Joan Hoff headed off to Puerto Rico for a much-needed vacation. He had run the longest and most intense race for governor by any Vermont candidate up to that time, and she had been with him almost every step of the way. Both were exhausted and welcomed the break from the campaigning and from the raw November cold. The Caribbean sunshine also helped Joan rebound from the bout of pneumonia that had knocked her out of the last days of the campaign. On their way back to Burlington they stopped in Washington, where President Kennedy had invited them to the White House and where—still awed by the glamour of the Kennedys—they were thrilled by the warm reception they received. In his own campaign, Hoff had tried to portray himself as a politician in the Kennedy mold—young and energetic and looking to lure talented people into public service by promising that they could change things for the better. Both he and Joan had left the White House with increased enthusiasm for the president and eager to begin the "bold new approach" to government that Hoff had promised.

Reality set in soon after they returned to Vermont. Hoff thought he had a good sense of what the problems were, and for the most part he did. He had spent more than a year telling Vermonters that a century of Republican rule had left them with a government unable to deal with major problems and unwilling to steer needed change. He nonetheless was stunned by some of what he found. He wouldn't actually set foot in the governor's office until the day he was inaugurated (Keyser never invited him in for transition discussions, an omission Hoff made sure wasn't repeated for his own successor, Deane Davis), and he would get there to find that all the filing cabinets had been totally cleaned out. Even the "black book" listing all the crackpots and nuisances who tended to hound public officials—most of them more annoying than dangerous—had been removed. But in the time between the election and the inauguration Hoff had moved into a temporary office in Montpelier and had begun assessing the situation and getting a better sense of the problems, starting with staffing. The governor's salary at the time was just $12,500 a year. No one else made more than that, although the commissioner of education came close. A salary of $10,000 was unheard of for anyone below the rank of a deputy commissioner. Even back in 1962, that wasn't a great deal of money, and one of the results of the low pay was that the people most concerned about job security tended to stay in government, while many of the more talented and confident moved on to other things. There were some very good people in government, of course, just as there were good people working as teachers, social workers, nurses, journalists, and in other jobs that, back in the '60s, were known for low pay. But it nonetheless was going to be hard to attract the quality of people he wanted with the salaries he could offer. An even greater problem was the structure of the executive branch of government itself.

In the late 1950s, a so-called Little Hoover Commission, headed by Deane Davis, the president of National Life Insurance Company, had studied the executive branch and concluded it was a cumbersome and inefficient structure that lacked some of the most basic management tools. It was called the Little Hoover Commission because it was modeled on the commission headed by former president Herbert Hoover that President Truman had appointed in 1947 to study the executive branch of the federal government. Despite its criticisms that the governor often had no control over his agencies or even any means of keeping in touch with them, and despite the high regard in which Davis and his commission members were held, many of the 135 recommendations for change hadn't been implemented. The result was that Vermont still had agencies clustered in a structure that was unresponsive at worst and unwieldy at best. While the top executives of many large companies didn't have more than seven or eight subordinates reporting directly to them, the governor of Vermont, with virtually no staff, had to deal with 126 boards, councils, and commissions, most of them autonomous, that separated him from his agencies. Since many of them had policy-making authority, and since the board and commission members were appointed for four- or six-year terms, a new governor came into office with his agencies in the control of persons appointed by previous governors and usually planning to stay there.

With the Republicans in power for more than a century, a tradition had developed in which a Republican commissioner usually could stay on the job for as long as he cared to. Governors came and went, but the commissioners remained in place, often cultivating their own support in the legislature and creating power bases of their own. In the case of Perry Merrill, the commissioner of forests and parks, Hoff had an important agency controlled by a man who had been appointed by Governor John Weeks in 1928. Merrill had been an ambulance driver in France during World War I who later studied forestry in Sweden, saw the passion for skiing there, and became convinced that the revenues from a booming ski industry could provide for an extensive system of forests and parks in Vermont, which he worked diligently to make happen. In that sense, he was a visionary and a great boon to the sate. But he also had been running the department since Hoff was four years old, had served under and outlasted eleven different governors, and had become such an independent force that Montpelier insiders muttered that he was the last dictator left in state government. A joke in Montpelier was "The leaves don't turn red until Perry gives them the word." He was the most extreme example, but many other commissioners also ran their departments with an autonomy that sometimes verged on independence. The result was that although the governor was elected to run the government, he couldn't be held fully responsible for it because he didn't have full control of it. If the commissioners and their boards were hostile to a new governor—as some of the Proctor faction had been to Ernest Gibson—they could ignore him during his whole time in office. It could take four years for a governor to appoint a working majority to most of the boards, and no Vermont governor since 1840 had served more than two terms.

"I knew he was going to have a hell of a time getting his own people in place," Phil Savory recalled. "He wasn't going to be able to appoint a lot of new department heads, and he wouldn't be able to find enough qualified Democrats if he could." Savory himself had no interest in working in government. He had been enthusiastic about helping Hoff get elected but wasn't interested in staying. "I wanted to get back to journalism," he said. Soon after the inauguration, he took a job with the *New York Herald-Tribune* as its Albany bureau chief, and then became the managing editor of the *Bennington Banner*. Before he left, he convinced Hoff that the single most important job he needed to fill quickly with a dependable ally was the commissioner of administration. Savory's friend and predecessor at the Morning Press Bureau, William F. Kearns Jr., was a deputy commissioner of institutions, and Savory told Hoff that Kearns was the best choice for the job.

The Department of Administration—a relatively new agency whose creation had been the principal recommendation of the Little Hoover Commission—had no oversight board, so it was a job that the governor could fill as he chose, with the consent of the Senate. Kearns was a straight-talking Irish Catholic who had grown up in Bennington. He had been a marine in the South Pacific who had survived banzai attacks on Tarawa and been wounded on Saipan, coming out of the war with a sergeant's stripes, a Bronze Star, and a Purple Heart. The Sixth Marine Regiment that he had served with was widely known as the "Pogey Bait Marines," because back in 1931, when sailing off for duty in Shanghai, it supposedly had put in a requisition for supplies that asked for ten thousand candy bars (sometimes called "pogey bait" in the rural South) and just two bars of soap. He had covered state government for eight years as a reporter for the Morning Press Bureau and was one of just a handful of officials in the entire executive branch to list himself in the state government handbook as a Democrat. Most of the other Democrats on the payroll, perhaps prudently, listed themselves as Independents. Hoff and Kearns didn't know each other. Kearns, in fact, later recalled that his chief impression of Hoff as a freshman legislator was simply that he had introduced so many bills that "I wondered how in the hell he was going to keep track of them."

"I introduced Bill to Phil and Phil to Bill," Savory recalled. Hoff picked Kearns to run the department, and he was confirmed by a Senate vote of 28–2. One of the two votes against him was cast by Irving Eastman, a Republican from Addison and a former telephone company executive who thought that a telephone company executive or someone with similar management experience should be running the department. He later told Kearns that his vote had been a mistake. The other was Republican George Morse, a seventy-year-old Caledonia County dairy farmer and coal dealer who had served in the field artillery in France in World War I, returned home, and stayed there surrounded by his family and his cows, becoming a staunch Republican even by Vermont standards, fiscally tightfisted except when it came to state aid for farmers. He told Kearns (whom he had known for a long time) that he knew he was a good fellow but that "I ain't voting for any Democrat." Kearns quickly became one of Hoff's most important and trusted aides.

Savory's departure had been delayed by a New York City newspaper strike, during which his new employer wasn't publishing. But on April 5 Hoff staged a farewell party for him in the apartment that he and Wes Grady shared on Terrace Street. The apartment was so sparsely furnished that folding chairs had to be brought in from a nearby funeral home. Charles Delaney and Noel Viens, both Democratic state senators and restaurant owners, cooked steak dinners. The State Liquor Board, as was common at the time, obtained liquor from a compliant salesman, a sort of widespread and low-level extortion that had fueled all kinds of political, legislative, and press parties for years and that would continue into the Davis years, when it finally was banned as the inappropriate practice it was.

The party lasted into the early morning hours, and then—with just a handful of people remaining, including Hoff, Savory, Delaney, and *Burlington Free Press* reporter Vic Maerki—Kearns announced it was time for a serious meeting. After a number of other issues were dealt with, it was agreed that Wes Grady, whom Hoff had named secretary of civil and military affairs, wasn't working out in the job. He had been one of Hoff's hardest-working and most loyal aides during the campaign and was a genial man who worked well with people. But he had no experience in state government and no real understanding of the nuances, power centers, protocols, and customs of the legislature. Kearns and the others said that someone else was needed to quickly change what was becoming a rocky relationship with the legislature. Hoff said he agreed and would ask his friend and roommate to resign. Hoff offered the job to Maerki, who—somewhat to Hoff's annoyance—refused it. The next day the decision was made to offer it to James (Doc) Kennedy, a former Democratic representative from Island Pond with many legislative friends in both parties. Kennedy would hold the job until July, when he would swap jobs with Thomas Kenney, the executive clerk, who would stay in the job and become a principal gatekeeper for Hoff during his first two terms.

Compounding the structural difficulties was the reality that there was little cooperation or coordination among agencies whose responsibilities overlapped. Even the most casual observer could spot numerous cases of inefficiency and waste and of departments working at cross purposes. For years, for example, the Fish and Game Department had spent a healthy part of its budget trying to stock and maintain Vermont's trout streams, while at the same time the Highway Department was dredging them for gravel for road construction, eliminating the pools that the trout needed to spawn in. At the same time that the Water Resources Department was sending its agents throughout the state persuading towns to build sewage lagoons rather than pump waste into rivers, the Health Department had its own workers out condemning sewage lagoons as health hazards. And when the Department of Motor Vehicles redesigned some forms in the early '60s, it did so without consulting with the Department of Public Safety, which maintained the forms. The result was that the Department of Motor Vehicles forms wouldn't fit into the state police files. In the summertime, three different state agencies—the Highway Department, the Fish and Game Department, and the Department of Forest and Parks—all had trucks traveling the same overlapping routes collecting trash from picnic areas, parks, beaches, and fishing access areas. The lack of communication among state officials was so great that when Hoff held two large dinner parties at his home early in 1963 for department heads and their wives, he found himself introducing many of his guests to one another, even though Montpelier was a small town and many of them worked in the same buildings.

He would begin to deal with that later, but his main focus late in 1962 was selecting a personal staff, preparing an inaugural address, and developing a budget. It was during the budget preparations that he got his biggest shock. This was when he went to the Department of Administration, which was housed in the former National Life Insurance Company building just north of the Capitol, to meet with the department head, Frank Free, about revenue projections. Free had been in charge of purchasing before being named commissioner of administration, and one of his colleagues recalled him as a thoroughly decent person and an excellent purchasing director, but someone with no grasp of long-term planning.

"I'll never forget the budget hearings that I held before the inauguration," Hoff said later, referring to the meeting with Free and his aides. "I didn't have a single person I could rely on, except for Phil Savory. I went into the [meeting] and asked for a ten-year projection, and they looked at me in complete bafflement and said they didn't have that. So I said I'd like a five-year projection, and they looked at me in complete bafflement again. Finally, I said 'Well, how about a projection for this coming year?' and they didn't have that either. I was flabbergasted." Hoff had known that the machinery of government was broken in many ways. It had been a major theme of his campaign. But the lack of information about something as basic as revenue projections and expenses nonetheless stunned him, and he left the meeting wondering "what in hell I was going to do."

What he did, in effect, was to call a "time out," and he did it on his inauguration day in a way that surprised both his supporters and his opponents. It was 2:15 P.M. on January 17, 1963, a bitterly cold day, when the Vermont General Assembly, which was overwhelmingly Republican, was gaveled into joint session by the Republican lieutenant governor, Ralph Foote of Middlebury. Hoff was sworn in to office by Chief Justice Benjamin Hulburd of the Vermont Supreme Court, who like all the other members of the Supreme Court was a Republican. A National Guard artillery unit on the State House lawn fired a nineteen-gun salute (the head of the National Guard, Francis Billado, who survived combat in World War II only to later choke to death on a roast beef sandwich, also was a Republican), causing the outgoing Governor Keyser to quip, "It isn't necessary to *shoot* me out of office."

In his farewell address to the General Assembly earlier in the day, Keyser also had shown signs of humor despite his deep disappointment in losing the election. "I am told this is a historic occasion," he said. "Frankly, I would like to disclaim any credit for its occurrence—it wasn't exactly as planned by me." At his own inaugural two years before, he had acknowledged that governments had taken on an enlarged role, no longer acting mainly as "policeman and umpire" to protect citizens from harm but increasingly being called upon to implement "newer ideas of social justice strongly tinged with humanitarianism." He applauded this trend, he said, but cautioned that Vermont simply couldn't afford any social programs that would require more taxes. "New taxes will stagnate and could destroy our potential development," he said.

Hoff had made clear during the campaign that he welcomed the enlarged role of government and didn't share Keyser's concerns. His position papers on subjects ranging from school aid to employment security and programs for the elderly all had called for greater government assistance and were detailed enough that they could be converted quickly into proposed legislation. So the expectation was that his inaugural address would include a list of new programs that he intended to try to implement quickly. But it was only a few minutes into his speech, which had been written by Savory, when the audience began to realize that the "bold new approach" he had promised was being put on hold. He was asking the legislature to have just an abbreviated session in 1963, approve a caretaker budget, allow him to inventory state problems, and then return for a special session in 1964 at which major new legislation would be proposed. He said that the people of Vermont "have clearly said that they don't want to continue with the old ways" and asked the General Assembly to "join with me in preparing a solid foundation for the bold departure from the past." But he said that he needed more time to determine just what new approaches should be taken and just how bold the departure could be. "What I am saying to you is this," he added. "The time has come to sit down and take a good look at ourselves and try to analyze who we are, what we are, what we have in possible revenues, what we can raise and still make Vermont an attractive place to live." In short, he asked for a one-year moratorium on legislation while he set up study groups to examine state needs.

Hoff's decision to do more planning before acting was more criticized than praised. Reid Lefevre, a state senator from Bennington County, called the inaugural address "a pleasant coma of indecisive confusion." Lefevre, a large and egg-shaped man whose size and jovial manner reminded some people of the storybook drawings of Old King Cole (he in fact ran a carnival called King Reid Shows and listed his occupation as "showman"), was considered one of the best orators in the legislature. He was often critical of Hoff's public speaking, which he considered self-assured but pedestrian, and later reacted to another Hoff speech by saying "I haven't been so excited since I had my last dish of tapioca pudding." But when he died of a heart attack a few years later, his widow asked Hoff to give the eulogy at his funeral, which Hoff did. Dick Levine, a reporter for the Morning Press Bureau and not as partisan as Lefevre, also dismissed the speech privately to his colleagues as "a mass of glittering generalities." And the *Barre-Montpelier Times-Argus* accused Hoff in a blistering front-page editorial that same afternoon (the paper in fact was on the streets even as the speech was being delivered) of failing to confront pressing problems. It said that the new governor was acting with the "courageous resolution of a maiden aunt, checking fearfully under her bed before retiring."

Hoff's closest supporters felt it was a wise decision or at least a practical one. Within weeks Hoff in fact had established numerous task forces of legislators, government officials, and citizens to review the state's problems and inventory its needs. At their peak, there were more than five hundred people—Republicans as well as Democrats—studying problem areas such as education, conservation, human resources, and fish and wildlife management. The work that they did during the spring, summer, and fall of 1963 resulted in serious and substantial legislative proposals for the 1964 session. And Hoff later said that it was his session with Frank Free and the Administration Department that had forced his hand. "It became quite apparent to me [during] the budget hearings that we were just plain lacking straight information," he said. "There wasn't any data at all."

He blamed Republican predecessors for ignoring basic research and planning, saying, "We must plan for the future, but we don't have the knowledge on which to base a plan. Vermont's importance as a dairy state has declined, but we don't know how much. The recreation industry has increased, but we don't know how much. We need additional money, but we don't know where best to find it. I'm just trying to find out what in hell we've got so we can decide what to do about it."

Many Democrats were disappointed by this approach, and some were angry that he hadn't attempted to quickly implement their party platform and oust whatever Republican officials he could. But the governor's office that Hoff returned to after his inaugural address was itself a reminder of another reality. The office and the corridors that led to it were lined with numerous portraits of past governors, many of them stern-faced and whiskered, looking down from the walls. There were lawyers, farmers, industrialists, bankers, Civil War veterans, and a serious robber baron or two. There were people of different religious faiths, political beliefs, personalities, and levels of competence. But there were no Democrats. That was the way it had been for more than a century, and the Republicans still dominated the legislature and ran virtually all the departments. Hoff knew that he was going to have to keep Republican support to get reelected and would have to work with the Republican legislature if he was going to get any sort of program enacted. The Democrats were still too small a minority to enact a program against even a reasonably united Republican majority, and Hoff knew that there would be a huge public outcry if he tried a quick and unceremonious removal of Republican department heads, many of whom had been in their jobs for a generation. Looking back to the governorships of Aiken and Gibson, he reminded himself that it had been "a combination of liberal Republicans and Democrats who historically have been responsible for the passage of all progressive legislation here in Vermont." And to party members who complained about a lack of action in his first months, Hoff began responding with a line that quickly became a favorite of his, telling them, "I'm the only Democrat in my administration, you know."

What in fact was the state of the state when Hoff took office?

In the months prior to the 1962 election, the U.S. Census Bureau had released its report for 1960. With a population of just under 390,000, Vermont had gained 12,000 new residents since 1950. Although that was a smaller gain than during the previous decade and well below the national average—and despite the fact that some of the brightest and most ambitious of the younger people were still leaving in troubling numbers—it showed growth in what had been a historically stagnant population. And more-rapid growth would soon follow. During the mid-1960s Vermont would grow by an unprecedented 55,000 people. Even by the time of Hoff's inauguration, just two years after the census count, the population had jumped to about 400,000, making it clear that the costs of education, welfare, and other government services would increase. Already, education—where close to 20,000 students had been added since 1950—was notoriously underfunded. But finding funding for more services wasn't going to be easy, because the $2,072 annual per capita income of Vermonters was $397 below the national average, and residents already bore one of the highest tax rates in the nation. Only residents of New York and Hawaii paid a higher percentage of their income in taxes.

The legislature was grossly malapportioned and dominated by small-town legislators who tended to oppose increases in state spending while funneling tax revenues into their often inefficient local governments in the name of "local control." The machinery of state government itself, harnessed to nineteenth-century concepts of minimal government, had become functionally obsolete, lacking the administrative ability, as Hoff became fond of saying, albeit with a bit of hyperbole, "to run a child's lemonade stand." There was little research and less planning, although the state was quickly changing in ways that required a good deal of both. Elbert (Al) Moulton, who became the commissioner of development in 1964, set out to remind everyone he could speak to anywhere he was invited to speak that the completion of the interstate highway would bring Vermont two hours closer to New York and an hour closer to Boston, making it much more assessable to skiers, tourists, businesses, and owners of second homes. "I spent most of the first year going all over the state talking to service clubs about the importance of regional planning," he recalled. "I kept telling them that there were going to be many more people coming to Vermont, and we had to have plans for what we were going to do with them and what we were going to let them do to us. . . . We had to plan for organized growth, not let ourselves be overrun with haphazard stuff."

A rotund man with a quick wit, ready smile, and the almost shameless boosterism of a carnival barker, Moulton had grown up in Maine and served in the navy as an enlisted man who helped program the firing of the five-inch guns on the USS *Rodman*, a Gleaves-class destroyer that landed troops on Omaha Beach on D-Day and that later, off Okinawa, was struck by three Japanese kamikaze planes on the same harrowing day while destroying six others. He had started out as a newspaper man but quickly found his talents more suited to promotion than journalism.

Eventually, he would work for four different governors (two Democrats and two Republicans), serve as chairman of the Vermont State Republican Committee, and become the executive vice president of the

Quechee Lakes Corporation, which was creating the sort of upscale and carefully planned development near Woodstock that he had worked as commissioner of development to bring to the state. It was a sign of the bipartisanship of the early Hoff years that Moulton was "never asked if I was a Republican or a Democrat" during the whole hiring process. It turned out he was a Republican, which would cause problems later. But he was hired to promote the state, not to develop Democratic policies, and he quickly became seen as a master of marketing. While he also worked to bring new industries to Vermont and to try to insure that the second-home market didn't develop in shoddy ways, he became best known for his efforts to promote tourism. Hoff was concerned that Vermont was losing out to New Hampshire and Maine in the battle for tourist dollars, and told Moulton to fix it. Moulton launched what was widely considered to be the state's most successful marketing campaign up to that time. Built around a glossy and beautifully illustrated booklet called *The Beckoning Country* (the idea for which actually had come from a young Burlington advertising executive named Bill Wheeler), it touted the virtues of Vermont for skiing, hunting, fishing, swimming, hiking, building businesses, and raising families; a place whose natural beauty, clear air, sparkling waters, and decent and hardworking people made it ideally suited for all those looking to relocate themselves or their businesses, vacation with their families, or buy second homes. In Moulton's "beckoning country" the skies were always blue, the waters sparkling and pristine, the snow deep and powdery, and the autumn foliage at its peak. All the sailboats had wind in their sails. Moulton advertised the brochure in *Reader's Digest* magazine, which was enormously well read and influential at the time, telling readers to send in a quarter and they would get *The Beckoning Country* in the return mail. His department was overwhelmed with requests for the brochure. "It did just what we wanted," he said.

The campaign would become particularly important because another reality facing the young governor was that the state's economy—and with it much of its traditional lifestyle and social order—was changing dramatically. For generations, Vermont's hilly landscape had been covered with farms, most of them small, and farming had been the principal occupation. During the years that George Aiken was governor, close to 30 percent of Vermonters had lived on working farms. By the time Hoff took office, the proportion was under 10 percent and shrinking fast. That meant that a way of life was changing as well.

In order to deal with those kinds of changes and problems, Hoff felt there was a need to reshape, coordinate, and better organize the 246 units of local government. In May 1963 he told a reporter for the *New York Times*, "With a population of less than 400,000 persons, Vermont has 800 school directors, 246 road commissioners, and 246 overseers of the poor. It's ludicrous, utterly ridiculous and wasteful. It may be political suicide but I am determined to end this sort of provincialism." He would come to find that 800 school directors, 246 highway commissioners, and 246 overseers of the poor, most of them with friends in the legislature, would prove to be a potent obstacle to change. But the bottom line was that Hoff in 1963 assumed the governorship of—but by no means the control of—a state that he believed needed to reapportion its legislature, reorganize its executive branch, and regionalize its local governments if it was to function in efficient and effective ways. And it also needed to do serious regional planning for forces that were threatening to change its economy, its demographics, and its very landscape.

Twelve days after his inaugural, Hoff sent his budget message to the legislature. Like Keyser before him, he cited the dilemma of limited financial resources and growing demands for services. Unlike Keyser, he made clear that he didn't think the scarcity of resources relieved the state from its "responsibility of providing services needed by our people." But he acknowledged the realities, which included a huge burden of fixed charges in areas like education, welfare, salaries, and retirement benefits that greatly restricted discretionary spending, as well as a substantial state debt. The debt service payments in 1963, in fact, would consume well over a third of the anticipated revenue increases. His immediate request to the legislature was for a caretaker budget and a quick adjournment. In effect, he asked it to give him the money needed to keep the government going for a year and then go home and let him and his task forces develop plans for action in 1964.

The legislative response wasn't what he had hoped for. Despite the fact that his former Young Turk allies had secured a great measure of control of the House (Franklin Billings had become the Speaker, and other Young Turks chaired most of the important committees), the legislature initially was as reluctant to defer to the Democratic governor as it had been to defer to Keyser. While legislative leaders ultimately agreed to return in 1964, they nonetheless rejected what they termed Hoff's "novel request" that they just go home, saying that they had a constitutional responsibility to enact a biennial budget and any legislation that went along with it. The legislature stayed in session for 175 days before adjourning on July 1. That was the shortest session in six years, but it was longer than Hoff had wanted and resulted in a larger budget than he

had asked for. At the end of the session, he rebuked the legislature, particularly the Senate, for "passing bills not in my budget . . . with little
thought of how they would be financed."

The Republican leadership saw things differently. Lieutenant Governor Ralph Foote of Middlebury, who had presided over the Senate
and was viewed as Hoff's most likely 1964 opponent, found agreement
with Republican national committeeman Edward Janeway (who also was
a state senator from Windham County) and Speaker Billings that "in
spite of the Governor's and some press protestations to the contrary, the
most significant [accomplishment of the session] was the spirit of absolute cooperation between the two political parties." The additional budget items, they said, were largely for education and mental health services that were widely considered, by legislators from both parties, to be
underfunded. The single largest budget increase had been the appropriation for the University of Vermont (another measure that had bipartisan
support), and all but two of Hoff's nominees had been confirmed. That
last was true enough, but Hoff noted that many of them had been Republicans to begin with and that he had appointed and reappointed so many
Republicans that it had provoked dissent within his own party.

The trio of Republican leaders were united in their response to
Hoff's rebuke but at the same time were different in their personalities
and their politics. Foote, a well-liked small-town lawyer, was a middle-of-
the-road Republican who still served as a captain in the Marine Reserves
and belonged to both the Veterans of Foreign Wars and the American
Legion. Among his other talents, at a political rally in Bristol in 1962
he had beaten all the other Republican candidates for Congress, governor, lieutenant governor, and attorney general in a corn-shucking contest. Janeway, tall and thin and patrician in both looks and manner, had
graduated from Yale, become a lieutenant commander in the navy, and
would have seemed as out of place at an American Legion or vFW club
bar (where Foote felt very much at home) as an Episcopal bishop playing
piano in a honky-tonk. A former New York investment broker, Janeway
had moved to Londonderry after the war, where he operated a dairy farm
and bred Guernsey cattle. He was still sometimes referred to by fellow
legislators as a "sun tanner," which is what people from away were often
called before the term "flatlander" came into wide use. He was somewhat
more liberal than the centrist Foote, while Billings was by far the most
liberal and least partisan of the three. Billings also had the more historic
Vermont roots. His father, Franklin Swift Billings Sr., had been a Speaker of the House, lieutenant governor, and then governor, and his uncle,

Frederick Billings, had gone west with the Gold Rush, opened the first law office in San Francisco, made a huge fortune from law and railroads, and then come back to Woodstock to buy the George Perkins Marsh estate that today is part of the Marsh-Billings-Rockefeller National Historical Park and also the Billings Farm and Museum.

Both Foote and Janeway had been a part of the Little Hoover Commission and thus were keenly aware of the structural defects in the executive branch. And all three understood that Hoff's call for dramatic change was resonating well with Vermonters. But giving Hoff and his programs the great exposure they would get in a special session could hurt Republicans in an election year, Foote in particular. So it was a striking manifestation of bipartisan cooperation when they agreed to have the legislature fund at least a part of the cost of the task forces and to reconvene "when it is decided what the study groups reveal in the way of legislative needs."

The previous March, Hoff had applied for and obtained a federal grant of $297,000 to help finance his one-year study program. To oversee the planning groups, he had picked Paul Guare, a native of Montpelier, a World War II veteran who had served with the Sixteenth Armored Division of Patton's Third Army, and a former reporter for the *Montpelier Evening Argus*. An amateur actor with the Montpelier Theater Guild, Guare also had worked as a location manager in Craftsbury and Stowe for the 1956 Alfred Hitchcock film *The Trouble with Harry*, and at the time was a lobbyist for the Vermont Petroleum Industry. Initially, he was recruited to become Bill Kearns's deputy in the Administration Department, but after the Democrats came into office the Republicans in the legislative appropriations committees cut the job out of the budget. So Hoff and Kearns put him in charge of coordinating the planning programs and paid him out of the federal grant. One of Guare's little-known but lasting legacies is that he first proposed lighting the State Capitol at night. He worked out a plan with Bob Burley, a Waitsfield architect who acted as the chief architect for the Capitol complex, to get the floodlights installed during Hoff's governorship, and the lights have been showcasing the building and its golden dome—proclaimed by John Gunther, the author of *Inside U.S.A.*, to be the most beautiful state capitol building in the nation—ever since. Guare's eight-person study council and the task forces it oversaw eventually would spend more than a million dollars and elicit testimony from a great number of Vermonters, which not only would help provide Hoff with the research and recommendations he needed but also would cause thousands of Vermonters to become more involved with their government. A minor downside for Hoff was that in his opening the process to new faces and a broad political spectrum, some Democratic insiders felt left out, particularly those Hoff aide Arthur Ristau liked to call "prenatal Democrats," born into families with a long history of party allegiance and, in many cases, rather conservative views. Many of those were working-class Democrats with strong union ties, and Hoff managed to placate some of them by resolving the Rutland Railroad controversy in a way that allowed the state to buy the 130-mile section of line from Bennington to Burlington and lease it to a private operator who would maintain at least some of the jobs.

At about the same time that the railroad controversy was being resolved, Hoff proposed a special two-day session in November to set priorities for dealing with some of the more important proposals from his study groups that would be introduced in the 1964 session. His proposal met with universal Republican disapproval. State Senator Asa Bloomer of Rutland had died during the regular session, and John Boylan of Island Pond, who succeeded him as Senate president pro tem, dismissed it as not having much worth. Foote used the occasion to attack Hoff for having reproached the Senate for passing bills without making provision for financing them, given that Hoff had refused to even consider a sales tax. He also criticized Hoff as "unprepared to govern." Even Billings, whom Hoff had singled out for praise when the 1963 session adjourned, condemned the idea as politically motivated and said that Hoff should present his whole package of proposals at one time, not offer them up piecemeal. U.S. Senator Aiken contributed to the anti-Hoff chorus by responding to Hoff's criticism about the state's education system by saying that "no one who runs down Vermont for any purpose is going to get any credit from me," a comment that suggested that even valid criticisms should be muted if they embarrassed Vermont. Hoff abandoned plans for a November session, both because of the opposition and because he suddenly had other concerns.

By the autumn of 1963 it had become apparent that west central Vermont, particularly Addison County and to a lesser extent Chittenden County, was experiencing a major drought, which it lacked sufficient manpower, equipment, and financial resources to deal with. On November 20, Hoff's request that Washington declare the region a disaster area was denied. The federal government had concluded that the drought wasn't serious enough to warrant a declaration or to spend federal money to deal with it. Hoff felt that the White House Office of Emergency Planning, which was headed by Edward McDermott, an Iowa Democrat who had managed Kennedy's Iowa campaign, didn't fully appreciate the situation. It didn't understand, Hoff said, that farmers in the area "were digging wells 400 feet deep and getting just a teacup full of water." He sent a telegram to President Kennedy asking him to reverse the decision. Kennedy in turn summoned McDermott to his office and told him to look into it personally.

McDermott recalled the Kennedy phone call in an interview with Associated Press reporter Chris Graff twenty years later. He had been surprised to receive a call on his direct line to the White House, he said, and the moment remained frozen in his memory. Kennedy ordered McDermott to hurry over to the Oval Office. When McDermott got there, he found the president packed and ready to leave for Texas. "He told me that the governor thought [Vermont] qualified for disaster relief and he said: 'You run up there and see Hoff. He's a good fellow. And I'll talk with you when I get back.'" Kennedy turned as he was still speaking, picked up his briefcase, and walked out of the office and through the Rose Garden to the waiting helicopter. McDermott was in Vermont the next day, and by the time he arrived back in Washington the day after that Kennedy had been murdered in Dallas. McDermott reported to President Johnson that Vermont indeed was experiencing a state of emergency, and Johnson quickly signed the forms declaring Addison and Chittenden counties disaster areas, setting in motion what became known as Operation Water Wagon. By the time it had concluded after seventy-six days, it had hauled in and pumped out almost 22 million gallons of water at a cost of about $127 million, of which 75 percent was paid by the federal government. It also caused Aiken to sponsor a Rural Water Bill that had a Vermont focus, and which Lyndon Johnson praised when he visited Vermont in 1966 to survey the results.

Drought relief operations for Addison and Chittenden counties were still in full swing when the special session convened in January. In a speech to the legislature that was written mainly by Kearns, Hoff laid out his plans for reorganization, reapportionment, and regionalization in ways that, much more than his inaugural address had, spelled out his vision for Vermont's future. In many ways, 1964 would prove to be the single most important year in Hoff's six-year administration. His first "bold new approach" program for the state, steeped in the concept of regionalization, would be rejected by the legislature, but he would go on to win a landslide reelection over Foote. Those two events would provide the leitmotif for the Hoff years, in which the public would be quicker to endorse and embrace him and his programs than the Republican-dominated legislature would be, and would underscore that support by giving him major victories at the polls.

The Hoff plan called for regional programs—as the alternative to what he said would have to be ultimate state takeovers—proposing regional schools, courts, highway districts, and tax assessments. He insisted he believed that "government is best that is closest to the people." But he also argued that many Vermont towns were so underpopulated and impoverished that they couldn't finance the services they were obligated to provide or that their citizens required. He proposed regionalization as a preferable alternative to having the state assume the funding and administrative functions. He also argued for countywide property appraising and assessment, not only because he believed it would bring in greater revenue but because he felt the existing system was plagued by unprofessionalism, guesswork, and favoritism. His arguments fell on deaf Republican ears. Many of the seventy-six bills introduced were killed outright, and many of those that passed were amended almost beyond recognition.

The strongest opposition was to his bill for regional schools, which flowed out of the recommendations from his task force on education. It called for the mandatory redistricting of Vermont's 254 local school districts into 12 districts, each with its own taxing power and superintendent. The bill was first shipped off to the Municipal Corporations Committee, where it was given an adverse report, and then to the House Education Committee, where it died. The bill was fiercely opposed by many small-town legislators, who saw it as the ultimate loss of local control. It also was opposed by the State Education Board, which was Republican dominated. The only floor debate came on the last day of the session, when Representative Richard Schmidt, a liberal Democrat from Burlington, tried to force the bill out of the committee for a floor vote and lost by a 125–75 margin.

The failure of the legislature to approve a regional school plan was one of Hoff's greatest disappointments. In his farewell address at the end of the session, he spoke about the defeat of this and other regionalization proposals, saying, "I regret that such a gulf of difference has opened between some of us. I know—I like and I respect many of you. But we can't seem to agree on the proper direction of Vermont's future." But while he failed to achieve reorganization of schools through a state-mandated method, his proposals stimulated discussions and debates about regional education that eventually brought about much voluntary consolidation of districts. By Hoff's last year in office, the Vermont Superintendents Association was adopting a resolution calling on school districts to reorganize on their own by 1974 or have it forced on them by the state, which was a striking change in attitude. While unsuccessful efforts to mandate consolidation of school districts would continue into the twenty-first century, many of the union school districts that eventually came into existence owed their creation to some degree to the efforts of Hoff and his task force. Most of his proposals for reorganization of state agencies would be enacted after he left, with the Republicans quickly putting into place things they had refused to do during his tenure. And the regional planning that he launched eventually became not only accepted but routine.

One of the successes Hoff did have during the 1964 session was the creation of a college loan guarantee program for Vermont students, and like much that he accomplished, Hoff did it by sidestepping the legislature and going directly to the people. The bill, the precursor of the Vermont Student Assistance Corporation (VSAC), initially went to the Republican-dominated House Banking and Corporations Committee. It was killed there by a 4–1 vote, with the committee barely looking at it, let alone studying it. But Hoff then generated enough pressure from school officials, teachers, education groups, and citizens that the legislature backpedaled like a bear cub that had run into a porcupine. The bill was revived in the Senate and passed. Eventually, Hoff would take great pride in the VSAC, which he had instigated, saying that without it there would have been "thousands of Vermont kids who could not have gone to college." Another success was additional funding for state aid to education, which raised Vermont's per-pupil spending closer to the national average.

Despite his distress about the defeat of the bill to consolidate school districts, Hoff said the "most tragic loss" in 1964 was the legislature's refusal to pass a bill that would have regulated the use of land in the state. Prompted by recommendations from the Scenic and Historic Sites Review Panel, the bill was intended to protect Vermont's scenic countryside from sprawling junkyards, unsightly road signs, and other clutter by imposing uniform standards of zoning. Hoff argued that this was necessary to help preserve the "untouched quality" of Vermont that was luring "hundreds of thousands of visitors" every year and that was going to be important to the economic future of the state as a whole. The defeat of the bill reinforced for Hoff the importance of reapportionment, since he felt it had been killed by small-town legislators putting the parochial interests of their individual towns—and their insistence on local control—ahead of the interests of the state.

During the session, Hoff received support for most of his proposals from such former Young Turk Republican allies as John Downs of St. Johnsbury and Anthony Farrell of Norwich. Billings wasn't totally supportive, but never provided the polarizing opposition that would mark the speakership of his successor and fellow Young Turk Richard Mallary of Fairlee. Hoff's closing remarks to the House, in fact, were full of kind words for Billings. In the Senate, where Foote presided, Hoff pointedly refrained from mentioning the lieutenant governor. When asked about this omission at a press conference afterward, Hoff said tartly, "He's just like all the other Republican candidates for governor." And when a reporter noted that Foote hadn't yet officially announced that he was running, Hoff lifted an eyebrow and said rather disdainfully, "Yes? Well, you'd think he had by the way he's been talking."

So the session ended with the battle lines drawn. Hoff had spelled out clearly his vision for Vermont's future, and it had been rejected overwhelmingly by the Republican legislature. Hoff now intended to carry the fight to the electorate, making the Republican rejection of his programs the chief focus of his reelection campaign and casting Foote as a chief villain. And while most Vermonters didn't yet know it, the adjournment also marked the end of an era. The previous October a three-judge federal panel had begun hearing testimony in *Buckley v. Hoff*, a suit that had been brought in hopes of forcing reapportionment of both houses of the legislature. The court was still deliberating in June 1964 when the deliberations were made irrelevant by the U.S. Supreme Court decision in the case of *Reynolds v. Sims*, in which the Court declared that both houses of state legislatures needed to be apportioned by population. So while reorganization had been stalled and regionalization had been defeated, legislative reapportionment was very much at hand.

Except for the first seven years under the Vermont constitution (when towns with eighty or more taxable inhabitants elected two delegates and all smaller towns elected one delegate to the state legislature), all towns, irrespective of population, historically had been guaranteed a single vote in the legislature. Until 1835, Vermont had a unicameral legislature, but in 1836 it added a thirty-seat county-based Senate apportioned by population, with each county guaranteed at least one senator. This system, in which Vermont had a House membership based on geography (in this case, townships) and a Senate membership based on population, was just the reverse of the federal system, where the House membership was based on population while the Senate membership was based on geography. In the beginning, Vermont's towns were created as arbitrary boundaries cutting up the countryside without regard for economics or geography. In fact, most towns had been laid out before they had any people living in them and had remained unchanged through nearly two centuries of development and shifting populations. Over time the disparities in population widened, and by the time Hoff reached the legislature in 1961 he represented more people in Burlington alone than representatives of the 107 smallest towns combined.

The Senate, particularly after it complied with the court ruling in the *Mikell v. Rousseau* case in 1962, closely reflected population. With 47 percent of the senators representing a popular majority, it ranked third among all the upper houses of state legislatures in terms of true representation by population. The House, in contrast, was the third-most-malapportioned legislative body in the nation. It was more rural, more Republican, and had a much greater percentage of farmers in it than the state as a whole. It was dominated by small towns, including some that had too few residents to even fill all the legally required town offices, meaning that some individuals had to hold multiple offices if the town was to function. Before it finally was disincorporated by the legislature in 1937 as not even a pretense of a municipality, the town of Glastenbury had been featured in Robert Ripley's syndicated newspaper cartoon *Believe It or Not!* as having every single public office held by Ira Mattison, his wife, or his mother. That was close to the truth but not exactly, because Rowland Hazard, a wealthy Rhode Islander who owned land there, also held several posts. But Ira Mattison in fact was the town clerk, as well as an auditor, selectman, lister, road commissioner, grand juror, fire warden, and health officer. He also was the state representative, although he seems never to have shown up in Montpelier for the 1937 session. That was a loss for the Democrats, because in addition to everything else, Ira Mattison was a Democrat, as were his wife and mother. All three of Glastenbury's presidential votes in 1936 had gone to Franklin Roosevelt.

Hoff and like-minded critics of the system argued that one consequence of the malapportioned House was that it consistently voted to divert an excessive share of state revenues to towns that were too small to function efficiently. In point of fact, in the 1961 legislature the representatives from forty of the smallest towns received more money in salary and expenses than their constituents had paid to the state in income taxes that year. Although he technically was the defendant in *Buckley v. Hoff*, no one expected Hoff to put up a defense, and in the end it was the real opponents of reapportionment, mostly small-town legislators, who created the "Committee to Defend the Vermont Constitution" to try to block it.

Buckley v. Hoff had been brought by T. Garry Buckley of Bennington and A. Luke Crispe of Brattleboro on behalf of the Vermont Independent Party. When they had formed the party in 1962 as a means of helping Hoff get Republican votes, they decided that a party needed a platform, even if it was a limited one. "We decided we would go to federal court and sue to have Vermont properly apportioned," Buckley said. "It was the only plank in our platform. We may have been the only party in history that kept all its campaign promises, because we only had one."

Unlike *Mikell v. Rousseau*, which argued in a Vermont court that the Senate's failure to reapportion violated the state constitution, *Buckley v. Hoff* was a federal suit charging that both houses of the Vermont legislature were so malapportioned that they violated the equal protection clause of the U.S. Constitution. The arguments were heard by a three-judge tribunal presided over by Second Circuit Judge Sterry Waterman, a St. Johnsbury attorney who had been a prominent member of the Aiken-Gibson wing of the Republican Party. He had managed George Aiken's gubernatorial campaign in 1936 and had been the assistant secretary of the Vermont Senate when Ernest Gibson Jr. was the secretary. When Aiken first proposed Waterman for a federal judgeship, President Dwight D. Eisenhower hesitated and asked for other nominations. But Vermont's other Republican senator, Ralph Flanders, who didn't agree with Aiken on many things (he was more conservative and more pro-business on many issues but had been more aggressive in fighting McCarthyism), joined Aiken in pressing for the appointment, and Waterman was named to the federal bench in 1957.

Waterman's tribunal was still deliberating the issue when the U.S. Supreme Court, in *Reynolds v. Sims*, ruled that both houses of any state legislature had to be apportioned by population. And so on July 19, 1964, Waterman's panel voided those sections of the Vermont constitution that guaranteed every county at least one senator irrespective of population and that guaranteed every town a representative no matter what the size of its population. It also rejected the argument that since the "time-lock" provision of Vermont's constitution required ten-year intervals for proposing amendments, immediate reapportionment itself was unconstitutional. It ruled, as almost everyone who had ever taken a college class in constitutional law assumed that it would, that "when there is unavoidable conflict between federal and state constitutions, the supremacy clause controls" and the federal constitution prevails.

The court further determined that since Vermont election law required persons seeking nomination to the House or to the Senate to file their petitions on or before July 29, just ten days away, the election had to proceed as scheduled "to avoid too much sudden disruption of the State's political way of life." In short, it ruled that the legislature could be elected in November 1964 as planned, but that it would have a term of only one year and that its only legislative business would be to reapportion itself, adjourn by March, and then hold elections for the newly reapportioned legislature in November 1965. It did, however, allow for a hearing later that month at which contending attorneys would submit plans for implementing the ruling.

Some hard-line opponents pledged an appeal. Chief among these was Samuel A. Parsons, the twelve-term Republican member from Hubbardton (population 238), a town that had been losing population since 1820. Parsons, who also was the Hubbardton town clerk and town treasurer, had been in the legislature since 1939, and the House Conservation and Development Committee that he chaired—a committee consisting mostly of members from such tiny communities as Rochester, Victory, Whitingham, Morgan, and Mount Tabor—had become the clearinghouse for small-town pork-barrel legislation. Parsons had argued before the three-judge panel that small towns were crucial to the national security because they could continue to function in the event of a nuclear attack, while the more complex urban areas would be paralyzed by the destruction of their power, water, and highway systems. But it was to the anti-reapportionment Committee to Defend the Vermont Constitution that he expressed his real concern, warning that if the small towns lost control of the House, they wouldn't be able to shift the public works programs away from the cities any longer.

Hilton Wick, the Burlington attorney for the anti-reapportionment group, asked the court to allow the legislature to have at least until July to reapportion itself. Hoff, who had promptly formed a committee to study and recommend reapportioned districts, concurred, and the court amended its ruling to authorize a longer session and also to permit the conduct of any other "necessary" business. And with that, the main focus of public attention turned to the upcoming state and national elections.

Under usual circumstances, presidential election years in Vermont boded ill for Democrats. Anticipating a difficult campaign, state chairman Jack Spencer had announced back in the autumn of 1963 that the Democratic Party strategy for 1964 would be to concentrate on Hoff's reelection, even if it meant paying little attention to others. There was evidence of this early in the campaign. Folk music had become popular in the country in the early 1960s, and the husband-and-wife folk-singing duet of Sandy and Caroline Paton had moved to the Burlington area, where they and a financial backer, Lee Haggerty, had created Folk Legacy records. In addition to producing folk-music albums, mostly from Appalachia, they wrote and sang a song for the Hoff campaign that was broadcast endlessly from a sound truck that Maxine Kenny, a young Michigan transplant and liberal activist, drove around the state to county fairs, local festivals, political gatherings, and other kinds of public events. The song focused on Hoff and no one else.

> Philip Hoff is the man
> The man with the plan
> For our great Green Mountain state
> So in 1964
> Send him back for two years more
> Together with his running mate

If genial Jack Daley, the mayor of Rutland and the candidate for lieutenant governor, objected to not even being named in one of his party's most popular and most repeated promotions, he kept it to himself. For a time, there was speculation that Hoff was considering asking Luke Crispe to be his running mate, in hopes of once again getting Independent Party support. Jack Spencer's 1963 emphasis on Hoff and Hoff alone had been based on his concern that the party still lacked the resources to run multiple campaigns. But by 1964 circumstances were changing, including those of Spencer.

Back in December of 1963 President Johnson had phoned Hoff, asking him to be part of a delegation from the United States attending celebrations to mark the independence of Zanzibar. Hoff had quickly agreed, although he "hadn't the foggiest idea" where Zanzibar was. As soon as the conversation ended he "ran to the atlas" and found that it was an island nation off the east coast of Africa, one of the so-called Spice Islands and a major exporter of cloves, nutmeg, cinnamon, and pepper. Spencer, who was a heavy drinker, wanted to go on the trip, but there wasn't another seat on the plane. "Jack wanted to go very badly, and the fact that he couldn't be part of the party set him off on a fatal binge," a Hoff aide recalled. "He simply couldn't accept not being chosen. There was some talk that he felt he had earned it as a reward for his part in bringing about Phil's election." The aide recalled that for a time Spencer would call in to check on things but wouldn't come into the office, and then even stopped calling. Then they got word that he was in a treatment facility. In January he resigned his position, issuing a statement saying "The facts are I am an alcoholic. . . . Since alcoholism is a major social malady, if we are to meet our responsibilities we must be willing to speak openly of these things with the candor and honesty they demand." Hoff acknowledged that Spencer had lost his battle with alcohol but predicted that he would "win the war and return to the fold." That didn't happen. Spencer spent time in a sanatorium and then died the following year in a Massachusetts hospital. He was just forty-seven.

Others were more aggressive in their thinking, insisting that Hoff no longer needed the Vermont Independent Party and urging broader and more intense campaigns by the whole ticket. The choice of Daley, who was Irish and Catholic, a World War II Marine Corps veteran, and the mayor of the state's second-largest city, played to the party's core constituency. Daley was a graduate of Norwich University and the father of eleven—two sons and nine daughters. He didn't have the vision of Hoff or the sharp mind of Richard Snelling, who would be the Republican nominee for lieutenant governor, but he had a pleasant and endlessly upbeat manner, a good deal of common sense, and was well liked personally even by people who opposed him politically. And by the time Hoff formally announced in July that he would seek reelection, the Republicans were mired in internecine warfare, making the Democrats more optimistic than when Spencer had cautioned against high expectations.

Both Foote and Janeway had endorsed the presidential candidacy of New York governor Nelson Rockefeller, a leader of the liberal Republicans, and Janeway had specifically rebuffed a request by the conservative Arizona senator Barry Goldwater for support. The fight between Rockefeller and Goldwater for the GOP nomination spilled over into the Vermont campaign. Foote was the chairman of the Vermont delegation to the party's national convention in San Francisco, where Goldwater won the nomination without receiving a single Vermont vote. Foote came home with a candidate whose politics he didn't share heading the national ticket and quickly found himself embroiled in a tougher primary fight than he had anticipated. Usually the state Republican primaries had been between moderately liberal and seriously conservative Republicans. But in 1964 the centrist Foote found himself challenged both by Robert Babcock, a UVM professor and former lieutenant governor who often seemed more of a Democrat than a liberal Republican, and Roger McBride of Halifax, who arguably was even more conservative than Goldwater. Babcock had been a football, basketball, and baseball player at the University of Rochester (he would later be named to the school's Athletic Hall of Fame, mostly for his heroics on the football field), and then a Rhodes Scholar at Oxford. A fellow Rhodes Scholar at the time, Penn Kimball, a journalist and teacher, later told one of his students at Columbia, knowing that he was a Vermonter, that after a night of heavy drinking and angry debate in a British pub, Babcock once had pounded his fist on the table and insisted to his fellow scholars, "Wait and see. Hitler will flower into something finer!" As the provost of the state colleges, a position he would be put in by Hoff, he would go on to play a key role in transforming the state's three "teachers colleges" at Castleton, Lyndon, and Johnson into a more serious and far more prestigious state college system. McBride, a cherubic-looking man with a pink, round face who favored three-piece suits even in summertime, later would become a Libertarian candidate for president, piloting his own campaign plane, a propeller-driven DC-3 that he called "No Force One." A graduate of Princeton and Harvard Law School, McBride had inherited the estate of an old family friend, Rose Wilder Lane, that included the copyrights to the books of Lane's mother, Laura Ingalls Wilder. This eventually made McBride very wealthy when he turned one of the books, *Little House on the Prairie*, into the hugely successful television series by the same name. But that would come later, and in 1964 McBride's main focus was campaigning against Foote and organizing efforts to fight reapportionment. Foote eventually won, with 42.8 percent of the vote. McBride got 21 percent and Babcock 36.3 percent. But the primary underscored the fact that Foote wasn't as liberal as many of the state's liberal Republicans and couldn't be counted on to fight reapportionment in ways that conservative Republicans wanted.

The Democrats had primaries of their own for the U.S. House and Senate, but both Hoff and Daley ran unopposed. The fact that almost two and half times as many votes were cast in the Republican primary as in the Democratic contest was encouraging to some Republicans, who thought the state ticket might survive even if Goldwater went down to defeat. Foote was well liked, and in later years, when he no longer was a threat, Hoff would describe him as having been an excellent legislator.

But Hoff was determined to "prove that 1962 was no fluke" and campaigned as intensely as he had two years earlier but with far more people to help him and more resources to work with. For the most part, the campaign was focused on issues, with Hoff stressing the need for reapportionment and regionalization and criticizing Republican efforts to block reorganization by not letting him combine state agencies (he wanted to reduce the number from thirty-three to twelve) and eliminate many of the boards and commissions. Foote argued that he would be a better manager and more prudent steward, while accusing Hoff of trying to force his progressive programs down the throats of citizens who didn't really want them.

Then, on October 21, just twelve days before the election, it turned nasty. Foote created a political firestorm by charging that "offices of public trust have been bought and sold within the Hoff administration," without saying which offices had been bought and sold or whom they had been bought by and sold to. It wasn't until the next day that Burlington attorney Clark Gravel, a Foote backer, drove down to Montpelier for a news conference to detail the charge. What it came down to was that Stephen Vince, a Democrat and an unsuccessful candidate for a rural postal carrier's route in North Bennington, had claimed that the appointment had been given to John Powers and not to him after someone (who never was named) gave someone (Vince said he didn't know just who) $2,000 to secure it. And Vince said that he had told this to Hoff when he complained about not getting the job.

The plural "jobs" had turned out to be one, and instead of being "in the Hoff administration" it turned out to be a job that Hoff had no direct control over and said he had never gotten involved with. Hoff acknowledged that Vince had complained to him but said he had told Vince that he had nothing to do with such appointments in the past and didn't intend to start trying to involve himself now. And he lashed back furiously at Foote, calling the allegations "a pure smear" and evidence of Foote's "bankrupt leadership and the desperation of his campaign." He also said that if Foote really thought that offices had been bought and sold he should have taken his evidence to the attorney general, Charles Gibson, and had been "derelict in his duty" for not having done so.

Immediately after Gravel detailed the charge, Hoff met with Kearns, Guare, his secretary of civil and military affairs Thomas Kenny, and Benjamin Collins, another former journalist who had joined Hoff's staff, to craft a rebuttal. Hoff was going to be on television that night, and he wanted to make the strongest possible immediate response to the charge.

Even through the closed doors, reporters waiting outside could hear Hoff shouting "I don't want to blame the *Republicans*, I want to blame *Foote!*"

What Hoff eventually said was "The job in question here is a job I have absolutely nothing to do with. If you will look at his original statement yesterday you will discover what he said was 'offices of public trust were purchased and sold within the Hoff administration.' I think that we then had a right to think he was going to talk about some appointment made by me. Instead, he talks about a Federal job that I have nothing, absolutely nothing, to do with. These jobs are strictly the province of the Democratic party and I have told people who have come in to complain to me as people did in this instance that this was not my province. I kept my hands off it completely. I had never interfered with even one of them."

The reality, of course, was that while civil service tests were a part of the process, politics had always played a major role in postal appointments, and the people who got them were expected to, at the least, make political contributions to the party that awarded them. Fred Fayette, who in this same election was running for the U.S. Senate on the Democratic ticket, would later be charged and convicted of receiving $3,000 for his promise to try to arrange the appointment of a postmastership in St. Johnsbury. Fayette's trial wouldn't take place until 1966, but the payment had been accepted (and later returned when someone else got the job) in 1963.

In this case, the attack by Foote backfired. The state's two largest newspapers, the *Burlington Free Press* and the *Rutland Herald*, criticized Foote for having overstated his case, and the *Bennington Banner*, where Phil Savory now was working, said in an editorial, "We can only conclude that unless Foote provides more substantial evidence to back up his original charges . . . that he has embarked on a deliberate strategy to win the gubernatorial election by campaign tactics of smear, innuendo and distortion."

When Hoff realized the extent of the backfire, he used a tape recording of Foote making the charge in radio commercials that strongly rebutted the charge and ended with Hoff saying, "Is this the kind of man you want for governor?"

Hoff defeated Foote by almost 50,000 votes, which by the standards of Vermont was a landslide of epic proportions. Robert Stafford, running for reelection to the U.S. House, and Winston Prouty, running for reelection to the U.S. Senate, were the only major Republican candidates to escape defeat. Hoff collected more votes than any previous gubernatorial candidate of either party, despite there being fewer total votes cast in

1964 than in 1960. Lyndon Johnson, who outpolled Hoff by 1,500 votes, became the first Democrat to capture the state's electoral vote for president and did so with only 2,000 fewer votes than Eisenhower's 1956 record total.

These were startling results from what had hitherto been a Republican stronghold, but even more startling was the fact that the Democratic tide pulled the entire slate of statewide candidates—lieutenant governor, attorney general, treasurer, secretary of state, and auditor of accounts—into office. Foote and Snelling didn't even carry their hometowns. Ousted were David Anderson, who had been auditor since 1941; George Amidon, who had been treasurer since 1949; and Howard Armstrong, who had been secretary of state since 1949. The new treasurer was eighty-one-year-old Middlebury banker Peter J. Hincks, who had first run for treasurer in 1938 and had been a fixture on the Democratic ticket (although always an unsuccessful one) ever since. In an interview given right after his election, he told a reporter that Amidon had been a good treasurer who had deserved reelection and it had never been his intention to beat him. Harry Cooley, the newly elected secretary of state, told Ron Cohen, the United Press International reporter who tracked him down for an early morning postelection interview, that he didn't have time to talk about it because he had to finish milking his cows.

Hoff saw his reelection and his 50,000-vote margin as both a personal vindication and as a mandate to press ahead with his vision for change. And the huge victory in a presidential year meant that there would be no more need for Democratic "still hunts" in which they would sneak up on and try to ambush unsuspecting Republicans. The victory was so large and so sweeping that even the "Sam Miller Rule" for focusing on just one strong Democratic candidate in an off-year election now seemed superfluous. Four years after he was elected to the legislature and two years after he was first elected governor by the narrowest of margins, the real "Hoff Era" had begun.

CHAPTER 3

THE HOFF ERA IN FULL FLOWER

It was just after 3:30 on the afternoon of Friday, May 14, 1965, when the vote to reapportion the Vermont House of Representatives came to an end. The temperature outside was in the high eighties, and the sun was shining brightly off the Capitol's golden dome. Originally the dome had been painted a dark terracotta red to suggest Tuscan tile. That had been changed to gold leaf in the early twentieth century, but much of the interior of the State House still looked much as it had back in Victorian times. The House chamber had an ornate red carpet, a huge gaslight chandelier that had been electrified, and, above the Speaker's chair, the large portrait of George Washington that was one the few things rescued from the fire that had gutted the building back in 1857. The floor rose at a slight incline from the well of the chamber to the rear and side walls, creating a legislative amphitheater in which the seats in the back rows were higher than those in the front. Spittoons were still positioned around many of the black-walnut desks, although tobacco chewing was largely a thing of the past. Representative Fred Westphal, a Republican from Elmore and a conservative contrarian who had once boasted "I don't ask my constituents to vote for me—I dare them to," was one of the few who still used them for their original purpose. Most of the other legislators used them as ashtrays. It was, in many ways, a nineteenth-century building housing a legislature that Hoff had criticized as not having yet moved entirely into the twentieth.

The votes had been counted, but House Speaker Billings was waiting for several lawmakers to explain their votes before announcing the official tally. His delay didn't add to the suspense. After four months of spirited and often-contentious debate, and after a tense and close vote two days earlier in which opponents had come very close to a victory, it had been a lopsided final vote, and the expressions on the faces of people in the chamber left no doubt which side had won. Up in the balcony with the spectators, Governor Hoff was looking down with a satisfied smile.

By tradition, governors never entered the House or Senate chambers unless invited in by the members, and Hoff later said his going there as a spectator had been a mistake. But it was a day in which a far more important tradition was ending, and Hoff wanted to be there when it happened. To the left of Billings and five rows away, sitting in seat number 191, Republican representative Frank Hutchins, a sixty-six-year-old farmer from Stannard, had tears in his eyes.

Stannard was a town of just 113 residents in Caledonia County, located north of Danville and west of Wheelock. It had three cemeteries but no stores. Originally it had been called Goshen Gore No. 1, but it had been elevated to town status after the Civil War and had been named for Brigadier General George Stannard, a hero of Gettysburg, who had ordered two regiments of his Second Vermont Brigade into a crucially timed and well-executed flanking maneuver whose devastating fire had helped break Pickett's charge. Hutchins was the chairman of the town's temperance committee, as well as the state representative. The tears had begun flowing down his cheeks as his small and uncomplicated world came crashing down. When he stood to speak, he said he regretted it deeply "when outsiders come into this parlor and tear us to pieces," and then—having vowed never again to run for election—implored the legislators who would be returning, "Don't forget Stannard."

Thomas Salmon, the freshman Democratic House member from Rockingham and later a two-term governor, found Hutchins's speech very moving. But his admiration that day was for Vivian Tuttle, the fifty-two-year-old town clerk and Republican representative from Stratton, which, with a population of thirty-eight, had fewer residents even than Stannard. It had a church but no schools, gas stations, or grocery stores. Most of the homes were owned by summer residents, and the town was so heavily forested that it may have had more bears than people. She was "a little lady," Salmon recalled many years later, "very short, diminutive, a very slight build, with her hands literally quaking—she wasn't a public speaker." His lasting memory of that day was of her bravely getting up to explain "why she was going to vote in favor of reapportionment and vote herself out of a job."

Hutchins was the last to speak from the floor. As soon as he sat back in his chair, Billings banged his gavel and announced, "Now listen to the result of your vote. Ayes, 163, nays, 62. The bill passes." Twenty-one members had abstained, but the Vermont House—after having been warned by a federal court that the court would impose a reapportionment plan of its own if the legislature didn't approve one that gave all Vermonters equal votes—had voted to reapportion itself from 246 to 150 members, with each of the 150 representing roughly the same number of people. Edward J. Conlin, a Windsor Republican, stood up and said rather solemnly, "Time marches on." Hoff was less solemn. He spun around in the balcony, brushed through the curtained doorway, let out a series of exclamations that sounded like "Whoa! Whoo-o-o-oa! Wowz!" and bounded down the stairs and back to his office.

The 1965 legislature had organized itself knowing that its main business would have to be reapportionment. Despite the record number of Democrats in both houses, the Republicans still retained large majorities. In the House, 173 of the 246 members were Republicans, more often than not representing small towns. The House membership included eighty-one farmers or retired farmers, forty-five women (eighteen of them listing themselves as "housewives"), four lawyers, four restaurant owners, three carpenters, a school bus driver, a stonecutter, a geologist, a radio and television repairman, and a paperhanger. The first business of the House was to elect a Speaker, and although it wasn't much commented on at the time, Billings became the first Speaker in more than fifty years to be reelected to a second term. He pledged to "preside impartially" and—knowing that reapportionment would require scores of Republicans to vote themselves out of office—began the reapportionment process with two moves that seemed questionable at the time but that later came to be seen as strategically wise. The first was to ask Hoff to remain quietly on the sideline so that reapportionment wouldn't be seen as a partisan Democratic effort. If the Republicans had to vote themselves out of office, Billings thought it would be better to have it seen as being done with Republican leadership and mainly by the Republicans themselves. Hoff agreed to do this, so long as the process stayed on track.

Hoff had never been on the sideline in the past, and in the end he wouldn't be here. When Buckley and Crispe had first brought their suit in federal court in 1963 to try to force reapportionment, Hoff had been named as the defendant, but in fact it had been his Burlington law firm that had done most of the legal work for the plaintiffs. And as soon as the federal court had ordered the legislature to reapportion itself, Hoff had assembled a group to begin planning the size and shape of the new legislature. Reapportionment had been a major issue for him from his very first days in the legislature. But during the first part of the 1965 session he agreed to keep a low profile and let Billings take the lead.

The second move by Billings was to name Emory Hebard, a very conservative Republican from the small town of Glover (population 683), to head the newly formed House Committee on Reapportionment, which would be charged with developing a plan. Hoff was stunned by Billings's choice, since Hebard not only was a conservative but someone who had carefully cultivated an image as a rusticated Vermonter committed to thrift in government and small-town values. In fact, he had been born in Maine, had a Phi Beta Kappa key from Middlebury College, and hadn't settled in Glover until 1952, where he ran a small country store and was a real estate broker. But he had developed the persona of a ninth-generation native whose outlook on life—and advocacy of self-reliance, staunch patriotism, and minimal government—might have been shaped by two centuries of living on hill farms, with time out to help fight the nation's wars. He had a sharp mind and a quick wit and had used them not just to advocate his own causes but to ridicule things he opposed, including much of Hoff's "bold new approach" for Vermont. The more Hoff stewed about the appointment, the more angry he became. But Billings believed that Hebard would be uniquely able to persuade fellow legislators that they should adopt a reapportionment plan of their own rather than have one imposed by the federal court, saying that he was sure Hebard "would do the right thing because he didn't want the federal government to do the wrong thing." He later recalled trying to mollify Hoff by telling him, "Emory Hebard can get the small towns to realize this is the law, even though they're voting themselves out of office. And we can't get them. I can't get them and you can't get them. And it'll work out."

The new twenty-five-member committee that Billings set up for Hebard to chair was itself a work of legislative shrewdness. It included some of the fiercest and most-vocal foes of reapportionment, including Sam Parsons, the Hubbardton Republican, who insisted "cities aren't healthy-minded. . . . You lose sight [when you live in a city] of what's honorable and dishonorable"; Representative Kenalene Collins, Republican of Readsboro, who argued in an anti-reapportionment floor speech that—despite all evidence to the contrary—the state's cities were financially "busted" and just wanted reapportionment passed so they could force the small towns to foot the bills; and Representative W. Clark Hutchinson, a Republican from Rochester (population 879), who had urged fellow legislators to chain themselves to their chairs and refuse to give them up to any new representatives elected under a federal court order. If anyone had the nerve to do it, it probably would have been the sixty-seven-year-old Hutchinson. A former cow puncher in Texas, apple picker in Oregon, and lumberjack in Washington, he had served in both the world wars, as a marine in the first and in the Coast Guard in the second, and had a manner that was both forceful and confident. He also was no fool. Born in New York City, he had been a Phi Beta Kappa graduate of Princeton and earned a law degree from Columbia. He said on the day of the reapportionment vote, "We know there is such a thing as honor and the sanctity of an oath, and we intend to preserve it. We know that forced reapportionment is the loss of self-government, and we intend to fight it, and we intend to vote against it now and forever." But he didn't chain himself to his seat. Instead—along with fellow Princeton graduate Roger McBride—he set out to wage a spirited but unsuccessful court fight to have reapportionment reversed. The Hutchinson-McBride suit would drag on as spring turned to summer and summer turned to fall, and finally Chester Ketchum, a deputy attorney general charged with defending the state, pulled McBride aside in a courtroom and told him, "Roger, I don't mind doing this now. It's your right to be here, and it's my job to represent the state. But if this thing drags on into November and I have to stay in court during the deer season, then, by God, I'm going to get mad." The McBride-Hutchinson suit finally was rejected by the Vermont Supreme Court on November 18, and Ketchum went off to deer camp.

A casual look at the membership of the reapportionment committee created by Billings suggested a major tilt toward the small towns. It had members from Glover, Cornwall, Weybridge, Hubbardton, Proctor, Stratton, Norwich, Berlin, Sherburne, Vershire, Rochester, Townshend, Bloomfield, Alburg, Irasburg, Lyndon, Milton, and Elmore. But a careful examination of the list showed that Billings had stacked the deck, or at least crafted the committee in a way that there was good reason to think an acceptable bill would result.

One of the Republicans was Cornelius Granai of Barre, whose city clearly would benefit from reapportionment. So would St. Johnsbury, which also had a Republican representative on the committee. The tiny community of Weybridge was represented by a thoughtful and liberal Republican, Arthur Gibb, while the member from Cornwall (population 756) was another thoughtful Republican who had taught at Middlebury College. When the six members from cities were combined with a Democrat from tiny Alburg, the liberal and moderate Republicans, and the nervous but courageous Vivian Tuttle from Stratton, there were thirteen

likely votes for reapportionment right from the start, not counting Hebard, whom Billings had confidence in while Hoff still had his doubts
about.

Given their different starting points, it was assumed that reapportionment of the thirty-member Senate would be fast and relatively pain-
less, and it was. If the Senate were to retain the requirement that each
county be guaranteed a senator, reapportionment would require adding many members. In fact, the Senate would have to nearly double its
size. Among other things, that would require the Senate chamber itself
to be redesigned or relocated, because there wasn't enough room for sixty desks, even if some of them were pushed back into the visitors gal-
lery or moved up into the balcony. That was never considered. Instead, it
was decided to keep the thirty-person size and the Civil War–era desks
and chairs and reapportion by removing the stipulation that every county had to have at least one senator of its own. The decision was to combine the most thinly populated counties with larger ones, specifically by
combining Grand Isle with Chittenden and Essex with Orleans.

From the very start, calls for House reapportionment had assumed
there would be fewer members, not more, and that many incumbents
from the smallest towns would lose their seats. But the debate over just
what the size should be ended up being both protracted and fierce, which
was why reapportionment didn't proceed as expeditiously as Hoff and
Billings had hoped it would.

Early in the session the House passed an advisory bill supporting the
idea of a 210-member House, which Hoff was quick to oppose. "This is
not the time to engage in nostalgia," he said. "It is a time to embrace the
realities of the present and hopes for the future." He believed that a majority of Vermonters not only favored a smaller House, but felt strongly
that a House of 90 to 150 members "would better meet the needs of our
state." Certainly he knew it would be one in which Democrats and liberal Republicans could exert more influence when working together. He
warned that if a bill passed for a 210-member House, he would give "serious consideration" to vetoing it. But the House came close to doing just
that in the last days of the debate.

Some legislators, noting the makeup of the federal government itself, argued that there was nothing in the U.S. Constitution to prohibit
a state with a bicameral legislature from having one chamber based on
something other than population. The U.S. Senate, of course, had two
members from every state, no matter what the size. Early in the session,
more than seventy representatives sponsored a resolution petitioning the

Congress of the United States to call a convention of state legislatures to amend the Constitution to specifically permit such a structure. Billings was among the sponsors, as was Hebard. Some of this may have been just posturing—a last stand of resistance before final compliance—and indeed two of the most adamant opponents of reapportionment, Sam Parsons and W. Clark Hutchinson, didn't bother to sign it.

Nonetheless, opposition remained strong and passionate, and Billings finally gave up on his efforts to push through reapportionment as a wholly Republican effort. About midway through the session he turned to Hoff and said it was time to join forces, and they met with legislative leaders from both parties at the Venetian, the Italian restaurant that Vergilio Bonacorsi operated in Barre's North End. The Venetian was a family-style restaurant, with checkered tablecloths and very large portions. While Bonacorsi prided himself on his veal dishes, most people went there for the less expensive but filling spaghetti and meatballs. The participants agreed over dinner that a Republican-Democratic coalition would be formed to support a bill for a 150-member House.

Tom Salmon said that both Hoff and Billings had argued forcefully that moderates in both parties needed to come together and agree on a single bill "so we could move on with our life and not find ourselves embarrassingly in violation of the Federal order to get reapportionment done." He said it never would have happened without the close cooperation between Billings and Hoff, and that "the success story of reapportionment, getting the job done, was truly bipartisan." But there were doubts about the 150-member House plan right until the end, with Daulton Mann, the liberal Republican from Peru, gloomily predicting just a week before the vote that it would never get a majority.

The opponents included Parsons, Collins, Hutchinson, and Royal B. Cutts, a Republican tree farmer from Townshend who insisted they were trying to "preserve the rights of minorities." The critical vote came on May 12, when—after two days of fiercely passionate debate—the House defeated two amendments by conservatives calling for a reapportionment plan that would create a 210-member House. The amendments differed in that one would have allowed a maximum of 15 percent in population differences between districts, while the other, offered by Hutchinson (who said he would still vote against any reapportionment plan even if his amendment was adopted) would have allowed deviations of up to 27 percent. The key vote was on the Hutchinson plan, which had the all-out support of conservatives and the backing of a handful of small-town Democrats. It was rejected by just 10 votes, 124 to 114, causing jubilation among the Democrats and those moderate and liberal Republicans who favored the 150-member House plan. "It's wonderful to be wrong once in a while," Mann said.

And then, on May 14, as Hoff watched from the balcony, a Hebard-sponsored bill calling for a 150-member House with multimember districts was brought to a vote. By this point, everything that could be said on the subject already had been said, and the final arguments were the expected and obvious ones. Rural opponents argued that reapportionment would mean the death of small towns and the end of Vermont's history, tradition, and way of life. Twenty-four years later, in fact, Hebard would say that he still felt that "Vermont ceased to be Vermont" with the vote. "To this day I feel it is one of the worst things we did to the state of Vermont," he said. But in the end he had done what Billings had told Hoff that he would do, namely, tell the House members it was better to "do the job ourselves and keep the courts out of it." Backers of the bill said again that while 200,000 Vermonters elected just 21 delegates, 200,000 of their more rural neighbors elected 225, and that this was a wholly undemocratic and unfair situation that couldn't be allowed to continue. The final vote, while historic, was in many ways anticlimactic. By the time it came, everyone knew what the outcome was going to be, and everyone knew that nothing that was going to be said in the floor debate was going to change anyone's mind. In the end, both Sam Parsons and Kenalene Collins voted for it.

The House bill was quickly agreed to by the Senate and signed by the governor, and on June 30, 1965, Vermont's last one-town one-vote House was adjourned. When the new House returned in 1966, it would have 150 delegates from 106 districts. The formula had been shaped by a House committee headed by Representative Sanborn Partridge, Republican of Proctor, who had spent much of the 1965 session surrounded by graphs, charts, statistics, and maps. It generally divided the more heavily populated towns and cities that voted Democratic into districts with multiple representatives while consolidating the more numerous smaller towns that voted Republican into single-member or two-member districts. Burlington and Winooski, previously with one delegate each, would have eight districts and fifteen representatives between them. Rutland City and Rutland Town would have four districts and eight representatives. Conversely, nine Northeast Kingdom towns would be combined into one district. Glover, Emory Hebard's home town, would be combined with four other towns into a two-member district. Woodstock, the home of Franklin Billings, would be united with five neighboring towns into a two-member district. Billings would announce his retirement from the legislature and wouldn't be back. Instead he would go off to a long and distinguished career as a jurist. Hebard would be reelected to five more terms, and then would be elected for six terms as state treasurer. The State Office Building in Newport later would be named for him. Kenalene Collins of Readsboro would be reelected, although as part of a two-member district made up of Pownal, Wilmington, Whitingham, Readsboro, Stamford, Dover, and Searsburg. Parsons, Hutchinson, and Tuttle would not return. Parsons announced early that after thirty years in the legislature he was calling it quits. "The cities will run everything. The Democrats will have a control stronger than the Proctor Dynasty," he warned. "I don't think it would be fun any more." The century would end without another representative ever being elected from Stannard.

Reapportionment was the most pressing business, but it wasn't the only business of the 1965 session. Back in 1964, Hoff had persuaded the federal court to lift its order restricting the legislative agenda in 1965 to reapportionment alone. And after his landslide win over Foote, he felt he had a strong mandate to push ahead with his programs. His January 1965 inaugural address had included an ambitious legislative agenda, some of the most important parts of which Billings had agreed with. While Billings's speech was framed as advice to the legislature rather than as a specific program for the House majority, it resembled Hoff's in urging increased state aid to education, raising the salaries of state employees, and reorganizing the court system. He also urged Republicans not to oppose Hoff's programs just because a Democrat had proposed them. "Let Republicans be constructive and let us legislators regardless of party approve legislation on its merits and for the best interests of Vermont," he said.

Hoff and many of the former Young Turks agreed on the need for a legislative council to act as a research and bill-drafting staff for the legislature. Before such a council was enacted in 1965, there had been only five assistants to help the 246 representatives and 30 senators draft bills. That meant that some of the most important drafting was in fact done by lobbyists. The lack of legal advisers meant that almost any bill with a legal question ended up in the House or Senate Judiciary committees, which became legislative logjams. That was particularly true of the Senate Judiciary Committee, which was chaired by George W. F. Cook, a Republican from Rutland who tended to move glacially (he would have said "thoughtfully") on most everything. His committee spent huge amounts of time reviewing bills—critics said that it wasted huge amounts of time reviewing bills—that could much better and more quickly have been handled by the Fish and Game Committee or the Agriculture Committee or any of the other Senate committees, if the committees had legal staffs. The lack of research staffs also meant that lapses or mistakes—some of them fairly astonishing—slipped through the process without being caught. In 1959, for example, the legislature approved a major statute revision and later learned that it had repealed all the laws regulating maple syrup and maple sugar production. The approval of the Legislative Council not only helped professionalize the bill drafting and review process but was an important step toward giving the legislature an ability to set and shape programs of its own, instead of mainly reacting to proposals by the governor. Without something like it, Mallary had complained, the legislature was reduced to being "not an innovator but [just an] editor of plans submitted by the governor."

The legislature also agreed to abolish the death penalty except for persons found guilty of killing police officers. Some who had argued for the exception were glad that they did when, just two months later, a Lyndonville barber was charged with shooting the police chief. The minimum wage was increased from $1 an hour to $1.25 an hour, and pay raises of 10 percent were approved for state employees. Hoff's proposal to consolidate court districts also was passed, although only after being so watered down by Cook and his Judiciary Committee that Hoff immediately announced he would introduce it again in its original form in the 1966 session. The Hoff bill would have reduced the number of municipal courts from seventeen to eight and put all the judges on full-time status. The Cook version reduced the number from seventeen to twelve and put just five judges on a full-time basis.

There were setbacks as well. Hoff's efforts to consolidate schools was defeated for the second year in a row, with the legislature spending more time discussing deer than schoolchildren. Deer hunting was something most legislators thought they knew something about and were quick to speak up about and at great length. The 1965 session was no exception, and—as they had been doing since the 1920s—they again refused to transfer control of the deer herd from themselves to the Fish and Game Department, insisting on maintaining control over decisions about who could hunt what kind of deer where, when, and with what sort of weapons. The attempt to repeal the poll tax as a voting requirement was defeated for the fifth time in five years. There was a dispute between Hoff and his lieutenant governor over the appointment of Belmont Royce Pitkin as chairman of the Fish and Game Board. Pitkin, a teacher at Goddard College and an adviser to Hoff on conservation matters, was opposed by veterans groups that showed up at the Capitol handing out red, white, and blue pocket handkerchiefs and demanding that Pitkin be rejected because he had been a conscientious objector during the Korean War. Hoff stood by Pitkin, but Daley, a combat marine in the South Pacific, sided with the veterans, and the Senate refused to approve the nomination. And there were growing public differences between Hoff and Richard Mallary, the chairman of the House Appropriations Committee, who would emerge as the Republican leader in the next session. The differences at first seemed more testy than serious, but were warning signs of the sharp and bitter divisions that would develop between them.

But in the main, it was a good year for Hoff and for the state. The fiscal year ended with a $2.4 million general-fund budget surplus, much of which was pumped back into the state's education fund. Federal money started flowing into the state in greater amounts than before. In addition to the state surplus, another $2.4 million for education came from the federal Elementary and Secondary Education Act. The passage of the federal Medicare program guaranteed adequate health insurance for 44,000 Vermonters, while another 12,000 on welfare rolls were brought under the health-care benefits of the Kerr-Mills Bill. More federal funds came in for roads, Head Start programs, and for expansion of parks.

A steady influx of light industries, coupled with a sudden boost in tourism and recreation, pushed the state gross product to an estimated $1 billion, which was nearly $200 million higher than it had been in 1960. Employment Security Commissioner Stella Hackel issued regular reports saying that employment was up, take-home pay was increasing across the board, and that seasonal drops in employment were lower than at any time since the Korean War. An estimated four million tourists had visited the state in 1965, and on the last week of the year more than ten thousand skiers had elbowed their way onto the lifts at Killington alone, filling up nearly every motel, hotel, and rooming house within thirty miles of Rutland.

And Hoff was putting more of his own people in place as department heads: Edward Kehoe in Fish and Game, Reed Rexford in Agriculture, Richard Gibbony in Education, James Malloy in Motor Vehicles, and Gerald Witherspoon as tax commissioner. He also would have liked to replace the commissioner of highways, Russell Holden, who was seen by Hoff aides as "not being on the team" and as having an agenda of his own. But Holden didn't want to leave, and Hoff, who had taught one of Holden's sons in Sunday school, had an admitted weakness when it came to sticky personnel matters. He didn't like to give people bad news. "I hate to hurt people," he said. He would finally summon Holden into the office on a winter's day in 1966 with the intention of firing him and putting budget director John Gray into the job. But Holden, who was heading off for a day of skiing, brought his Sunday school pupil son with him, and Hoff found that he couldn't go through with it. He told Kearns right after the meeting that Holden in fact had offered to resign. "Well," Kearns told him curtly, "*that* was your chance."

Hoff also was getting a very good press. The state's biggest newspaper, the *Burlington Free Press*, and its only television station, WCAX in Burlington, were run by politically conservative owners who were generally hostile. And historically, most of Vermont's larger newspapers had sided with the conservative Republicans. One exception was the *Rutland Herald*, whose turn-of-the-century owner, Percival Clement, had been a serious business and political rival of the Proctors and whose managing editor, Howard Hindley, was thought by some to have been the model for the crusading small-town Vermont editor Doremus Jessup in the Sinclair Lewis novel *It Can't Happen Here*. Under later owners, the *Herald* had been supportive of both Aiken and Gibson. But at bottom the *Herald*, which also owned the *Montpelier-Barre Times-Argus*, was dependably Republican on its editorial pages and had endorsed Keyser in 1962 and Foote in 1964. The important reality for Hoff was that news stories were generally considered more important than editorial page opinions when it came to shaping public perceptions, and most of the news coverage was being generated by a handful of young reporters who for the most part liked Hoff personally and, while not open about it and while insisting that it wasn't reflected in their work, shared his politics and his activist approach to government. There also suddenly was a lot more coverage of the government than there had been in the past.

For many years, the *Herald* and *Free Press* had shared a common news operation in Montpelier called the Morning Press Bureau. It usually had consisted of one reporter assigned to cover government the year round, supplemented by one or two others when the legislature was in session. The Associated Press and United Press International also had one-person bureaus in the State House. The *Herald–Free Press* partnership had started in 1919, with Hindley of the *Herald* covering the legislative session with Edward F. Crane of the *Free Press*. In 1935 that arrangement was expanded to keep the bureau functioning year-round. The first bureau chief under that arrangement was Robert W. Mitchell, who in 1965

Phil and Joan Hoff in 1960. In his successful campaign for the state legislature, Hoff ran such a minimalist campaign that he didn't even have any campaign literature of his own. He handed out brochures touting John Kennedy's campaign for President instead.
Hoff Family Collection

With his victory in 1960, F. Ray Keyser Jr., shown here with his wife, became—at age 33—the youngest person ever to be elected governor of Vermont. His defeat by Hoff in 1962 marked the end of more than a century of Republican rule. Vermont Development Commission

The theme of Hoff's 1962 campaign for governor was that it was time for a change—a time for new vision, a time for new approaches to government, and a time to end a hundred years of one-party rule. Carr Studios, the Hoff Family Collection

T. Garry Buckley of Bennington, an anti-Keyser Republican, was a co-founder of the Vermont Independent Party in 1962. This was a largely paper organization that allowed Vermonters to vote for Hoff without doing it on the Democratic line, and in the end provided Hoff with his margin of victory. *The Bennington* (Vermont) *Banner*

The mill town of Winooski, adjacent to Burlington, was a Democratic stronghold in one of the most Republican of states. After the votes from Winooski insured Hoff's victory in 1962, he drove there for a boisterous late night celebration.
Hoff Family Collection

People still sent telegrams back in 1962,
and Phil and Joan Hoff received a flurry of
them on the morning after his 1962 win.
Hoff Family Collection

Newly elected Gov. Philip Hoff was surrounded by
his happy daughters on the morning after his win.
Hoff Family Collection

The Hoffs were invited by President John Kennedy
to visit the White House en route back to Vermont
from a post-election vacation in Puerto Rico.
Associated Press

Hoff invited Vice President Lyndon Johnson to visit Vermont, and LBJ and Lady Bird arrived for a two-day visit in the autumn of 1963.
Hoff Family Collection

Young Vermonters greet Hoff and Vice President Johnson on the steps of the State Capitol in the autumn of 1963.
Hoff Family Collection

Hoff and his family were enthusiastic skiers, and he put a big priority on touting the state as the ski capital of the East. He's shown here with Walter Foeger, the Austrian who founded the Jay Peak ski area, and with a poster promoting skiing in Vermont. The man Hoff charged with launching a major effort to promote tourism in Vermont was his energetic and enthusiastic Development Commissioner, Elbert G. (Al) Moulton. (a) Hoff on Skis, Hoff Family Collection; (b) Hoff with ski poster, Vermont Development Department; (c) Al Moulton (with pointer), *The Bennington (Vermont) Banner*

a

b

c

In 1964, Hoff scored a landslide re-election victory over Republican Lieut. Gov. Ralph Foote of Middlebury (right) and his running mate Richard Snelling of Shelburne (left). They're shown here with William Miller, who was campaigning for Vice President as Barry Goldwater's running mate.
The Bennington (Vermont) *Banner*

Phil and Joan Hoff campaign with a donkey, which was provided by Williamstown farmer George McCarthy who was a staunch Hoff supporter.
Hoff Family Collection

Hoff is sworn in for his second term as Governor by Chief Justice James Holden of the Vermont Supreme Court. Looking on are the Catholic Bishop of Burlington, Robert F. Joyce, and Lieut. Gov. John Daley of Rutland.
The Bennington (Vermont) *Banner*

All through the Hoff years as governor, U.S. Sen. George D. Aiken remained a hugely popular figure in Vermont. He and Hoff were rivals who rarely confronted one another and never ran against one another. In addition to being a Governor and U.S. Senator, Aiken had been a nurseryman in Putney, specializing in fruits, berries, and wildflowers. He also was the author of *Pioneering with Wildflowers*, a book so popular that it went through five printings over the course of four decades.
Tyler Resch, the *Bennington* (Vermont) *Banner*

The Hoffs attend a Democratic victory party and fund-raiser at the Rain Barrel Restaurant in North Bennington, April 10, 1965. Chef and owner of the restaurant and a French national who had served in the French Underground in WWII, Alain Midiere baked the cake.
The Bennington (Vermont) *Banner*

WILLIAMS COLLEGE

HINNEY BAXTER   GOV. PHILIP HOFF   TELFORD TAYLO

In the 1960s, the College Bowl was a popular television quiz show that pitted students from two colleges against one another. This variation had three prominent alumni from Williams in a show that was broadcast from New York in 1963. J. Phinney Baxter (right) was a former president of Williams, and Telford Taylor (left) had been a prosecutor at the Nuremberg War Crimes trials.
Hoff Family Collection

Republican Richard Snelling of Shelburne, shown here working the streets of Bennington, was a tireless campaigner in 1966, but Hoff defeated him to become the first three-term Vermont governor in modern times.
The Bennington (Vermont) *Banner*

After he became the Republican House Speaker and thus a major force in the Republican party in 1966, Richard Mallary of Fairlee managed to block or delay several major Hoff initiatives. He and Hoff had been allies while in the House together, and they would become friends again after Hoff left office. But there were times, when Hoff was governor and Mallary was speaker, when there was much warring between the two.
The Bennington (Vermont) *Banner*

"King Reid" Lefevre, a carnival showman as well as a Republican legislator, stage managed one of the most important pieces of Hoff-backed legislation, which shifted all of Vermont's welfare programs from the local towns—where they had been administered in very uneven ways by 246 different Overseers of the Poor—to the state.
The Bennington (Vermont) *Banner*

The von Trapp family singers—the subject of the wildly popular Broadway musical and movie *The Sound of Music*—moved to Stowe, Vermont, after WWII. When both Hoff and Development Commissioner Elbert Moulton saw Montreal (like New York and Boston) as a potential source of tourist dollars, they persuaded the family to appear at a "Vermont Night" during the Montreal Expo of 1967. The von Trapps' appearance drew the biggest crowd of the Expo, except for that of Queen Elizabeth.
Hoff Family Collection

Winston Prouty, the Republican U.S. Senator from Newport, Vermont, already had served three terms in the U.S. House and two in the Senate when Hoff challenged him in 1970. He defeated Hoff soundly, ending Hoff's hopes for national office. *The Bennington* (Vermont) *Banner*

Hoff was the first Democrat elected Governor in 109 years, but Patrick Leahy (left) was the first Democrat from Vermont ever elected a U.S. Senator. He's shown here with Hoff and with his mother, Alba Zambon Leahy.
Hoff Family Collection

was the publisher and co-owner of the *Herald*. It had been an arrangement that worked well for both papers for a very long time. But when Kendall Wild, the *Herald*'s managing editor, had a discussion with his *Free Press* counterpart in December 1964, he was told that the Burlington paper intended to send its chief political reporter and columnist, Vic Maerki, one of the best reporters in the state, to supplement the bureau in 1965, with the promise to him that—as Maerki had insisted—he would cover reapportionment and nothing else. Wild erupted in anger, saying that he wasn't going to have the *Free Press* reporter skim all the cream and do only what he wanted to while his own people would be left with all the scut work. Wild himself had been a former *Morning Press Bureau* bureau chief and had been looking for ways to increase coverage, saying often that "anyone who ignores state government is just contributing to the sorry shape that it's in." He persuaded Mitchell to dissolve the partnership and create an independent three-person bureau for the *Herald* and *Times-Argus*, to be called the Vermont Press Bureau. The *Free Press* then committed three people of its own to what was going to be a mini newspaper war. WCAX announced plans for expanded coverage; radio station WDEV in Waterbury did the same; a new paper in Springfield with liberal leanings added a staffer; a freelancer set up shop to provide coverage to radio stations and small weekly papers; and suddenly there were a dozen reporters covering the government pretty much full time, where in the immediate past there had been only three. There also was the odd situation in which Kenalene Collins doubled as a stringer for the *North Adams (Massachusetts) Transcript*, which covered her town. It was common for her to make a speech on the House floor and then climb the stairs up to the "Crow's Nest," a cluster of small offices just under the dome where the press operations were located, borrow a phone, and dictate a story to the *Transcript* beginning "Rep. Kenalene Collins, R-Readsboro, said today . . ."

Hoff himself tended to be open and friendly with reporters. He seldom complained about coverage, although he once ordered the *Herald*'s bureau chief, Jon Cottin, out of a news conference when he felt Cottin was snickering at something he said, and told him not to come back "until you learn how to behave like a human being." It also worked to his advantage that some of his closest aides—Bill Kearns, Paul Guare, and Ben Collins—were former reporters. (They would be joined by another, Arthur Ristau, in 1966.) All of them understood that reporters appreciated having their phone calls returned quickly, as well as inside information and candid assessments. These aides tended to be helpful—but of

course in ways that also were intended to be helpful to Hoff—by providing all three. Moreover, Hoff and his people were in Montpelier year-
round, while the Republican legislators usually went home in early summer. The result was a closeness between the reporters and Hoff and his
team that worked to Hoff's advantage. Hoff generally was able to get his
message out to the voters in the ways that he wanted, despite the open
hostility and Republican leanings of some of the state's media barons.

Reapportionment was regarded as a major Hoff victory and was expected to work to the immediate advantage of Democrats. Hoff had said
privately that he hoped to see the Democrats get at least sixty House
seats and ten Senate seats. That didn't happen. Democrats failed to turn
out in large numbers for the special election, and—despite Sam Parsons's
prediction that the Democrats would end up running everything—the
Republicans increased their majority in the Senate, winning 23 of the 30
seats, and also won a surprising 114 of the 150 House seats. Whereas Republicans had controlled 70.3 percent of the seats in the malapportioned
House, they now controlled 76 percent of the seats in the reapportioned
one. The results were a blow to Hoff and also were the source of some
critical mutterings by Democrats, who complained that instead of campaigning locally for Democrats, as he had vowed to do, Hoff hadn't even
been in the country during the last weeks of the campaign.

Back in May, Hoff had voiced strong support for Johnson's handling
of the war in Vietnam, and in July he had attended a Washington, D.C.,
briefing on plans to escalate U.S. involvement. Shortly afterward, he had
predicted a long war and had expressed an interest in visiting Southeast
Asia. In August, along with nine other governors, he was invited to participate in a trade mission to Japan, and Johnson decided that the trade
mission should be extended to include a five-day inspection tour of Vietnam. Hoff had never been to Japan and was eager to make the trip. Thus
for several weeks before the election he was out of Vermont, touring Asia
rather than campaigning for local Democrats. And even when he returned he found much of the news media (including the NBC television
news show *Meet the Press*) more interested in his views about national issues and Vietnam than Vermont politics. His view on the war—which
had broad public support at the time—was that there would be no negotiated peace and that it would be a long one. He also took the opportunity to express disapproval of antiwar protests and to voice his support
for the president's policy, which was escalating U.S. involvement by com-
mitting larger numbers of combat troops.

In fact, however, some seeds of doubt had been planted. The administration had tried to keep the governors on a short leash, led from one briefing to another intended to impress them with statistics showing how air power and additional ground forces would ensure that the war would be won. But during the trip Hoff had met a young army officer from St. Johnsbury who offered to take him on a quiet and unsupervised tour of the countryside. The officer came back the next morning well before dawn, in an unmarked jeep and wearing a uniform without any badges of rank or unit identification. He took Hoff and Governor John Chafee of Rhode Island, whom Hoff had persuaded to come along, out to meet Vietnamese. "We got to talk with a lot of people, and it became clear that they really wanted everyone—the Americans, the South Vietnamese Army, the North Vietnamese and the Viet Cong—to just go away and leave them alone," he recalled. "I didn't see how we could win a war that way."

Republicans were gleeful about the election results, with one Republican House victor saying that it would teach Hoff not to "trade his campaign hat for a kimono." Hoff himself felt that criticisms that he didn't do enough to help fellow Democrats were unfair and overstated. But he didn't dispute that it provided him with a strong incentive to abandon the Vermont tradition of not having governors serve more than two terms and to run for a third term in 1966. He also would argue that while reapportionment didn't quickly bring more Democrats into the legislature, it did produce a legislature that was much more activist, progressive, and willing to make changes than the one it replaced.

Hoff, in fact, opened the 1966 legislative session fully expecting much of his program to be rejected, not just because of the Republican numbers but because Mallary had indicated early on that he intended to be a very different Speaker than Billings. Mallary wanted the Republicans to have a legislative agenda of their own—not just react to Hoff's agenda—and intended to impose party discipline by removing committee chairmen who didn't toe the line. That in fact would start happening in 1967, when Mallary would begin the session with a Republican caucus that committed itself to a ten-item program of its own to rival Hoff's and stripped several Republicans of their chairmanships for having been too independent in 1966.

"My feeling ever since Phil Hoff was elected was that the Republican Party was deficient in merely being the party of opposition or cooperation or what have you," he said in a 1981 oral history interview for the University of Vermont. "I thought it was important for the Republican Party to evidence that it stood for something, rather than merely be for some of the things that Hoff wanted and against some of the other things." And he wanted to end the notion that committee chairmen could do "whatever they damn well pleased." So in 1967 he "removed a couple of committee chairmen from their positions and put them elsewhere because they had not worked cooperatively and consistently, not just with me, but with the general political and philosophical positions that had been taken by the party." In short, Mallary's view was that if Vermont in fact was going to become a two-party state, not just a state dominated by two different factions of the Republican Party, the Republicans were going to have to have real party programs and real party discipline.

Hoff considered Mallary to be the "most interesting" of the Young Turks because he was "a real fiscal conservative" who nonetheless had a strong commitment to civil liberties and civil rights. As a congressman, he later would vote to disband the House Un-American Activities Committee. "He's the sort of fiscal conservative who could support a single-payer health plan," Hoff said. He also called Mallary "one of the brightest" people in the legislature, although adding that as House Speaker "he became a kind of a pain." That was a moderated assessment long after both had retired from public life. At the height of their legislative warring, Hoff had called Mallary "the greatest obstacle to progress in Vermont." Mallary himself later said that he hadn't been too upset by the criticism because "my nature is that I don't particularly get infuriated by anything" and because he had come to expect "a certain amount of hyperbole from Phil."

Mallary had been born in Springfield, Massachusetts, in 1929 and started coming to Vermont as a child when his parents bought a summer camp on Lake Morey. They spent the bulk of the year in Springfield, where Mallary's father was a prominent lawyer, but also bought a dairy farm in Vermont that others worked and managed for them and which provided milk to Dartmouth College. After the war broke out, the Mallarys decided that they should do hands-on working of the farm as their part of the war effort. Mallary's father and older brother stayed in Springfield so that the brother could finish high school there, commuting to Vermont on weekends. But in the fall of 1942 Richard Mallary and his mother moved to the farm in Fairlee. Mallary milked cows and worked the farm all during his high school years at Bradford Academy, and then went off to Dartmouth intending to become a lawyer. But during his senior year in college, after already having been accepted in law school, he decided that "I didn't want to live in the city and I didn't want a country law practice, so I decided to turn to farming instead."

Mallary's mother, Gertrude, had been elected to two terms in the House and one in the Senate, so by the time he first ran in 1960, the Mallary name was well known and highly regarded in the region. He was elected to the 1961 legislature without a Republican primary or a Democratic opponent—"I had a free ride all the way," he later said—and found himself drawn into the group of new legislators that became known as the Young Turks. He later said that he wasn't sure just how he got pulled into the group, most of whom—except possibly for Sanborn Partridge of Proctor—were politically more liberal than he was and all of whom were older than he was. But he had known Tony Farrell and Byron Hathorn as fellow farmers, and knew Billings slightly. And while his politics were somewhat different from those of most of the others in the group, he shared what he said was their "willingness to be somewhat iconoclastic, willingness to look at new approaches and not be bound by traditions."

In 1967 Mallary would say, "When I entered the House in 1961, I was labeled as a 'Young Turk' and considered something of a 'dangerous liberal.' By 1965 I had been labeled as a 'conservative' or 'traditional' Republican, apparently indicating a shift to the right in my thinking. The odd thing is that I am not aware of any major changes in my basic political philosophy." Mallary was not being coy in this. He had generally portrayed himself as a sort of nineteenth-century liberal, and over time would come to be seen as favoring abortion rights, opposed to Sunday "blue laws," opposed to prayer in schools, and—much later—in favor of civil unions for same-sex couples, all the while remaining fiscally conservative and wary about government-mandated programs, whether designed by Montpelier or Washington. But the fact that he was being seen as a conservative in 1965 was yet another sign of how rapidly Vermont itself was changing, becoming more politically liberal and socially progressive than it had been just a few years before. And there were signs of this change in the 1966 legislature.

Hoff opened the 1966 legislative session by urging it to look beyond "petty affairs" of partisanship and to "unshackle our institutions and yes, even our minds from the chains of negative thinking that have dominated much of the past." But not even he anticipated the feverish pace at which the legislature, roughly divided between freshmen and veterans, would work over the next ten weeks. At times, the 150-member House seemed flushed with the excitement of doing things that were new, untried, and even daring. Hoff found that many of the first-time legislators were following his lead, rather than—as had usually been the case in the past—the recommendations of the legislative committees, and particularly their chairmen, voting for his bills even when House committees had rejected or proposed altering them. Mallary labeled this almost wholesale abandonment of committee steering as a frightening time for Vermont government.

The legislature repealed the payment of the poll tax as a voting requirement, something that Russell Niquette of Winooski had first tried to have done twenty years before. It gave up its management of the deer herd, deciding that if the state was going to have a Fish and Game Department, that department should be allowed to manage fish and game. The legislature had taken control of the herd after the department had authorized a doe-hunting season back in the 1920s that had killed so many does that hunters complained it had ruined deer hunting for the next decade. Ever since then, the legislature had rejected attempts to return control to the department, often being scathingly critical of the department and its game wardens in the process. But in 1966, the votes weren't even close. The legislature also approved bills making it easier for cities to start urban renewal programs, and putting yet more funding into local schools. It approved a package of penal reform bills that started the state on a course of rehabilitation for criminals, not just incarceration. And, over the angry and persistent objections of Stuart (Red) Martin, the head of Burlington television station WCAX, it finally—after a ten-year battle—authorized an educational television network (ETV) to be operated by the University of Vermont. Hoff saw educational television as another major commitment to improving education statewide, along with more funding for local elementary and high schools (which happened with bipartisan support and with Republicans sometimes voting more money than he had asked for), proposals for mandatory consolidation of school districts (which didn't happen, although much voluntary consolidation began taking place), and the strengthening of the state college system, transforming the three former "Normal Schools" at Castleton, Lyndon, and Johnson, which had mainly trained schoolteachers, into more-robust liberal arts colleges, with former lieutenant governor Robert Babcock as their provost.

Hoff withheld his formal support for the specific ETV plan until a Broadcast Council created to study it gave a favorable report. But in fact he had worked closely with UVM officials to insure it would happen. Red Martin, whose angry and constant interruptions of Broadcast Council discussions were labeled as "harassment" by Ralph Nading Hill, the

Vermont author and council member representing the general public, went so far as to try to block construction of the ETV broadcast tower on Mount Mansfield by dumping truckloads of rocks and sand on the narrow road to keep workers and equipment from the site. Hoff was "livid" when he heard the news, and first ordered bulldozers to open the road and then went to court to block Martin from doing it again.

The legislature also implemented a federal Rural Water Act program that Aiken had helped shape after the drought in Addison County in 1963. It would be the first program in the nation to be put in place, and its completion would be celebrated in Addison County when President Johnson visited Vermont and along with Aiken and Hoff turned on the spigots that brought water along a hundred miles of pipe to three hundred families.

Republicans differed on the causes and merits of the legislative outcome. Sandy Partridge lamented that "everything we do he [Hoff] takes credit for. And he blames us for everything bad." Emory Hebard was even less happy, complaining that the sheer volume of the legislation and the added cost had been inflicted on the state because "all those farm boys who used to vote no, they aren't here any more." He later said of the 1966 session: "Hell, those weren't legislators, they were reformers."

Even reformers could vote no, however, and a fair-housing bill was rejected by three votes, although it would be reintroduced and enacted the next session.

The organized Republican opposition that Hoff had expected didn't take place. There were still sharply divided factions in the party, with Daulton Mann, the liberal Republican from Peru, openly referring to the conservatives as the "Cro-Magnon wing." The tradition of committee chairs going their own way was still strong. And Mallary's efforts to unite Republican legislators collapsed in a fight over a highway appropriation that was caused by his own fiscal conservatism. The issue was a $34 million program to improve roads in the southwestern part of the state that had been bypassed by the interstate system. The interstate (I-91) had been built along the eastern side of the state, from Brattleboro to Newport, with a four-lane section (I-89) jutting off to the northwest from White River Junction to Burlington. This was a particular sore point in Rutland, in the west, where the major links to the rest of the state and to New York and Massachusetts were the east-west Route 4 and the north-south Route 7, both of them narrow, twisting, and in many places dangerous two-lane roads. Hoff's highway commissioner, James Marro of Rutland, complained that the federal government with the support of Vermont's two U.S. senators had built a four-lane road "from Aiken's front door" in Putney "to Prouty's front door" in Newport. Four governors in a row had promised better roads for the western part of the state, particularly between Bennington and Rutland, but not much had happened. Senator George W. F. Cook, Republican of Rutland County, complained that he had been waiting eight years in the Senate for governors to keep their promises. "We're the gateway to the west," he said of Rutland County, "but there's no gateway." Improving roads for that part of the state also had been a major editorial page crusade of the *Rutland Herald*.

Hoff had called for $34 million in bonding to improve Route 7, expand Route 4 into a four-lane road from Rutland west to New York state, and to build a beltway around Burlington. It had wide support in southwestern Vermont. Six of the eleven members of the House Highways and Bridges Committee in fact were in Rutland on January 26 inspecting Route 7 when Mallary called a quiet after-hours meeting with three powerful legislators and told them he didn't want to approve the bonding, which—because it was fast-track road building and not a part of the federal program—would require 100 percent state funds. He wanted a less-ambitious improvement plan, stretched out over a longer period and funded in part with an increase in the gas tax. A Vermont Press Bureau reporter who saw State House lights burning in a back office when they shouldn't have been followed them into the meeting and then wrote a strong but straightforward story about it. What showed up on page one in the *Herald* the next morning was far from straightforward. A three-column headline at the left top side of the page read:

HIGHWAY BILL EVISCERATED
ON ORDERS FROM MALLARY

There were pictures of Mallary; Reid Lefevre; Republican Walter Kennedy, the chairman of the Highway Traffic Committee; and Lawrence Franklin, the House majority leader. The headline over the pictures read: "No Better Roads, They Say." The captions under the pictures of Kennedy and Franklin each said "Hatchet-man." The caption under Mallary's photo said "Gave the order," and the one under Lefevre's said "Route 7 or the bush," which no one understood and even the editor who wrote it couldn't later explain.

The news story, rewritten by S. Kendall Wild, the managing editor, began

Montpelier—A bill calling for faster revamping of twisting western Vermont highways was eviscerated Wednesday on orders from House Speaker Richard W. Mallary, of Fairlee-on-the-Interstate.

Even as the majority of the House Highways Committee was touring Route 7 Wednesday, a secret meeting of four House bigwigs decided in Montpelier to eliminate faster repair of the very road the committee members were looking at.

Republican Mallary's henchmen in the secret meeting here Wednesday were Rep. Lawrence Franklin, R-66, of Guilford—also on the Interstate—Rep. Walter Kennedy, R-35, of Chelsea in Orange County, between two Interstate roads, and Rep. Reid Lefevre.

A small box in the middle of the story directed readers to an editorial "critical of Mallary's position," which was written by Seargent P. Wild, who was Kendall Wild's father and the paper's chief editorial writer. Lefevre complained angrily to *Herald* reporters the next day about his treatment by "Wild and his father—I'm told that he has one." He said he had been summoned to the meeting to be asked about his overall views on road construction and because his Ways and Means Committee would have to approve an increase in the gas tax that Mallary thought preferable to 100 percent bonding, but that he hadn't even been there when Mallary's decision had been made. Hoff was furious and weighed in heavily. Republicans, particularly from Bennington and Rutland counties, broke ranks. The GOP House members caucused and rejected Mallary's plan. In the end, Hoff got the $34 million authorization, much of Route 7 between Rutland and Bennington was improved, the Burlington beltway was half built, and Route 4 from Rutland west to New York was turned into a four-lane road.

But later in the session Hoff would lose to Mallary and the Republicans in his attempt to create a nonprofit corporation to import and sell Canadian hydropower, and it was a defeat that he would never forget or forgive.

The plan was to import as much as two million kilowatts of power at a rate slightly above four mills (or four-tenths of a cent) per kilowatt hour from Churchill Falls in Labrador. The power would be transmitted from Labrador to Vermont through Hydro-Québec for distribution in the state and elsewhere in New England for an initial period of twenty years. The chief architect of the plan was Democratic senator Frederick

J. Fayette, of Burlington, who also was the attorney for the state's rural
electric cooperatives. The key to the plan was the creation of a nonprofit
corporation, backed by the state, to buy and sell the power, and a commitment by the state to prepay $450 million to help with the construc-
tion of the Churchill Falls project. The bill sailed through the Senate by
a 23–2 vote.

The House, however, was a different matter. The state's private utilities, particularly Albert (Bert) Cree of the Central Vermont Public Service Corporation (CVPS) and his lobbyist, John Carbine, weighed in heavily. Freshman representative Luther (Fred) Hackett of Burlington, a
conservative Republican, orchestrated an intense opposition. And there
were whisperings—never stated openly or specifically—that Fayette, who
by this time had been charged criminally with influence peddling in connection with the St. Johnsbury postmastership, stood to somehow benefit personally from the deal. Hoff acknowledges that there were questions about Fayette, saying that some people saw him as an "Arab trader"
and didn't fully trust him. But he was very knowledgeable about power
issues, Hoff said, and the plan was a sound one. Hoff also noted that Fayette had been hired by the state's Public Service Board and its highly regarded chairman, Ernest Gibson III, as a special counsel on Canadian
power issues, and said that he was persuaded to back the plan not just by
Fayette but also by Walter Cook, the head of the Vermont Electrical Co-
operative. Hoff complained that "much of the anti-hydro power lobbying was of doubtful probity" and that Cree was making dubious promises
about much-cheaper power from a nuclear plant that CVPS and the Green
Mountain Power Company intended to build—not only saying that it
would be less than the four mills per kilowatt hour that Churchill Falls
was promising, but that it would be "too cheap to meter"—promises that
Hoff couldn't refute at the time but that never were realized in the forty-
five years afterward.

There were complaints from Republicans that the bill was a form
of socialism. Hackett insisted that the costs would be greater than what
the administration projected. Mallary questioned whether the nonprofit corporation would qualify for the low interest rates the administration anticipated, and doubted that Wall Street would put up the needed
money. The controversy became personal when Fayette charged Mallary
with operating from financial self-interest because Mallary's father was a
CVPS board member. Fayette later retracted the charge. Years later, Mallary himself became a vice president of CVPS and Hackett a CVPS board
member.

For many, Senator Aiken's statement that he didn't support the bill because of his reservations over financing was the final blow. Aiken was a longtime champion of public power, so his opposition was critical in many ways. This happened when a South Burlington legislator, Republican Theodore Riehle, decided to ask Aiken's opinion and then read Aiken's letter of response on the House floor. The letter not only brought Aiken's prestige into the debate on the side of the power companies, but also gave cover to Republicans who wanted to oppose it but didn't want to be seen as having been arm-twisted, bought off, or otherwise swayed by the utility executives and their lobbyists. Hoff later regretted he hadn't gone to Washington to try to line up Aiken's support, but remained angry about Aiken's move—and the fact that Aiken hadn't warned him that it was coming—many years later, saying that it helped kill a plan that would have been a huge economic boon to Vermont because it would have lured businesses to the state by offering the lowest power costs in all of New England. Aiken never wavered in his belief that nuclear power offered the best long-term benefits, and he may in fact have felt that Cree's promise of low-cost nuclear energy was real. But Hoff was still insisting forty-five years later that Aiken's action had cost Vermonters billions of dollars.

The House didn't actually vote the bill up or down, but instead steered it to a Legislative Council study committee that effectively killed it. The committee issued a report on June 28 saying it would be unwise "to create an organization hostile to the privately owned systems of the state" and that in any event Canadian power was "not likely to be lower in cost" than the nuclear power plant that the CVPS and Green Mountain Power intended to build. By the time the report was issued, the legislature had adjourned, which is what Mallary and Hackett had intended.

The legislature ended its business on Saturday, March 12, with a flurry of last-minute activity and considerable partying that stretched from the preceding Friday into Saturday afternoon. On Friday afternoon many legislators had gathered on the front steps of the Capitol to watch a scene that seemed bizarre at the time and even more so in retrospect, in which Hoff gave a spanking to Kenalene Collins. He had warned her during the session that if she didn't stop voting against his bills he was going to spank her for being an obstructionist, and he did. The sergeant at arms placed a chair on the Capitol steps, someone found a large wooden paddle, and Collins was summoned to the site where Hoff bent the forty-seven-year-old grandmother across his knees and spanked her. She seemed to go along with it as a joke at the time but later wrote a scathing letter to the *Bennington Banner* saying that it was only her respect for the office of governor that had prevented her from kicking his shin or slapping his face, and that she didn't try to get out of his clutches because she was too busy trying to keep her skirt down.

Inside, many Senate committees were still frantically at work. The Senate Judiciary Committee tabled a Hoff plan to further consolidate district courts and approved, with revisions, another plan to improve the selection process for picking municipal and county court judges. The bill for a one-cent increase in the gas tax that Mallary had coaxed through the House was killed in the Senate. Another $1.5 million in state aid to education was approved, intended to reward towns already making extra efforts at education by spending more than the average per-pupil cost. As afternoon turned to evening, many parties formed in different committee rooms, with recorded music, considerable alcohol, and platters of food. It became a movable feast with a Mardi Gras mood, with legislators wandering from one place to another for food and drink, following the sounds of spirited discussion and laughter. A particularly well-stocked bar, provided by the lobbyist for the state brewers association, was set up in the House Highways and Bridges Committee room, and late into the night legislators drifted in and out, telling one another that they were "building bridges." A newspaper reporter who walked into another committee room found not bridges being built but a female political activist on her knees performing fellatio on a portly committee chairman.

The legislative session finally came to an end at 3:43 P.M. on Saturday. The Senate, which had been loaded down with bills that the House had passed weeks before, worked until the very end, passing a $474,466 supplemental appropriations bill, authorizing $5.3 million in bonds for school construction and municipal sewage plants, and finalizing legislation requiring all junkyards and dumps to be at least one thousand feet from interstate and primary roads—something it had to do or risk having the state lose $2.5 million annually in federal highway funds.

While the senators kept working, the House members, as reporter John Mahoney recounted in the next day's *Herald*, continued their partying. Someone wheeled a piano into the well of the House chamber, and Kenalene Collins flexed her fingers and sat down at the keyboard. Bob Smith, a freelance reporter, unpacked his fiddle. Representative Hubert Brooks, a Republican of Montpelier, put his mouthpiece on his trumpet. Songbooks were passed around. House members gathered around and sang as the trio played "Dixie," "Show Me the Way to Go Home," "Nearer My God to Thee," and other familiar songs. From time to time the Senate would vote and message a bill back to the House, and Mallary would bang his gavel for the music to stop. A vote would be taken, and then the music would start again. When Joan Hoff joined the group around the piano, Representative Herman Hoyt, a Republican from St. Johnsbury, peered over the tops of his glasses through a cloud of cigar smoke and asked her, "May I have this dance?"

"Why thank you. I'd love to," she said. And they circled out of the well and down the aisle.

Hoff was angry about the defeat of the Canadian power bill but had reason to be happy about the session as a whole. Among other things, it had ended the poll tax as a voting requirement, turned the management of the deer herd back to the Fish and Game Department, opened the way for cities to take advantage of Great Society urban renewal projects, approved funding for major road improvements in southwestern Vermont, created an educational television network, increased state aid for education, passed legislation intended to produce prison reforms, and brought the benefits of Aiken's federal water program to Addison County. Hoff's personal popularity was high, while the Republicans remained a party divided. And, although the formal announcement was still a few months away, he had made up his mind to seek a third term.

CHAPTER 4

THE THIRD TERM

B efore Hoff's formal announcement that he would seek a third term, U.S. Senator George Aiken warned that public opposition to third gubernatorial terms in Vermont was so strong that if Hoff ran for one, "everything that anyone has against him will come out." It's not known just what Aiken meant by that or just what he expected might come out. He didn't elaborate, and no one asked him to. Except for the one charge in 1964 by Ralph Foote about offices having been "bought and sold," which had backfired against Foote, Hoff's administrations had been virtually free of allegations of political corruption or personal gain. He was becoming known as a heavy drinker (he favored gin martinis), and there were whispers that he was being seen too often drinking too much in public. But even this wasn't widely known outside political circles, in part because it hadn't yet become as serious as it later would, and in part because the journalism of the time seldom dealt with personal behavior unless it became very public, like an arrest for drunk driving or an acrimonious divorce suit. Very few New Yorkers, for example, knew what almost every reporter in Albany knew—that when the Governor's Mansion in Albany caught fire late one night in 1961, state troopers had smuggled Nelson Rockefeller, who had been elsewhere, into the mansion from the rear so that he then could be seen "escaping" from the front. Very little was known publicly about John Kennedy's many extramarital affairs until after his death. And most Vermonters in 1966 had no sense that when it came to deciding when cocktail time began, Hoff was taking the view that it must be five o'clock somewhere in the world.

Hoff had enough concerns of his own about this break with tradition—no Vermont governor since 1835 had sought more than two terms—that just four days after announcing he would run for a third term he also pledged not to run for a fourth. He eventually came to feel that this promise had been a mistake—"a bad move" was the way he put it—because even before the ink was dry on the newspaper headlines announcing his defeat of Republican Richard Snelling he already was being seen as a "lame duck" governor, with all the erosion of political clout that the term implies. And in the end, despite Aiken's warning, nothing came out. Snelling ran a campaign that very much stuck to what he considered the issues, and a third term wasn't one of them. The reality was that neither Aiken's warning nor Hoff's concern had been warranted to begin with. The break with tradition proved to be no issue at all. It was yet another sign of just how quickly and dramatically Vermont was changing that a deep-rooted tradition could be discarded like an old coat, with neither the state's senior U.S. senator nor its young governor realizing the degree to which the voters no longer cared.

Hoff ran and won with almost 58 percent of the vote. The Democratic candidates for lieutenant governor, treasurer, secretary of state, and auditor of accounts also won, and the Democrats made impressive gains in the legislature. They won 13 of the 30 seats in the Senate and 54 of the 150 seats in the House. Not even in the days of a 246-member House had so many Democrats been sent to Montpelier. But the 1966 election was a Democratic victory that didn't play out in the usual non-presidential-election-year manner. In 1966, the Democratic falloff was far greater than the Republican. Hoff's total vote declined by more than 25,000 from 1964, while Snelling managed a thousand more votes than Ralph Foote had gotten in 1964. It is not clear just what the reason for this was, although Snelling ran a much more aggressive campaign than Foote had, booking himself into an exhausting schedule that often had him leaving his Shelburne home in the darkness before dawn and not returning until midnight or later.* And Democrats may have been lulled by news stories and polls that suggested right from the start that Hoff would win and win easily. Republican Robert Stafford, with 65.6 percent of the votes for Congress, was the biggest vote-getter, and Republican James

*Snelling would go on to great political success in later years, being elected governor in 1976, 1978, 1980, and 1982, and then—after losing badly in a 1986 attempt to win the U.S. Senate seat held by Patrick Leahy—to a fifth term in 1990. (His wife, Barbara, would herself be elected to two terms as lieutenant governor and was running for governor in 1996 when a cerebral hemorrhage caused her to withdraw.) He died in the seventh month of that last term. The cause was a heart attack while having a swim in his pool. He was just sixty-four. Snelling always remained a fiscal conservative but over time became increasingly progressive when it came to conservation issues and women's rights. During some of Vermont's most economically challenging years, he increased taxes but at the same time insisted on also increasing spending for human services, something that Hoff, by then back in the legislature as a state senator, applauded him for. He seemed to become more open-minded and less dogmatic as time went by, moderating the self-assuredness that many took for arrogance and that to some degree was. Friends attributed the change in his persona in part to the influence of his four children—two sons and two daughters—who challenged him to open up to different ways of thinking and to embrace changing times.

Oakes of Brattleboro, a former clerk to Sterry Waterman and a particular favorite of Aiken's, was elected attorney general. The voters had reelected a popular Democrat as governor along with four of his five ticket mates, and had elected more Democrats than ever to the state legislature. But they also had reelected a popular Republican congressman, kept solid Republican majorities in the legislature, and elected a Republican attorney general. All of which suggested that Vermont had become—or at least was well on its way to becoming—a two-party state.

The 1966 campaign would take place against a backdrop of great changes in the political, social, and economic landscape of the state. It would result in another strong endorsement of Hoff's "bold new approach" for Vermont, which future governors, including Snelling, would never attempt to reverse, and would mark an important change from the way that political campaigns had been waged in the past.

Richard Arkwright Snelling was thirty-nine years old in 1966. A native of Allentown, Pennsylvania, he had attended college at Lehigh, moved on to Harvard, served in the army in 1945 and 1946 as an enlisted man (he was a military investigator and editor of an information bulletin with the rank of T5, the equivalent of a corporal), and then returned to Harvard, graduating cum laude in 1948. He and his family had settled in Shelburne in 1953, where he had founded Shelburne Industries and had become a millionaire at a time when many Vermonters (including some working for Shelburne Industries) were earning less than $55 a week. Although he had come from a well-to-do family (his father was a chemist and explosives expert who discovered propane as a volatile component of gasoline and sold his patent to the Phillips Petroleum Company), he stressed often that he had made his own fortune, not inherited it, saying that he had gotten "not a sou" from his family. At the same time, he often expressed annoyance at news stories describing him as a "wealthy industrialist," feeling they were evidence of reporters' trying to portray him as removed from the concerns of ordinary Vermonters. At the time, he owned factories in Vermont, Massachusetts, and New Jersey, employed more than 250 workers, and in fact was quite wealthy by the standards of the day. But as an "industrialist" he wasn't Andrew Carnegie. Shelburne Industries twisted small bits of wire into cup hooks, and also made can openers. It later branched into making ski racks.

During the 1966 campaign, Snelling insisted repeatedly that he was a businessman, not a politician, and his approach to campaigning in fact was organized and disciplined. He also proved to be very adept in his extensive use of television, which had been more of a novelty than a serious part of earlier campaigns. He was an effective speaker and a good debater. He also involved himself in every detail of his campaign, perhaps too much so, writing many of his own speeches and press releases, doing much of his own scheduling, sketching out the layouts for his newspaper ads, and spending many hours each week on the sort of routine campaign scut work that Hoff generally left to others. This was in spite of the fact that one of the consultants he hired, and seemed to pay only marginal attention to, was Doug Bailey, who would go on to be a major figure in GOP politics by helping shape the presidential campaign of Gerald Ford and the U.S. Senate campaigns of Edward Brooke, John Chaffee, Richard Lugar, Charles Percy, and many others. Another consultant who didn't last long with Snelling but went on to become a major force in Republican political campaigns was Robert Goodman of Maryland, who helped get Spiro Agnew elected governor and would eventually work on more than a hundred campaigns. Jon Margolis, a longtime national correspondent for the *Chicago Tribune* and later the creator of the Web blog Vermont News Guy, recalled that Snelling liked to say he had fired Goodman after about a month because "He gave me only one good idea and that was to blow-dry my hair."

That, in fact, was good advice, and Snelling did it until he died, twenty-five years later. But his protestations that he wasn't really a politician were mocked by some Democrats. John (Jack) O'Brien, the fiery Democratic senator from Chittenden County, liked to remind crowds that after serving one term in the House, Snelling had never stopped running for office. O'Brien was short, irreverent, and given to hyperbole, with elfin looks (he resembled the leprechauns in the Walt Disney movie *Darbie O'Gill and the Little People*) and the pugnacious manner of a boxing promoter, which he in fact once had been. "Mr. Snelling says he's not a politician—a statement refuted by the fact that he is a perennial office seeker," O'Brien would shout, jabbing his ever-present cigar for emphasis. "In fact, Mr. Snelling appears to be climbing the ladder of successive defeats.

"He ran for [reelection to] the House, and he was defeated.

"He ran for the Senate, and he was defeated.

"He ran for Lieutenant Governor and was beaten by 300 votes in his own home town.

"And he will fall flat on his face in November and come back and run for the U.S. Senate two years from now."

Snelling in fact had lost Shelburne in 1964—when he had set an endurance record of sorts by campaigning in every town in the state—but only by 13 votes, 459 to 446.

Snelling was a big man, and for a time in the early '60s had put on considerable bulk. He had gone on a crash diet in the months before his official announcement, dropped forty-two pounds, and started his campaign as a big man wearing a bigger man's clothes. His suits often seemed several sizes too large and his shirt collars too wide. He liked to remind people that he had been a blocking back on the Harvard football team in 1943, which also gave him a chance to define himself politically by adding, "Bobby Kennedy and I were on the same team then, but we haven't been on the same team since." Harvard back in those days still played what was considered big-time football, but the team Snelling played on was a highly informal wartime team. With only about 1,000 students left on the campus and most of them either freshmen who hadn't yet reached draft age or upperclassmen who had been found unfit for military service and thus were classified as 4-F, the school had canceled a regular season that would have included games against Yale, Princeton, Pennsylvania, and other such schools. Instead, it decided to play a limited schedule, against local teams, which wouldn't require any train travel: the Camp Edwards army team, which it played twice and beat both times; Worcester Polytechnic Institute, which it lost to 13–0; Tufts, which it lost to 13–7; and Boston College, which it tied 6–6. The only preseason scrimmage had been against a high school team, Medford High, just north of Cambridge. Yet the appetite for even that level of college football was so strong that 45,000 fans crammed into Harvard Stadium to see the team play Boston College in the last game of the season.

Snelling started off knowing he was a serious underdog but hoped that with a unified party and an aggressive campaign he could do better than most expected, possibly upset Hoff, and at the least project himself into a leadership role in the party. The party unity never developed. He was challenged in the primary by Thomas Hayes, a longtime aide to Winston Prouty who had been working in Washington for the past fifteen years. While Snelling defeated him handily, he had to spend weeks focusing on Hayes rather than Hoff and found himself having to defend his "tax reform" proposals—the core issue of his campaign—from a fellow Republican, not just from Democrats. Even earlier, back in the fall of 1965, Franklin Billings had dismissed Snelling as a "no-win loser," and both Billings and fellow Young Turk Daulton Mann of Peru would openly endorse Hoff in the fall of 1966. Mann said that Hoff was "a better man than his Republican opponent" and that Snelling's past advocacy of right-to-work laws and his current advocacy of a sales tax made him the candidate of special interests. The Republican candidate for lieutenant governor, Perry Merrill, began handing out brochures telling voters how to split their ticket if they wanted to vote for Hoff for governor but for him as lieutenant governor. And the Republican candidate for secretary of state, Byron Hathorn, never put a Snelling bumper sticker on his own car, although he kept a couple in the trunk, he told reporters, just in case anyone should ever ask him for one.

Snelling had said at the start that his chief campaign expenses in 1966 would be for "shoe leather, gas and tires." That may not have been literally true—he would spend much more on television than any Vermont candidate had up to that point—but he did travel the state extensively, usually in a reconditioned bus that had been transformed into a moving campaign headquarters, complete with work tables, typewriters, several benches long enough to catnap on, and an electric outlet that allowed him to use an electric razor to shave himself late in the day. A loudspeaker system blared Sousa march music to attract crowds and allowed Snelling to make impromptu speeches to small groups that local party organizers managed to assemble around gas stations, village greens, and general stores. The bus, which was painted white, had a large campaign poster of Snelling on the back and a destination sign over the front windshield that said "State House." It was driven by Tony Thompson a young Dartmouth graduate and Vietnam veteran, who served as Snelling's principal aide, and it got about six miles to the gallon. Since a typical day for Snelling might have him going from Burlington to Poultney to Springfield, Bellows Falls and Brattleboro and then back, it was common for the bus to use a hundred gallons of gas during just two days' campaigning. One of the few times Snelling—who prided himself on his businessman's attention to detail—allowed himself to be seen publicly angry and embarrassed during the campaign was one cold morning at 6 o'clock when the bus ran out of gas in Charlotte, just a few minutes after leaving his home. He was still fuming about it hours later when the battery went dead. On days that ended far from home, Snelling sometimes would be met at the local airport by his friend, Shelburne neighbor, and state party chairman Derick Webb, and flown back to Burlington in Webb's Cessna Skywagon, while Thompson, who got even less sleep than Snelling did during the campaign, would drive the bus back to Shelburne.

Hoff also had a hectic schedule, but Snelling probably saw the sun rise more often than Hoff did during the last month of the campaign and probably subjected himself to more aggravation as well. Hoff found himself so annoyed at Snelling's repeated claims that as a successful businessman he could better manage the state that he stopped listening to them and reading about them, knowing that if there was anything he really needed to respond to, his aides would alert him. But Snelling spent hours on his bus reading as many of the news stories as he could get about the campaign, underlining facts he felt were wrong, characterizations he felt were misleading, quotes that he felt were incomplete (some of them were, since he tended to be so long-winded that it was difficult to quote him fully or paraphrase him precisely), and passages that he felt were slanted against him or toward Hoff. He often used a ruler to measure the newspaper column inches devoted each day to Hoff and himself, readying himself to confront reporters and editors at any and every opportunity about what he felt were their insufficiencies and biases.

Snelling had plenty of chances to do it, because the 1966 campaign was the most heavily covered of any Vermont campaign up to that time. In the past, most coverage had been from afar—by rewrites of press releases supplemented by phone calls. But at the instigation of *Rutland Herald* managing editor Kendall Wild, Robert W. Mitchell, the publisher of both the *Herald* and the *Montpelier-Barre Times-Argus* (who although having endorsed first Keyser and then Foote in earlier campaigns would endorse Hoff in 1966), agreed that the three reporters from the Vermont Press Bureau—John Mahoney, Tony Marro, and Steve Terry—would cover every public event held by both the candidates every day for the last six weeks of the campaign. Wild wanted his reporters to be with the candidates from the time they left their driveways every morning until they returned every night. Daily coverage of candidates was standard for such big-city papers as the *Chicago Tribune*, *New York Times*, and *Boston Globe*. But nothing like it ever had been attempted in Vermont, and even the big-city papers didn't seek or expect to get the sort of intimate access to the campaign that Wild wanted his reporters to have. The *Burlington Free Press* quickly responded by increasing its own coverage, although it never attempted the sort of saturation coverage that the *Herald* did. Both candidates were remarkably accommodating, allowing the Vermont Press Bureau reporters to ride in their cars and buses with them, fly in their small planes with them, eat meals at the same tables with them, and often eavesdrop on their phone calls. During the first week of such coverage, Snelling said to Marro, "We're flying down to Bennington tomorrow. Do you want to come with us?"

Marro had never been in a plane before and wasn't sure he wanted to start by flying in a small one. But he had been told that his job was to stick as close to the candidates as he could, wherever and whenever he could. "Sure," he said, only to be told, "Don't ever say that." Snelling, himself a pilot, then went on to warn him that he should never get into a small plane without first asking who the pilot was and what his credentials were. He then turned to his wife and, nodding his head back toward Marro, said, "Can't you just hear him? 'Sure I'll fly with you, Orville. You're the best bicycle maker in Dayton.'"

It turned out that the pilot would be Derick V. Webb (the "V" was for Vanderbilt), the GOP state chairman, as well as a state senator from Chittenden County and the heir to the Vanderbilt-Webb property that later became the National Historic Landmark called Shelburne Farms. Webb was tall and ruggedly handsome. No one in the legislature looked better in a blue suit. A graduate of Yale, he had served as a sergeant in the Ninety-seventh Infantry Division in World War II and was the president of the Vermont Dairy Council. He was friendly and down-to-earth, and eventually would leave Vermonters a great public treasure when instead of breaking up his 1,400-acre property—with its handsome nineteenth-century country house and stunning five-story brick barns, all showing signs of past glory but in serious need of repair, and its magnificent views of Lake Champlain and the Adirondacks—and selling it for what could have been a huge amount of money, he helped his children transform it into a nonprofit environmental education center. But he didn't have the mental quickness or agility of Snelling, and that was sometimes seen when Snelling suddenly would say, "Derick, what would you do if your engine cut out right now?" Webb would look very slowly over to his left, scan the landscape, and then even more slowly move his gaze to the front of the plane and then over to the right, until Snelling finally, sometimes impatiently, would suggest a distant pasture, a strip of beach by a lake, or an uncommonly straight stretch of road. If the emergency drills by Snelling were intended to inspire confidence in passengers, they didn't.

Snelling had intended from the start to make major use of television. By 1966, WCAX, a CBS affiliate and the state's only Vermont-based station, reached twelve of the fourteen counties and was going into 90,640 of a potential 103,500 homes in those areas. It didn't have viewers in Bennington County (which was part of the CBS Albany market) or Windham County (which was reserved for the CBS Boston market). And because of the mountains, reception was spotty in parts of Rutland and Windsor counties. But Peter Martin, the president and general manager of WCAX in 2010, said that by 1966 "We had revolutionized politics in the state because for the first time you could reach [almost] the entire state with your message." Snelling may have been more attuned to this rapidly changing reality than Hoff because Red Martin, Peter Martin's father and head of WCAX at the time, not only was a friend and backer but sat in on many of the Snelling campaign's strategy sessions. Hoff's main advisers—including Kearns, Collins, Ristau, and Guare—all were print people who focused on the reality that, for the moment at least, most Vermonters were still relying on newspapers for most of their news.

Snelling also felt that television gave him a chance to speak directly to the voters without his words being filtered through or challenged by reporters, who he believed were mostly Hoff supporters to begin with. During the last six weeks of the campaign, he aired five-minute talks—most of them taped in advance—five nights a week, and also had three half-hour "telethons" in which Vermonters could call in their questions for him to answer. His campaign likely planted some of the telephone questions, but Hoff's probably did also, given that, one night, back-to-back callers, using almost exactly the same words, asked about the supposedly low wages being paid at Shelburne Industries.

Hoff claimed he disliked using billboards (he had about thirty of them across the state proclaiming "Hoff Prosperity") but said he needed them because he couldn't afford all the television time that Snelling was buying. Snelling said that Hoff's billboards were costing more than his own television advertising did. Whatever the case, Snelling used television more widely and more effectively than any candidate up to that time, and every candidate in the future would follow that lead. At the same time, because he also realized that he was less well known outside the WCAX core market, Snelling set out to focus his personal campaigning in places that weren't served by WCAX or that didn't have the sort of high household penetration by WCAX that Chittenden, Franklin, Addison, and Washington counties did. These, of course, tended to be the places farthest away from his Chittenden County base, which made most of his days very long ones. His goal was to have personal contact with a thousand voters a day, mainly through a combination of factory tours, women's club teas, service club lunches, and sidewalk campaigning. Both he and Hoff also visited many schools, even though none of the students could vote. Hoff loved children and as governor made it a point to visit as many schools as he could. When requests started coming in every spring for him as a commencement speaker he always started by picking the smallest school. Local schools at that time were not only willing to let candidates campaign inside the buildings but happy to have their school marching bands sometimes play at political rallies.

Snelling's speaking style was articulate and clear and radiated self-assurance. Some of the reporters who followed the campaign felt he bested Hoff in most of their one-on-one confrontations. Hoff and Keyser had never appeared at the same venue together, but Hoff and Snelling had several head-to-head debates and often appeared at the same forums at the same time. During the last weeks of the campaign, both candidates also did live early morning radio broadcasts by calling in from wherever they were at the scheduled time, whether still at home having coffee (which was seldom the case for Snelling) or—since this was back before car phones and cell phones had come into use—from gas station pay phones. Snelling often seemed to be better prepared for these as well. But Hoff himself was a poised campaigner and more charismatic, and the 1966 campaign was the one, he later said, that he most enjoyed. He went through it confident and upbeat, with his mere presence at an event generating an excitement that Snelling's seldom did. With his easy charm and movie star good looks (one woman in a Pownal factory where he was campaigning was overheard whispering to a co-worker that he could "put his shoes under my bed" any time that he cared to), he had the ability to make many Vermonters feel that he and they were setting off on a great adventure together. During the last week of the campaign, while he was being interviewed by a Lebanon, New Hampshire, television station that broadcast into Vermont, Hoff was asked what he felt the greatest accomplishment of his administration had been. He said that he thought it had been "helping to generate a new feeling of optimism about the future of the state of Vermont." That optimism was very much alive in the autumn of 1966, and it worked very much to the advantage of Hoff. The campaign had begun in earnest in mid-September, when the hills were already turning vibrant with color. By the time it ended, those same hills, as the *Herald*'s managing editor Wild noted in an introductory blurb to one day's campaign coverage, were feather gray, with occasional tufts of yellow and brown, and the skies had become slate-colored and damp. It had taken both candidates into every corner of the state and had reaffirmed for both just how much change was taking place. There had also been memorable scenes along the way of the familiar Vermont—a misty morning in Addison County, for example, with the rising sun slanting through the mountain gaps to the east, silhouetting picturesque churches against its pale orange glow. Hoff had bundled his trench coat against the passenger-side window in the backseat and was trying to catch a few more minutes of sleep. His car traveled down through the rolling Champlain Valley, past fields where the stubble of recently cut corn gave clear sign that fall was passing into winter, past lighted farmhouses and stone walls, the car rising and falling with the road, climbing out of and then dipping back into the fog. Suddenly there was a pale light ahead, and out of the mist came a farmer with an old-fashioned kerosene lantern leading a herd of cows across the frost-covered ground. It was a moment that seemed to capture an essence of Vermont. But the campaign showed that—like the statue of Ceres atop the State House dome—it was more a symbol of Vermont's agricultural past than its present or future.

What the campaign showed day in and day out was that Vermont was undergoing significant change. Some of the changes were obvious, like the sprawling new IBM complex at Essex Junction; the road-clogging influx of tourists; the concrete ribbons of interstate roads; the developments of thousands of condos and second homes springing up around ski areas, along with the strip-mall clutter of motels, restaurants, bars, shops, and gas stations that went with them; the clusters of trailer parks in Milton providing low-cost but slumlike housing for workers in the greater Burlington area; and the new union schools rising out of the pastures of Orleans and Lamoille counties. Other changes were more subtle, like the gradual march of forests back into what had been open land. Once while flying over Rutland County en route to Springfield, Hoff's aide Johannes von Trapp, a young member of the Trapp family of Stowe, pointed out site after site where pastureland from abandoned farms was growing up into scrub pine and brush. And many of the scenes that the candidates saw showed the need for the state to move quickly if it was going to be able to avoid being overrun by forms of urbanization—by billboards and strip malls and pollution and helter-skelter developments—without urban controls. Looking down from Webb's Skywagon, Snelling shook his head at the murky LaPlatte River, a shallow sewer that meandered through Hinesburg on its way to Lake Champlain.

"That's just a grubby administrative problem," he said. "We've got the laws we need on the books, but we can't hire pollution control engineers because the pay scales are way out of line. It's like insisting a man have a Ph.D. for a job, and then setting his pay at $4,000.

"It's just a grubby administrative problem."

In some cases it was, but in many cases it wasn't. Only about seventy of Vermont's towns had any zoning at all, and what controls they had tended to be very local and rather weak. Apart from the interstate, there was virtually no regulation of roadside billboards, and long stretches of roads, particularly leading to resort areas like Stowe, were cluttered with signs—many of them large, some of them garish, most of them offensive to people who cared about the natural beauty of the state, and more than a few of them falling into ruin—telling travelers what clothes to wear, what gas to buy, and what cars to drive; advising them where to sleep, eat, drink, shop, ski, and go to church. A section of Route 7 north of Brandon had close to a dozen huge red and white billboards, all of them taller and wider than most rural schools, urging drivers to pull into a tiny gift shop called Sea Shell City, which was located in the middle of the only state in New England without a seacoast. The LaPlatte wasn't the only river in Vermont that had become polluted and spoiled. From the air, candidates could see points where raw sewage was still being dumped into the Winooski, Lamoille, Missisquoi, Passumpsic and many others.

Snelling and Hoff both had plans for dealing with many of the changes they saw and the problems they recognized as they crisscrossed the state, but neither of them talked about them very much during the campaign. Snelling didn't because he found that he couldn't, and Hoff didn't because he decided right from the start that he could put Snelling on the defensive and keep him there by going out day after day and unleashing endless attacks on his tax plan.

The centerpiece of Snelling's campaign was a call for "tax reform," in which he proposed a 3 percent "limited" sales tax that he said would generate $15 million (Hoff insisted it couldn't generate more than $11 million) and allow him to reduce both personal income taxes and property taxes and to pump more money back to the towns in the form of state aid to schools. But one person's "reform" can be another person's "scam," and Hoff began his formal campaign with a charge that Snelling's plan was a "phony reform" that would benefit rich people and business owners (like Snelling and his businessmen friends) and hurt ordinary Vermonters by making "an already regressive tax structure even more regressive."

Jack Daley began calling Snelling "a Robin Hood in reverse," saying that his tax plan would steal from the poor to give to the rich. And peppery Jack O'Brien fired up partisan crowds by saying, with even more hyperbole than usual, that it would "transfer the cost of government to the poor, the blind, the crippled and the bed-ridden." Snelling later admitted he knew he was in trouble when he heard Democratic radio ads in which a clerk rang up purchases to the sound of a cash register and then, at the end, announced cheerfully that she now would have to add in Mr. Snelling's sales tax as well.

The Hoff attack on Snelling's plan was daily and relentless. He told a news conference in Montpelier that it would reduce taxes for nonresidents (who paid high property taxes on their second homes) while raising taxes for Vermonters (who would pay the sales taxes every day). He told a group in Bellows Falls that the plan was a part of Snelling's attempt to return control of government "to the hands of the privileged few." He said in a radio interview in St. Albans that it was "neither fair, just, decent, nor honorable." And he told farmers at a Morrisville Grange that "there is no group of Vermonters that would suffer a greater calamity under the sales tax than Vermont farmers."

Despite his tough talk, Hoff in fact wasn't ideologically opposed to a sales tax, although he insisted that one wasn't needed at the time. He later would endorse the one that Deane Davis would call for in 1969. His own tax commissioner, Gerald S. Witherspoon, had been working on a sales tax proposal since the summer of 1965, convinced that one could be crafted without the regressive features of most sales tax plans, and that if implemented might nip the rebellion against rapidly increasing property taxes that was springing up all across the state. But Bill Kearns was violently opposed to the Witherspoon plan, and Hoff also paid attention to the opposition of *Free Press* reporter and columnist Vic Maerki, who had considerable influence on his thinking.

Snelling, as was his wont, at first blamed his problems on the press, saying that people misunderstood what he was proposing because reporters kept focusing on the sales tax alone and not on his overall "tax reform" plan. But a review of the more than four dozen articles mentioning the plan that the *Rutland Herald* and the *Times-Argus* ran during the height of the campaign showed that every one of them described the sales tax proposal in the larger context of his promise to also reduce personal income and property taxes and to return more money to towns in the form of state aid. The simple fact was that Snelling failed to recognize that even in a state as small as Vermont, it takes a long time to educate large numbers of people about complicated issues. The result was that during the last week of his campaign, after months of careful and detailed explanations of his proposal, he was still fielding questions from many people, including business executives and Republican loyalists, who clearly didn't know just what it was that he was proposing, except that it would inflict on them some sort of a sales tax that currently didn't exist. As late as October 26, even Senator Aiken, when he made a joint appearance with Snelling to endorse him, responded to questions by saying that while he backed Snelling as a candidate, he still didn't know enough about the tax reform plan to support it. Which meant either that Aiken in fact didn't understand it, which couldn't be blamed on the press, or—more likely—understood it fully and wasn't prepared to embrace it.

Two days earlier, during a radio interview in Brattleboro on October 24, Snelling had complained that while it was only a small piece of his plan for governing Vermont, his tax reform proposal had been the focus of more attention that all the other issues combined. That was true, and it had been from the start. No matter what he set out to talk about on a given day, he ended up explaining, defending, and justifying his tax plan. And just a few hours later that same day, as Hoff was getting ready to address a crowd in Bellows Falls, a reporter asked him what he was going to talk about. "There's only one speech in this campaign," he said. And he went into the hall and launched yet another attack.

In his third inaugural address, Hoff called for further consolidation of the courts, for the transfer of welfare programs from the towns to the state, and called again for the kinds of regional planning needed for "controlled growth and planned development." He urged the legislators to help turn Vermont into a "showcase for democracy" and a "laboratory for progress" and reminded them that "the forward thrust of this program for Vermont and its people has three times been endorsed by the electorate."

All of Hoff's inaugural addresses were rather short, and his third took him only twenty minutes to deliver. But it was a long inaugural ceremony nonetheless, coming after a morning session that had been filled with hymns, prayers, homilies, and benediction, and a lunch that had included two former governors (Robert Stafford and George Aiken) and the widow of a third (William Wills). Hoff had developed close ties to many of the state's religious leaders, and while Episcopal bishop Harvey Butterfield and the Polish-born rabbi Max Wall of Burlington had taken part in earlier inaugurals, it was Catholic bishop Robert F. Joyce, who was known to his close friends as "Pat," who led the prayers at this one, along with clerics from Protestant, Jewish, and Greek Orthodox groups. Choirs from Saint Michael's College and Trinity College performed. There was much pomp and too few open windows, with the temperatures in the House chamber seeming to hover near the nineties. Two

National Guard howitzers on the State House lawn rattled the windows and shook the House Chamber chandelier with their blasts, which were intended as salutes to the governor but which also might have been symbolic of the legislative warfare to come. Snelling and Webb, still angry about Billings's endorsement of Hoff and about Hoff's subsequent naming of Billings to a judgeship, were intent on rebuking Hoff and punishing Billings by having the legislature remove him. And Mallary not only had put some anti-Hoff conservatives in key committee posts but had developed a legislative program of his own that made no provision for the $4 million that the plan to move town welfare programs to the state was expected to cost. Hoff praised Mallary's plan for the most part and told reporters, perhaps tongue in cheek, that he thought the missing $4 million for welfare reform might have been just "an oversight."

The third Hoff administration featured a shuffling of aides. Thomas Kenney, the secretary of civil and military affairs and thus Hoff's main liaison with both the legislature and the state agencies, left. Bernard Leddy had been appointed to the federal bench, and Kenney, the father of eight, was offered the chance to take over Leddy's lucrative law practice. A quiet and reserved man who favored bow ties and a low profile, Kenney had sought to protect Hoff in many ways, both by slowing down others who were trying to stampede him into quick decisions and by steering him out of social events before he had done too much drinking, even though Kenney himself, as a colleague noted, "wasn't bashful at a bar." He also was suspicious and wary by nature, asking the director of purchasing, Dick Raymond, to have the phones in the governor's office checked regularly to make sure they weren't being tapped, despite no evidence ever being found that they were.

"He was sort of my protector," Hoff said. "He wasn't more conservative [politically] than the others, but he was more cautious." At a boisterous party in Montpelier one night after Kenney left, with Ben Collins tugging at his sleeve to get him to leave, Hoff was heard to remark in a low-voice aside, "Tom would have had me out of here three-quarters of an hour ago." Kenney was the sort of political operative who believed in keeping positions vague for as long as possible. "Keep it fogged up," he often would say. In contrast, Benjamin McVicker Collins, the special assistant who replaced him, was, in Hoff's words, a "damn the torpedoes" sort of guy, pushing for rapid social and economic change and ready to take on any and all opposition. A graduate of Haverford College, a Quaker school just outside Philadelphia, Collins had been an army sergeant in Korea, a reporter for the *Free Press*, and, briefly, the editor of the *Caledonia Record*. He had a biting sense of humor, labeling some of the state's most resolute conservatives, including Vrest Orton, the founder of the Vermont Country Store, a "Kerosene Kult," who in their romanticizing of the past wanted to take the state back to the days of horse-drawn buggies and kerosene lamps. He had strong liberal views and could be combative in expressing them, causing Aiken to once note that he was "a good fellow, but pretty ferocious for a Quaker." In talking about Kenney and Collins many years after leaving office, Hoff said, "They were two very different people, but they both served me very well."

When Collins took the Kenney job, yet another former reporter, Arthur Ristau, moved into the Collins job as chief liaison with the press. That meant that during Hoff's third term, most of his chief advisers—including Kearns, Guare, Collins, and Ristau—were former newsmen. Since Collins and Ristau were ideologically very close, it also meant that there no longer was the differing viewpoint that Hoff had often been confronted with when Kenney had been in place. The important exception in the mix was Tom Davis, the son of Deane Davis, who had served as regional director of Vermont Community Action and moved up through the ranks to become the Vermont director of the federal Office of Economic Opportunity (OEO), a job he continued to hold during his father's administration. The OEO was a fundamental instrument of Great Society programs in that its funding came directly from Washington and did not require legislative approval. Since OEO funding required only a governor's signature, Hoff was quick to use it to bring more than eighty Great Society programs into the state. Many of these were obtained with the help of a federal Department of Agriculture official, James Woods, whom Kearns admired as a "can do" sort of official who rolled up his sleeves and did much of the detail work himself while "leaving the speech-making to others." The programs usually required state contributions as well, just as most federal highway building did, and by 1967 it was apparent that some unanticipated costs, such as the construction and maintenance of connector roads to the federal highway system, were going to require higher bonding limits. With little notice being taken of its action, the 1967 legislature voted to raise the state bond debt limit to $150 million, and it also passed a bill requiring that the Legislative Council be informed of all future state applications for federal funds. By the time Hoff was getting ready to leave office, the federal programs—while bringing many benefits to the state in terms of education, development, manpower training, and welfare initiatives—were contributing to a state deficit that would cause Deane Davis to call for a 3 percent sales tax in 1969 to help balance the books.

The 1967 session met from January 4 until April 15, and the legislature then adjourned until January 1968, when it reconvened until March 23. These final years of Hoff's governorship were marked by an increased involvement in national affairs and a painful break with President Lyndon Johnson, whom Hoff in fact both liked and admired, over the Vietnam War. They were marked by sudden deficits that would force him to order a $350,000 cut in general spending in 1968. And they also were marked by continued fighting with Mallary, who opposed enough Hoff initiatives that Hoff would later say that while they had been friends in the past and would again be in the future, "there were days when I was governor that I'd willingly have killed him." The first big battle of the 1967 session, however, had nothing to do with Mallary or Hoff's legislative agenda.

Back in May 1966, a vacancy had opened on the Superior Court bench. Since the legislature wasn't in session, the vacancy could be filled by gubernatorial appointment. Hoff had been prepared to appoint Franklin Billings, when Bob Larrow suddenly phoned to say he wanted to be a candidate. Billings's desire to be a judge was well known, while Larrow had not previously expressed any judicial ambitions. But as he had gotten older, Larrow, who was a large man to begin with, had developed a hip disorder that made movement painful. He would have made much more money in private practice, Hoff said, but when the vacancy occurred, Larrow decided that with his physical condition, a judgeship, which would allow him to sit through trials rather than constantly be moving around the courtroom, might be a better way to end his career. "I think he called me within five minutes" of making the decision, Hoff said. Given Larrow's role in the building of the modern state Democratic Party, Hoff was quick to give him the appointment. Both candidates were equally qualified, Hoff said, but he felt obligated to pick Larrow because "I owe it to my party."

In December, when a second Superior Court vacancy occurred, Hoff appointed Billings. While the appointment wasn't a surprise, it nonetheless sparked controversy. When Billings had endorsed Hoff the previous October, Snelling had grumbled that Billings was still harboring a resentment against him because he had voted for William C. Hill of Monkton instead of Billings in a 1959 legislative judicial election. After Hoff named Billings to the post, both Snelling and Derick Webb denounced it as a "classic example of political reward" and put out the word that they intended to try to unseat him. Not all Republicans agreed. Edward Janeway, the Republican national committeeman, was critical of Billings's defection but "not sure party discipline should be applied at that level." Byron Hathorn of Hartford, one of the Young Turks, said that Snelling and Webb were "proven losers," suggesting it was time for them to go back to making cup hooks and running a dairy farm and let others take control of the party.

In previous years, Superior Court judges had faced reelection by the legislature when their terms expired, or election if they had been appointed by a governor when the legislature hadn't been in session. There had seldom been any opposition to incumbents, and only in cases of serious dereliction of duty was reelection denied. In the rare cases when a rival candidate was nominated, it was a clear signal from the legislature that the incumbent shouldn't seek reelection. But the recently adopted Judicial Selection Act, which had been backed by Hoff, held that instead of such elections, the General Assembly would simply vote on a paper ballot on the question "Shall Superior Judge _____ be retained in office? Yes ___ No ___." That meant that instead of a contest between Billings and someone else, who could have been nominated by the Snelling-Webb forces, the decision would be simply a referendum on Billings himself. As a former secretary to the Senate, a former House member, a former Speaker of the House, and the son of a former governor, Billings had history, tradition, and many legislative friendships on his side. Despite his endorsement of Hoff in 1966, he still had the support of the legislative leadership, including Mallary, and on something approaching direct orders from Hoff he would receive the solid bloc of Democratic "yes" votes. He was retained despite thirty-nine "no" votes, which was a substantial number against him (the next largest number of "no" votes against a sitting judge was eight) but which did more to hurt party unity than his career. He would go on to such a distinguished career on the Superior Court that Snelling would appoint him to the Vermont Supreme Court and President Reagan later would name him to the federal bench. It was an important victory for Billings, but in some ways it was an even greater triumph for Hoff. It would be one of his last.

The up-or-down "retain" vote, such as the one on Billings, had been just one element of a broad package of judicial reforms Hoff had been working on since his first days in office. By 1967, big pieces of his package finally had been put in place, despite repeated battles with George W. F. Cook and his Senate Judiciary Committee, which had found ways to whittle away at the package year after year, managing to delay implementation, reduce its scope, and scale back the salary increases Hoff thought were needed. Hoff had been particularly distressed with the municipal courts, which were many in number but staffed largely by part-time judges who were paid minimal salaries, supplemented by fees, and who maintained private practices on the side. Over time, Hoff managed to reduce the number of courts, increase the pay, and make the positions full time.

Hoff also disliked the selection process for Superior Court judges, who were elected by the legislature with no prior screening or review by the State Bar Association or anyone else. He criticized it as a "sort of a popularity contest within the legislature itself," which it was, and a dangerous one because tradition held that once elected, Superior Court judges could simply move up the ladder as a matter of mere seniority until they ended up on the Supreme Court. In effect, longevity became the principal qualification for becoming chief justice of the Vermont Supreme Court. It was considered a dramatic gesture of disapproval in 1964 when Hoff refused to appoint the senior Superior Court judge, Natt L. Divoll, to the Supreme Court, instead naming the father of the man he had defeated for governor, F. Ray Keyser Sr., to the post. Divoll, a Rockingham dairy farmer as well as the senior judge, had become the center of controversy in 1959 when he had directed a verdict of acquittal against a man charged in the death (many Vermonters considered it a vigilante lynching) of Orville Gibson, a Newbury farmer whose body had been found bound with ropes in the Connecticut River three months after he had left his house to do morning chores. The case had attracted a great deal of attention by the national media, which had depicted it as a Gothic tale of murder in the hills, in which neighbors had killed Gibson for having beaten a hired hand on Christmas Eve in 1957, and the whole town then had remained silent to protect the killers. Hoff later said that this decision by Divoll played "no role whatsoever" in his decision to keep him off the Supreme Court. Instead, he said, his decision was based on his own opinion of Divoll as a judge from back when he, Hoff, had been a practicing attorney. Divoll was well liked. He was a descendant of one of Rockingham's oldest families, had served as a navy officer on a PT boat during the D-Day invasion, and had many friends in the legislature, where he had been the secretary to the Senate. But he also had a reputation as a rather laid-back jurist who often came into court late, bringing his hunting dog (a retriever) with him, often left early for fly-fishing or skiing, and—in the view of some of the lawyers who practiced before him—tended to let cases wander around and drag on longer than they needed to, sometimes seeming to pay more attention to his dog than the issues before him. "He was a likable guy, but I wasn't alone in thinking he shouldn't be on the Supreme Court," Hoff said. Hoff also said that Keyser was angry about the decision to name him because he was a strong backer of the seniority system, but he took the job because he knew that if he didn't Hoff would just give it to someone else other than Divoll.

By 1966 the legislature finally had raised the pay for jurists and established a selection board that included both members of the bar and nonlawyers to screen candidates. Whenever a vacancy occurred in a judgeship, applicants would submit their names to the board, and the board—after reviewing the applicants' qualifications—would submit at least three of the names to the legislature, or to the governor if the legislature wasn't in session. The 1966 legislation also had extended the term of office to six years (which along with the higher pay helped attract better candidates), and of course had added the "retention" clause. The 1967 vote on Billings was the first test of the reforms and ended up doing just what Hoff had intended.

The last two years of Hoff's governorship were years of turmoil in the nation, with urban riots, angry protests against the Vietnam War, and social confrontations involving race, feminism, and the counterculture's advocacy of drugs, radical lifestyles, and casual sex, along with the trauma of the assassinations of Bobby Kennedy and Martin Luther King Jr. Although spared the urban riots that set fire to Newark, Washington, Watts, New York, Detroit, and other places, Vermont was very much caught up in the turmoil of the time. Hoff himself became deeply involved in the debate over the war, which he had come to oppose, and in trying to help mend the country's racial divide, and as he did his popularity in Vermont began to drop sharply. They also were years in which he increasingly regretted the fact that he was too often removed from the lives of his young daughters, complaining to friends that the job wasn't allowing him to spend enough time with his family. And he was finding himself drinking even more heavily. It would be several years before he would acknowledge publicly that he was an alcoholic, but by the time his formal portrait was painted for the State House in 1968, the picture, by Peter Gish, showed him seated in a chair with his right leg crossed over his left, a cigarette in one hand and the other looking as though it should be holding a glass, which in fact it often was, at least late in the day. Many of the people who acknowledge that Hoff was drinking more than he should have been also insisted that they never saw that it influenced his judgment or his functioning as governor. And most of them noted that there was a great deal of drinking in Montpelier in the '60s, the main watering holes being the Morgan Horse Room of the Montpelier Tavern and the Brown Derby Restaurant. "That was quite a drinking group in Montpelier back then," Al Moulton recalled long afterward. "I did some of it myself. I never saw that it affected [Hoff]. I never saw it impair his judgment or cause him not to be able to make a speech." And Hoff seemed to have remarkable powers of recovery. Once early in 1967, reporters who had been drinking with him late into the night at the Morgan Horse Room showed up for an early morning news conference bleary-eyed and somewhat hung over to find a bright-eyed Hoff who moved briskly and sharply through the session, as though he had spent the previous night drinking ginger ale. When it ended, he said to one of the reporters who had lagged behind, "This state has probably had better governors, but I don't think any of them ever had as much fun." But by the time of the 1968 session he was drinking heavily enough that his efficient and loyal secretary, Priscilla LaPlante, was finding herself having to cover for him as he started showing up late for meetings; and he also was, he later conceded, totally exhausted from three campaigns and five years as governor. At the same time, he was watching his political clout slip away because of his self-imposed lame-duck status and because of his increasing involvement in unpopular causes.

There were important legislative victories in his last years nonetheless, including the shift of local welfare programs to the state from the towns, where they were being administered in highly inequitable, sometimes haphazard, and often arbitrary ways by local overseers of the poor. And his ongoing attempts to promote the state both for businesses and tourists had a huge success at the 1967 Expo in Montreal, where a "Vermont Night" featuring the Trapp Family Singers (which was arranged by Al Moulton, who in return had promised Maria Von Trapp that he would see that the dirt road to her Trapp Family Lodge in Stowe was paved, even if he had to do it himself) drew the biggest crowd of the entire World's Fair except for the appearance of Queen Elizabeth. Other successes included getting the state income tax linked to the federal income tax by making it a percentage of the federal tax. Instead of having the legislature set the income tax rate, which was the practice, Hoff and his tax commissioner, Gerald Witherspoon, wanted Vermonters to simply pay a percentage of their federal tax, which was far more progressive

than the Vermont version. The legislature also would impose a state capital gains tax for the first time. This was done with the help of James Jeffords, a Republican of Rutland, who later would become a U.S. senator
but who in 1967 was in his first year in the state Senate. Jeffords broke
with party leaders and cast the deciding vote that sent the bill out of committee and onto the floor, having concluded that by piggy-backing onto
the federal tax plan Vermont's tax structure would go from one of the
most regressive in the nation to one of the most progressive. Jeffords was
given what he later called "some talking-tos" by angry Republicans and
also was confronted before the vote by reporter Mavis Doyle, who "put
an index finger in my face and told me in no uncertain terms that I had
better vote for that bill." That was inappropriate for a reporter, of course,
but not unexpected. Doyle was known as someone who not only wore her
heart on her sleeve but who drove around with the bumper stickers of favored politicians on her car. Yet other successes included additional pay
increases for judges and other state employees, still more court reforms,
a minimum-wage increase, and—after years of rejection—a fair-housing
law prohibiting discrimination in housing, which was passed 74–56 after three days of angry debate and eight roll-call votes by House conservatives attempting to kill it, stall it, amend it into insignificance, or
tie it into procedural knots. The 10 percent pay raise for state employees
proved to be important in future years, helping Vermont attract a more
professional class of civil servants.

A measure that received little attention at the time but that Hoff took
great pride in was the creation of a Vermont Planning Council, which
Hoff chaired with William Kearns as his vice chairman. The council
included legislators, state commissioners, and citizens, but the driving
force was its clerk, Leonard H. Wilson, the 1960 Democratic candidate
for lieutenant governor, whom Hoff had lured back from Washington to
take a state planning job. In 1968 the council published *Vision and Choice:
Vermont's Future* and *Vision and Planning*, two reports that have been cited
as early giant steps toward Vermont's pioneering environmental legislation of the Deane Davis years. Hoff had started out as an advocate of industrial development,but had come to conclude that unrestricted growth
was detrimental to the environment and that maintaining the state's natural beauty was crucial to its prosperity. Reaching back to the 1777 state
constitution, which held that "private property ought to be subservient
to public uses when necessity requires it," he argued for "a new balance
between property rights and human rights" that would halt the spoiling
of Vermont and its resources. Although the Vermont Planning Council's

proposals were tentative and broadly drawn, Hoff came to treasure them as central to his legacy. That same year saw the first serious land-use legislation, allowing towns to enforce regional zoning, and it was Hoff's pressuring of Democrats in the 1968 session that finally gathered enough votes to pass the landmark legislation sponsored by Republican legislator Theodore M. (Ted) Riehle Jr. that banned most billboards from Vermont roads.

Hoff felt that much more could and should have been accomplished in the 1967 and 1968 sessions, and he blamed some of the failures on Mallary's attempt to unite the broad range of Republican House members by placing some anti-Hoff conservatives, particularly Emory Hebard, in key legislative posts. Hebard had been given the hugely important chairmanship of the Ways and Means Committee, an appointment that Hoff called "incredible." Hoff also labeled the conservatives "enemies of Vermont" and said that Mallary had created a spirit of divisiveness and partisanship by trying to make deals with them. Hebard shrugged off the criticism and dismissed Hoff late in the 1968 session by saying, among other things, that he himself didn't have any interest in anything that "a peacenik lame-duck governor" had to say. House Majority Leader Luther (Fred) Hackett rebuked Hebard for the remarks and disassociated himself from them. But the Republicans not only managed to block Hoff's final attempts to reorganize state government that year (the proposal would breeze through under Republican Deane Davis), but in the last weeks of the session a small group of conservatives headed by Hebard managed with just forty votes in the House and ten in the Senate to use parliamentary maneuvers to block action on a Capitol-complex plan for new building, increases in the minimum wage for public works employees, and many other bills supported by large majorities from both parties. They even managed to delay committee reports on appropriations and tax bills, until Mallary finally left the Speaker's podium to go to his floor desk and make an impassioned appeal that the bills be released.

Despite Hoff's criticisms, Mallary didn't see himself as being an obstructionist. With Vermont becoming a two-party state, he felt it was important for Republicans to develop legislative agendas of their own, impose a "winner take all" philosophy for the awarding of chairmanships (meaning that only members of the majority party in the House would get them), and enforce party discipline by denying chairmanships to House members who bucked him and other party leaders on important votes. He and Hackett felt such moves were necessary to create a balance of power by giving legislative leaders the ability to counter Hoff's vast use of executive powers, which in fact was setting the standard for a strong governor that would continue into the twenty-first century. In a news conference at the start of the 1967 session, they said that what Hoff was calling "partisanship" was nothing more than Republicans "coming up with responsible alternatives." The legislative program Mallary developed for 1967 called for more funding for regional vocational schools, pay raises for state employees, increased workmen's compensation insurance, increases in the minimum annual teachers' retirement benefits (up to $2,400 after thirty-five years of service), and a labor relations bill. Although Hoff at one point criticized the 1967 General Assembly as a "do nothing" legislature, it nearly doubled state aid to education, approved a statewide system of district courts with full-time judges, created the policy-making board for state planning, tightened up laws regulating dumps and junkyards, increased the minimum wage, and, of course, passed the hugely important bill transferring local welfare programs to the state.

The welfare bill, in fact, was a classic example of some of the important legislation of the Hoff years that got enacted in bipartisan ways, and a key player was the somewhat unlikely figure of Representative Reid Lefevre, Republican of Manchester. Although Lefevre was not a staunch conservative, neither was he considered a progressive. He was a mainstream Republican in many ways, but conservative enough that Emory Hebard had urged him to run for governor in 1966. "Historically, he hadn't been an advocate for social issues," Hoff later said. There had, however, been exceptions. Back in 1951 he had touched off a bitter legislative battle when he introduced a bill setting safety standards for school buses. At the time, many towns hired farmers to bus children to school, and some of them were hauling children in the backs of open cattle trucks.

"It was outrageous," Lefevre recalled many years later. "They were hauling those children like cattle in below-zero weather in trucks that had manure on the floor." There was strong opposition to his bill from legislators who feared it would unleash a flood of state controls over their local schools. But Lefevre capped his campaign by arranging for *Rutland Herald* photographer Aldo Merusi to photograph a group of schoolchildren being transported in midwinter in the back of an open cattle truck. Merusi's picture, captioned "The rigors of education in old Vermont," was sent to newspapers across the nation by the Associated Press, and Lefevre credited the embarrassment it caused many Vermonters with helping muster the support needed to pass the bill.

That sort of flair marked much of what Lefevre did and made him one of the most interesting figures in the legislature from the late '40s until the late '60s. A large man with a stomach that began at his chin, he owned a carnival called King Reid Shows that traveled from Alabama to Canada. It included rides, food concessions, bingo games, shooting galleries, carnival strippers, and what used to be called "freak shows," with a collection of midgets, fat people, sword swallowers, fire eaters, "seal boys" (with flippers instead of arms), and tattooed ladies. The son of a well-known and financially successful author, Wall Street investor, and ambassador, Lefevre had attended schools in Paris and Seville and later had studied at Yale, Williams, Columbia, and the University of Vermont. One of his first jobs after college was as a press agent for the fighter Jack Dempsey (it was Dempsey's trainer who first dubbed Lefevre "The King"), and he kept a picture of the heavyweight champion in the trailer that he used as his carnival headquarters. He later ran a stable of fighters out of Miami, Florida, and Troy, New York.

Considered one of the finest orators and wittiest members of the legislature, Lefevre once spoke against a motion to dock the pay of absent members by saying that "some of our members have contributed most generously on days when they were absent." He once characterized a legislator he considered not very bright as having "an insufficiency disguised as incompetence." He had long been one of the most influential legislators, but in the winter of 1967 he was angry and licking his wounds. Mallary, who considered him too independent, had stripped him of the chairmanship of the important House Ways and Means Committee during the first week of the session and had demoted him to the much less important Social Welfare Committee. Lefevre, saying that he had no experience in the field and was "totally ill-equipped" for the post, at first threatened to refuse it. But both Hoff and his welfare commissioner, John Wackerman, urged him to stay, in large part because the number-two man on the committee, who might move into the chairmanship if Lefevre declined it, was the very conservative Fred Westphal of Elmore, who had described the pending welfare bill as "the most foolish thing I've heard or seen." Westphal later described his philosophy about welfare as "Starve or get out and work." The idea of Westphal taking charge of the bill was a nightmare scenario for Hoff and Wackerman. "Good God, that would have been the end of it," Hoff later said. And Hoff said that for some time—well before Lefevre had been moved to the Social Welfare Committee—it had been Wackerman's plan to try to draw Lefevre into supporting the bill and taking a lead role, knowing it needed a respected Republican with great powers of persuasion if it were to pass. Wackerman was a Republican who had served with Lefevre in the legislature in the 1950s, and the two liked and admired each other.

The bill, which would allow the state to assume full responsibility for the administration and financing of all public assistance programs, was intended to end a situation in which Vermont's needy were cared for in very different and sometimes highly arbitrary ways, according to the different standards and mercies of 264 overseers of the poor. The bill had evolved out of a legislative study group, had been drafted by the Legislative Council in 1966, and had been made one of Hoff's major priorities for the 1967 session. The Democratic caucus had endorsed it unanimously, but while Mallary himself supported the bill, it hadn't been a part of his Republican agenda for the session because a poll had shown that forty-seven of the ninety-five House Republicans wanted to either kill it or delay it for another session. The opponents included the seventy-nine-year-old Arthur W. Simpson, Republican of Lyndon, who in the 1930s had been the head of the Old Age Assistance Commission, which later became the Department of Social Welfare. He and many others saw the bill as a last assault on the "local control" that had characterized Vermont in the pre-Hoff and pre-reapportionment era, and they were passionate in their opposition. Jeffords captured some of the mood of the time in his book *An Independent Man*, writing that Lefevre was distressed by the demotion but "there was no quit in Reid Lefevre and he was no fool," and that "in revenge for his demotion he entered into an unspoken alliance with the Democratic governor." Jeffords went on to say that many Republicans complained that the bill was yet another attempt to have big government take away local control, and that in the past Lefevre likely would have been complaining along with them. "But he felt wronged, and pretty soon it seemed the more Reid learned about the welfare changes, the more he liked them," Jeffords wrote. "Despite Republican protests, King Reid stayed on Hoff's side."

What Lefevre stage-managed during the winter months of 1967 was a legislative tour de force in which he crafted changes in the sixty-two-page bill in committee; lined up support in the House; spoke in articulate and passionate ways on the floor about the history of aid to the poor, about the needs of the blind, the crippled, children, and the mentally ill; orchestrated supporting speeches on specific aspects of the bill by Representatives Tom Salmon, Homer Ashland, Deborah Beattie, and others; and over three days of argument beat back attempts to have it tabled, radically amended, and subjected to a state referendum. The bill, officially known as Act 147 of the 1967 session, was so sweeping and the changes in state law so many that a special section of the so-called Green Book, the book of all state laws and their history, had to be printed just to deal with them. The final vote of 112–32, after conservatives had obtained two minor amendments and thrown in the towel, was no real sign of the depth of the opposition or the intensity of the debate. Representative George Van Santvoord, a Bennington Democrat, said Lefevre's leadership had been crucial, and it was "doubtful whether anyone else in the House could have done it."

It would be a last hurrah for Lefevre, who would die of a heart attack in January 1968. And, except for Ted Riehle's anti-billboard bill, which Hoff didn't initiate but had an important hand in, there would be no other such major successes for Hoff in the 1968 session. Riehle and the Republicans in fact had decided to exclude Democrats from the bill and keep it as a Republican initiative, which annoyed many Democrats to the point where they threatened to vote against it. But despite all the work Riehle had done to drum up support for the bill (among other things, he seemed to have spoken to almost every garden club in the state in 1967), the opposition of businesses that used them and farmers who rented land for them was so strong that in the end, despite the Republicans' huge majority in the legislature, they couldn't get enough votes. So Hoff weighed in and leaned on enough Democrats to get the necessary votes. "They needed some help, which I provided, I must say with a little bit of resentment because they had been so adamant about this being their baby," he later said. "Having said that, you have to give Ted Riehle real credit for the bill. It was a far reaching piece of legislation, very carefully thought through and crafted, and I think it served us very well." That aside, the three-and-a-half-month session in 1968 was a difficult and frustrating one for Hoff, not just because of the refusal of Republicans to approve his plans to consolidate and reorganize state agencies into a more manageable structure, but because of the success of a small minority of conservatives in using parliamentary maneuverings to block many bills that had broad bipartisan support. He was angry enough that he vowed to call an emergency session to reconsider some of that legislation, something Hebard said he wasn't worried about because Hoff wouldn't "have the guts" to call one. In the end Hoff didn't, saying long afterward that it wasn't a matter of guts but simply a matter of "not having the votes."

But by then, his mark already had been made. During the Hoff years, general-fund revenues had increased by more than 100 percent, and much of it had been sent back to the communities in forms of state aid. The Vermont Housing Authority and the Vermont Home Mortgage Credit Agency had been created to help meet the shortage of housing for low- and moderate-income families. State aid to education had increased from $5 million annually to $15 million. The legislature had been reapportioned. The poll tax had been abolished as a voting requirement. The death penalty had been virtually abolished. The Commission on Women had been created to investigate discrimination against women, document the needs of working women and their children, and support a more active role for women in the political life of the state. The Democratic Party had become revitalized. Scores of federal programs had been implemented, providing everything from water and roads to job training and education. A significant expansion of parks and recreation areas had taken place, new zoning and land-control measures had been enacted, and many natural areas, including Camel's Hump, had been preserved. A Legal Aid program had been established for low-income Vermonters, and a Consumer Protection Office had been created as well. A Council on Aging had been established, and nine senior citizen centers had been opened. The Vermont Student Assistance program had been launched to provide state-guaranteed college loans. The three teachers colleges had been transformed into much more robust liberal arts schools, and—despite the refusal of the legislature to mandate it—regionalization of schools was becoming a widespread reality. The reforms of the court and welfare systems would prove to be both significant and long-lasting. But Bill Kearns, who served with Hoff from the start to the end, argued that Hoff's impact wasn't just in legislation achieved and things done through executive orders, but in the leadership role that he assumed and the whole spirit of excitement and optimism about Vermont's future that flowed from it. "There was some criticism of Phil for not being a greatly skilled administrator, and of course he wasn't," Kearns said. "He recognized that the governor, to be effective, had to be a leader. That leadership was what the office was all about. . . . We felt as an administration that Hoff's very election was history. It made a statement that Vermont was ready for change. And that's what he set out to do."

CHAPTER 5

CIVIL RIGHTS IN THE WHITEST STATE

On October 25, 1964, Governor Hoff and Governor George C. Wallace of Alabama appeared on *Meet the Press*, the popular NBC Sunday evening television news show. It wasn't a joint appearance. Wallace appeared by himself and was questioned by the panel during the first half of the program. Hoff was questioned separately during the second half. A boxer in his youth and feisty in his politics, Wallace—who was still calling himself a Democrat at the time, although he later would become the presidential candidate of the American Independent Party—stopped short of flatly endorsing Republican U.S. senator Barry Goldwater for president, saying that if he endorsed him or anyone else the headlines the next day would shout "Racist Governor, Bigoted Governor Endorses So and So," and that he didn't want "my liabilities to be saddled upon any candidate in the country." But he spoke highly of the Arizona conservative and staunchly defended Alabama's attempts to maintain the segregation of its schools.

Hoff's appearance was intended to provide viewers with a sharp contrast—a northern liberal Democrat versus a southern conservative one—and it did. He offered a wholehearted support of President Lyndon Johnson and the recently enacted national Civil Rights Act, while projecting Vermont's self-image as a racially enlightened society. Asked by James J. Kilpatrick of the *Richmond (Virginia) News Leader*, "Wouldn't you say, Governor, that it is pretty easy to be virtuous about civil rights when less than one percent of your population is Negro?" Hoff replied, "Perhaps so, but I would remind you that the heart of Vermont went out in the Civil War, and we have been suffering those losses even to this date, so I don't see that anybody can say we don't have a concern in this whole question." At another point, he said, "We certainly don't stand in Vermont and say that we do not welcome Negroes. We like to think that we treat them on an equal basis. . . . I want to make it abundantly clear here and now that we do not in any way say that Negroes can't come to our state. They are welcome at any time."

Seven months later, in response to a San Francisco student asking about racial relations in Vermont, Hoff said, "Vermont has no significant racial problems" and attributed the absence to "Vermonters always believing in the equality of man and the dignity of the individual." He would have been more accurate to have qualified his statement by at least substituting "largely" for "always." Many Vermonters took pride in the fact that their constitution was the first to prohibit slavery, although there had been very few slaves in Vermont at the time. Census records afterward, in fact, showed that right up until the Civil War about 50 percent of the few blacks who did live in the state continued to live in white households, with the terms of their employment—or their servitude—often unclear or ill-defined. At the time of Hoff's comments, the fact that less than 1 percent of the population was black—the census of 1960 showed only 519 blacks in the state, which was just 0.133 percent—allowed many Vermonters to consider themselves far removed from the deep-rooted racism of the South and the growing racial tensions of the urban North. But fear and distrust of strangers also had been a part of Vermont history. In the late nineteenth and early twentieth centuries, a bias against immigrants in general and Catholics in particular had been widespread, and for a time in the 1920s the Ku Klux Klan had been active in parts of Vermont.

Klan operations in Vermont weren't particularly secret and seldom were violent. Crosses were burned in fields and in the hills, but there were no lynchings and little in terms of serious intimidation. The Klan in Vermont was mainly anti-Catholic, its Protestant members viewing Catholics as not entirely American and not fully patriotic because of their religious ties to Rome and the pope. "America for Americans" was a rallying cry, and many of the Vermont Klan meetings were—at least on the surface—rather celebratory affairs. John Cleary of Woodford remembered as a child going to a Klan meeting in Bradford in the early '20s that was much like a Fourth of July picnic. "The town band played at it," he said, which was why he had been taken there in the first place, since both his uncle and grandfather were members of the Bradford Brass Band. Many Klan rallies in fact took place in broad daylight and in very public places, like local fairgrounds, with robed and hooded (but usually not masked) men and women carrying picnic baskets and flags, local bands providing festive music, and fireworks later lighting the night sky along with the burning crosses.

A broadside poster for a KKK meeting near Poultney in the 1920s announced

> America is in Danger!
> Ku Klux Klan Lecture
> Sunday, October 3rd
> at 7:30 P.M.
> at the
> Howe Farm
> on Main Road between Wells and Poultney
> Fiery Cross and Ceremonial
> State Representative will deliver lecture
> All Protestants Are Welcome
> Kome—Rain or Shine—Kome

Klan rallies were held in Montpelier, St. Johnsbury, Barre, South Royalton, Hardwick, Rutland, and elsewhere. Credible numbers are hard to come by, but Maudean Neill in *Fiery Crosses in the Green Mountains* wrote that 5,000 men and women of the Klan attended a "konclave" at the Lamoille County fairgrounds in Morrisville on May 2, 1925, and that Klansmen claimed to have had more than 14,000 members in Lamoille, Chittenden, Orange, Washington, and Caledonia counties alone. There was no verification cited for the 14,000 figure, although Lamoille, Orange, and Washington counties were among the places where the Klan was most active. But whatever the numbers, the Klan activity in Vermont was mostly nonviolent and rather short-lived. In Rutland, the *Rutland Herald* printed the license plate numbers and owners of all the cars at a Klan rally, which helped end Klan activity there. And by the late 1920s, it was pretty much a thing of the past, although the underlying biases remained. In fact, a survey of Burlington banks in the late 1950s showed that—despite the city's large Catholic population—Burlington had no bank officials and only one bank teller who was Catholic.

Anti-Semitism also was common in Vermont, as it was virtually everywhere in the country, despite the small numbers of Jews in the state. This remained true well into the 1950s and early '60s. The University of Vermont (or UVM—from the Latin *Universitas Veridis Montis* or "University of the Green Mountains") had a much larger percentage of Jewish students (most of them from out of state) than Vermont had Jews, causing the school to sometimes be referred to derisively by Vermonters as

"JewVM." The authors of *Freedom and Unity: A History of Vermont* noted that in the early years of the tourist industry, Jewish travelers often found themselves excluded from hotels and guesthouses in Vermont (the Glenwood Resort in Hydeville, for example, said in its newspaper ads "No Hebrews entertained") and that French Canadians also "did not always receive a warm welcome." Some people who were active in politics in the '30s, including George Aiken, said that while it would have provided many jobs for Vermonters, part of the reason that a proposed 260-mile stretch of scenic road along the ridge of the Green Mountains, to be called the Green Mountain Parkway, was defeated on Town Meeting Day 1936 was concerns—very real but mostly unstated—that it would bring Jewish resorts and large numbers of Jewish vacationers to Vermont, just as the parkways north of New York City had brought Jews to the Catskills.

Raul Hilberg, the UVM professor who authored a seminal work on the Holocaust, *The Destruction of the European Jews*, recalled in a memoir that he initially had resisted going to Burlington to discuss a job at the college because he expected to find such discrimination against Jews that he wouldn't survive the first interview. "When I arrived in Burlington, I learned that I was safe," he wrote. "The discrimination was directed at Catholics." The Political Science Department that he joined had nine members—six Protestants and three Jews—and while there in fact were Catholics on the faculty, although not in great numbers, Hilberg later told writer Jules Older that he came to believe that in the late 1950s and early 1960s anti-Catholicism was a more serious problem at UVM than prejudice against blacks or Jews. But the anti-Semitism was real, and in 1959 Hilberg discovered that the school in fact had developed a policy of segregating first-year women students by religion. In going through the school directory, he found that all the female Jewish freshmen were assigned rooms with other female Jewish freshmen, and that female Catholic freshmen were assigned rooms with other Catholics. The school also, he found, paired off female students from rich families with other females from rich families, and short females with other short females. "This was social engineering!" he told Older. "If you were short and Protestant and poor, chances are you would be living with someone else short and Protestant and poor."

Hilberg wrote a letter to Lyman Rowell, then the dean of administration, demanding an end to "the segregation of Jewish freshman girls in the university dormitories." He argued that application forms should delete questions about race and religion, and that room assignments should be made without consideration of those factors. "You have my assurance that the results will be checked in the fall," he wrote. It's not certain that most freshman women objected to the pairings, or the degree to which Hilberg's protests brought about change. But in fact, the practice ended soon afterward.

So while ethnic, racial, and religious tensions weren't so open or so widespread for most Vermonters to consider them problems, Vermonters had their prejudices, as Hoff himself had experienced a few years before when he had gone to court to reverse a Rutland County probate judge's decision involving a home-grown form of bias. A Rutland minister, Frederick P. Miller, and his wife had taken in a foster child who was the daughter of a "half-black" mother. They already had adopted a two-year-old Puerto Rican boy and had asked the state Welfare Department for a girl of mixed blood because they knew how hard it was for the state to place such children with adoptive parents. When it became time for her to enter kindergarten at Rutland's Longfellow School, she had to have a birth certificate showing her age. The Millers, intending to adopt her, asked Probate Judge George Jones to grant her one with themselves listed as the parents. The Vermont law said that an adoptive child's birth certificate should be no different from one of any other child. In effect, it required the certificate to say that the child was a "natural" child and not an "adopted" one.

Jones said that what the Millers were doing was "a Christian act" and that "nobody is going to take the child away from them." But he refused to permit a birth certificate showing white parents for a black child, saying flatly, "I will not make birth records show a Negro child with white parents." He then defended his decision by telling *Rutland Herald* reporter Robert Bennett that he might have allowed it if the child had been fairer skinned, but that she was too dark for him to do it. "If I had ruled the other way, I'd have Orval Faubus [then the segregationist governor of Arkansas] and the Ku Klux Klan up here to scalp me," he said. "I wouldn't say this girl is as black as the ace of spades, but she's chocolate milk color." Hoff took on the case without a fee and in 1961 had the decision reversed in higher court. The story about Jones's decision was picked up by the Associated Press (which paid Bennett $10 for it) and appeared in newspapers all over the country. Jones, who was furious that the *Herald* had published the quotes but who never denied them, was a longtime judge who had been reelected easily to term after term.

But he was defeated when he next ran for election and blamed Bennett for his loss. Since the story had been accurate and not even Jones had claimed that it hadn't been, this bothered the young reporter not at all.

There had been other cases that attracted national attention, and while they had seemed limited and isolated, they nonetheless suggested deeper problems. The April 16, 1946, issue of *Life* magazine, for example, featured a story about the UVM chapter of Alpha Xi Delta sorority, which closed itself down rather than agree to a demand by the national headquarters that it not accept as a member a black student from Washington, D.C., Crystal Malone. The sorority had pledged Malone, one of only two black students on the campus at the time, after the Pan-Hellenic Society that oversaw the fraternities and sororities on campus had adopted new standards saying that racial or religious discrimination no longer would be allowed. The president of the Alpha Xi Delta national organization traveled to Burlington to try to persuade Malone not to join and also to try to persuade the local AXD chapter not to accept her. Malone refused and the local sorority burned its charter, knowing that the decision would force it to disband.

That was a dramatic stand for civil rights, and a laudable one. But rather than weigh in on the side of the sorority, the university, in a Pontius Pilate–like gesture, washed its hands of the controversy. John Schoff Mills, the president, said it was a matter between the local sorority and the national, not something for the school to get involved in. The dean of women, Mary Jean Simpson, likewise refused to offer support for the sorority, saying that UVM had no policy on the matter. So instead of taking a strong stand in support of civil rights and declaring that fraternities and sororities that discriminated would be banned on campus, the university chose to duck the issue. Peter Mallett, a student and war veteran, decried this in a letter to the student newspaper, the *Vermont Cynic*, complaining about "the pathetic indifference of the administration."

A decade later, another racial incident showed deeper problems. In February 1957, Leroy Williams Jr., the captain of the 1956 UVM football team and one of only seven blacks on the campus, reserved a motel room for his date for Kake Walk, the school's winter carnival. The reservation had been made by a white friend, both for Williams's date and three other women. One of the women (who was white) arrived on a Thursday night and was given a room. But when Williams's date (who was black) showed up on Friday, she was turned away after being told that "there was arrangement on Williston Road among motel operators to take no

Negroes." She eventually found accommodations in a tourist home, but this time there was greater outrage. The *Cynic* published a scathing editorial, saying in part,

> The captain of our team was not allowed to put up his girl at the motel because the color of his skin was not the same as ours. The man who led our team to so many victories, the fellow who gave his spirit and leadership to our team, the guy who symbolized the whole university as he struggled with our foes on the gridiron was "not allowed" because a small-minded inn-keeper didn't like his color.
>
> It is obvious that an injustice has been committed, an injustice which involves not only the people of Burlington but every member of this University and every member of this state. . . . There is a need of a Civil Rights bill in this state, so that a public licensed institution such as a motel shall not be able to legally bar anyone from use of their facilities because of race, creed or religion.

Protests were staged, a UVM Council on Human Relations was created, and the school's president, Dr. Carl W. Borgmann, condemned the action. The state legislature, acting with unusual speed, on April 23 passed a bill introduced by Senator Fred Fayette prohibiting discrimination in places of public accommodation. The legislation—"An Act Relating to the Full and Equal Enjoyment of Public Accommodation"— broadly defined "public accommodation" and made violations of the act a criminal offense punishable by fines of up to $500 or imprisonment of up to thirty days, or both. But at the time, little attention was paid to the racist nature of Kake Walk itself. It would be another decade before Kake Walk—the wildly popular centerpiece of the UVM winter carnival, and something that Hoff himself took part in as governor by presenting cakes to the winners—came to an end.

Just what was Kake Walk? At bottom, it was a dance competition based on dances performed by slaves in the antebellum South, usually on Sunday afternoons when little plantation work was being done. The best dancers sometimes would be given prizes by the plantation owners and their families who had come to watch, causing the dancing to be known as a "prize dance." When a performance of "prize dancing" was staged at the Centennial of American Independence exhibition in Philadelphia in 1876 as part of a display of Negro culture, the winners were given a huge cake, and the term "cakewalk" came into being. But at UVM it was much more than that, and it's hard looking back from a distance of four decades to describe the sense of excitement and anticipation that surrounded the event. It began in the 1880s as UVM's version of the "nigger shows"— variety-type minstrel shows done in blackface—that were common and very popular all across America at the time. Eventually, it turned into a dance competition, with Kake Walk being spelled with a "K" because early versions of the event had been labeled by students as "The Kullud Koon Kake Walk." Many colleges in the Northeast had winter carnivals, including nearby Middlebury and Dartmouth, but few if any of them had the sense of excitement that marked Kake Walk. In 1952, it was featured in *Life* magazine, in a totally upbeat picture spread that never suggested it was racist in any way. By the early 1960s it had become a three-day February festival with classes canceled, the library closed, and jazz concerts featuring such top performers as Duke Ellington, Coleman Hawkins, and Dizzy Gillespie; the election of a carnival king and queen; formal dances and sports competitions; serious drinking (much of it illegal, since the drinking age in Vermont was twenty-one at the time); fraternity skits and fraternity parties; snow sculptures; and, at the heart of it, "Walkin' Fo' De Kake," in which two-man teams of dancers from each fraternity—wearing blackface, bright satin minstrel costumes, and strutting to the music of "Cotton Babes" (a ragtime two-step written by Percy Wenrich in 1909)—competed for trophies and cakes, while a gymnasium packed with thousands of spectators, almost all of them white, cheered and applauded. It was so popular that many students tried to downplay or ignore its racist character, arguing that it was a celebration of black culture and tradition and that there was nothing racist about portraying black people as fun-loving and happy. The walking itself was described vividly—and in two very different ways—by James Loewen, a member of the UVM Sociology Department, in a chapter about Kake Walk that was included in the anniversary book *The University of Vermont: The First Two Hundred Years*:

> The crowd quiets, until an electric stillness fills the darkened auditorium. A pencil-thin spotlight illuminates a black-gloved hand holding a white handkerchief at shoulder height. The hand opens. The handkerchief drops. A band begins a catchy ragtime tune. A larger spotlight picks up two dancers, both men, who kick their feet high into the air, toes pointed, arms around each other's back, moving as one being, in perfect time. The pace is

rapid, the gestures staccato. The men move apart, still dancing. Then they slow, but their routine looks even more difficult.
They seem to hang in the air between steps. The dancers face
each other, link two feet, lean back at an impossible angle, leap
high, and push their white-gloved hands skyward. This performance is at once difficult and athletic, graceful and aesthetic.
The band, an integral part of the production, shows an uncan-
ny ability to anticipate each tempo change. Even the crowd gets
into the act, clapping and chanting rhythmically. It is like ice
dancing in its rapid changes of tempo and mood. It is like free-
form gymnastics, with certain steps that must be included in an
overall routine. It is like ballet. It is like no other. It is UVM Kake
Walk, an eighty-year tradition, the crowning event of the school
calendar.

Or, he continued, looking at it another way:

In a packed gymnasium, five thousand white people and perhaps
two or three people of color watch intently as two white college
students put on a caricature of African Americans. Their hands
and feet are white, exaggerating the fact that, to some whites,
blacks have large hands and feet, whose palms and soles are not
the same color as the rest of them. The students' faces are colored black but not a human color. Rather, like the "pickaninny"
dolls of the nineteenth century, this black is unnatural. Large
white eye and mouth sockets exaggerate the perception whites
have that the eyes and lips of African Americans are too big,
stand out too vividly against their skin color. Outlandish kinky-
haired wigs complete the effect, not so much comic as mildly re-
pulsive, although the audience seems to view it with affection.
The students now begin to strut and kick up their legs in a ritual
called "a-walking' fo' de kake." When they have finished, they
bow humbly to a white couple with crowns on, seated in a place
of honor. They shuffle off like Stepin Fetchit in the old Holly-
wood movies. The crowd shows its appreciation with wild applause. This too is UVM Kake Walk, an eighty-year fascination
with a stereotype of blacks in the whitest state in the Union.

The *Cynic* had first editorialized against the blackface aspect of Kake
Walk in 1954, creating a huge backlash of opposition against the paper.

It dropped its opposition for a few years but in the '60s again began calling for changes. In 1964 the National Association for the Advancement of Colored People (NAACP) formally criticized Kake Walk. Blackface and kinky wigs were eliminated in 1965, and various shades of green and gold (and in one case, purple) face colorings were substituted, a compromise that pleased almost no one. The rise of the civil rights movement brought increased calls for abandoning Kake Walk altogether. By 1969, the director of admissions, Harold Collins, was complaining that Kake Walk was making it difficult for the school to recruit black students, and both Governor Deane Davis and Hoff (now a former governor) were urging the school to end it. On October 30, 1969, Phi Gamma Delta fraternity, whose Kake Walkers in recent years had performed without makeup or wigs, announced that it no longer would enter walkers in the competition, saying that Kake Walk "is a degrading activity not fit for any winter weekend or celebration, particularly at this period of our nation's history." The next day, the Kake Walk directors voted to end it completely. By this point, as *The Vermont Encyclopedia* noted, "with civil rights, Vietnam, political assassinations, and the counterculture heating up campus debate, Kake Walk looked not only racist but increasingly frivolous and anachronistic."

The end also came in the aftermath of two incidents that had taken place in Vermont in 1968—the angry reaction to the creation of the Vermont–New York Youth Project that had brought minority youths to Vermont, and shots being fired at the home of a black minister in Irasburg—which had been troubling to many Vermonters concerned about civil rights, had been politically damaging to Hoff, and had exposed a latent racism in the state that was deeper and more widespread than Hoff and many others wanted to believe. As the *Rutland Herald* noted in an editorial on November 9, 1968, the Irasburg matter in particular had "brought Vermonters face to face with some extremely unsavory evidence of racial bias in the state." It was a situation that made the racial stereotyping at the state's university winter carnival even more objectionable, and further undercut the arguments (never sound to begin with) that Kake Walk wasn't racist because Vermonters themselves weren't.

Hoff's involvement in the events of 1968—he had launched the youth project, and he had ordered an investigation into the state police's handling of the Irasburg shooting—should not have surprised most Vermonters, since a commitment to civil rights had marked his entire career in state government. In some cases, Hoff's efforts had proved more well-meaning than effective, because much of the legislation passed during his time in office hadn't been backed up with the necessary funding to provide staffing or aggressive enforcement. But during all his years in government he had been an outspoken opponent of discrimination on the basis of race, religion, or sex. As a freshman legislator in 1961, he had introduced "An Act to Provide Freedom from Discrimination in Employment." There was strong opposition from legislators who argued that it was among the cures Hoff was offering for maladies that didn't exist, and it was defeated. The proposed act also had encountered strong opposition from labor groups, which feared it would interfere with union hall practices and would also—as had been the case in some other states—be used to advocate right-to-work legislation. Emory Hebard, in fact, tried to amend the bill to also prohibit discrimination against employees based on "membership or lack of membership in any labor organization or association." The amendment failed, after a spirited and lengthy floor fight, but the bill itself failed as well, defeated on the third reading in the House by twenty-five votes. But in his first term as governor Hoff backed a similar bill, this time with union support, that passed after a floor amendment—which in fact had been intended by opponents to help scuttle it—had been added to also prohibit "discrimination in rates of pay for reasons of sex." Because the law didn't give aggrieved parties the right to bring suit under the statute, and because no specific agency was charged with enforcement, it proved to be of limited value. But it was passed a year before the federal Civil Rights Act of 1964, and Hoff had cited it in his *Meet the Press* interview as evidence of Vermont's opposition to discrimination.

The Civil Rights Act of 1964 was landmark legislation in many ways, and Stephen M. Wrinn, in *Civil Rights in the Whitest State*, argued that it was the compromise crafted in large part by U.S. Senator George Aiken—the so-called "Mrs. Murphy's Boardinghouse" exception to Title II of the law—that made the bill acceptable to enough Republicans to allow it to be passed. The only way the bill was going to be passed in the Senate was with the use of cloture—which required approval by two-thirds of the Senate—to end a filibuster by southern Democrats that would have prevented a vote. With the twenty-one southern Democrats certain to vote against cloture, the support of twenty-two of the Senate's thirty-three Republicans would be needed.

Title II was the centerpiece of the proposed legislation, guaranteeing equal access to all public accommodations, including "hotels, motels, motion picture houses, theaters, sports arenas, stadiums, exhibition halls, retail shops, department stores, markets, drugstores, gasoline stations, restaurants, lunch counters, and soda fountains." Aiken believed that there should be equal access to public accommodations, but also felt that the federal government shouldn't blur the lines between clearly public accommodations and what were primarily private homes. The issue for him was whether any business that offered accommodations to the public should be covered by the law, no matter what its size, or whether exclusions should be made for operations so small that they should be considered private homes rather than interstate commerce. Aiken himself told a television interviewer in Washington on July 7, 1963, "I don't think it would be safe to force Mrs. Murphy, who took tourists perhaps down a country road, to accept anyone who comes along. . . . I think she should have the right to select the people she is willing to take into her house and rent rooms to them, or give them board."

There was, of course, no actual "Mrs. Murphy." The closest thing to a "Mrs. Murphy" near Aiken's hometown of Putney was Mrs. Carl Olsen, a boardinghouse operator who could lodge up to eighteen people at a charge of $5 a night, and her operation was too large to be excluded from the law in the compromise that resulted. But Aiken managed to turn the idea of a "Mrs. Murphy" into a national symbol of the public accommodations dispute. "Let them integrate the Waldorf and other large hotels," he said in June 1963, "but permit the Mrs. Murphys who run small boarding houses all over the country to rent rooms to whomever they choose." In the end, the compromise worked out by Aiken and his longtime breakfast partner, Senate Majority Leader Mike Mansfield, and accepted by Senate Minority Leader Everett Dirksen and many civil rights advocates, exempted from the law any establishment with five or fewer rooms for rent that also was occupied by the proprietor as his or her residence.

Not all Vermonters agreed with Aiken on this. Dr. M. Alfred Haynes, the head of the Vermont chapter of the NAACP, said that "when Mrs. Murphy is doing business with the public, certainly a Negro should be included in the public." And *Burlington Free Press* reporter and columnist Vic Maerki noted that Aiken was trying to protect Mrs. Murphy from federal legislation while Vermont's own public accommodations law of 1957 did not. He criticized Aiken's position as "another attempt to answer the Negro's appeal for equality with an offer of near equality." But Wrinn concluded that it was key to getting the necessary Republican votes, and thus made Aiken a key player in the law that "abolished racially segregated public accommodations on a large scale."

Just a month after the 1964 Civil Rights Act became law, a group of individuals and organizations committed to civil rights met to form the Vermont Civil Rights Union. Among the groups active in the organization of the VCRU were the Human Rights Council of Vermont, which was based in Rutland; the Burlington chapter of the NAACP; and the Rutland chapter of the National Conference of Christians and Jews. By January 1965, it had drafted a constitution; elected a Catholic priest, the Reverend Edward Fitzsimons, as its president and Paul Hackel, a Jewish businessman from Rutland, as its secretary-treasurer; and had adopted "Vermont in Mississippi" as its first major project.

The Vermont in Mississippi project had been proposed in 1964 by Ted and Carol Seaver, two newcomers from Wisconsin who had settled in Calais, taken jobs teaching in area schools, and spent the summer of 1964 helping register black voters in Mississippi. Their plan was to develop a community center in Jackson, Mississippi, that would help strengthen black leadership. Hoff backed the project, saying it was "in the tradition of Vermont's concern for civil rights," and it also had the backing of many Vermont clergy, as well as House Speaker Franklin Billings; Lieutenant Governor John Daley; the head of the Vermont Bar Association, Robert Ryan; and the president of the Vermont Labor Council, Ralph Williams. The VCRU pledged $7,600 to the effort.

According to Paul Hackel, Vermont in Mississippi was intended from the start to be just a two-year project, which was the time the VCRU estimated it would take to get it established and turned over to Mississippi residents. "We wanted to help the black community get organized, involved in the political process . . . and then have locals take it over," Hackel said many years later. "It was planned for two years and at the end of two years it was turned over." It wasn't without controversy in Vermont, and in February 1965—with the Seavers in Mississippi and intending to stay there for some time—the Montpelier School District ended Ted Seaver's contract. He and Carol remained in Mississippi for the two years, and among other things helped establish the first licensed integrated day care center in the state. But when the two years ended, they returned to Wisconsin, and the VCRU turned its attention to supporting enactment of a fair-housing law in Vermont.

Meanwhile, on November 23, 1964, Hoff had appointed a Governor's Commission on the Status of Women, which was authorized to research "how discrimination was occurring, how women's roles were changing and [to] document the needs of working women and their children and to support a more active role in the political life of the state." Madeleine M. Kunin, who would become Vermont's first woman governor, was a member of the commission, as was Barbara Snelling, who would serve two terms as lieutenant governor and two terms in the state Senate. Again, the effort was well meaning, but in the early years funding was lacking. Commission members operated without offices or staff, usually working out of their homes. It wasn't until the 1970s that staffing was provided and not until 2002 that the Vermont Commission on Women was made a permanent and independent state agency.

In September 1965 Hoff announced his intention to seek a fair-housing law that would make it illegal to refuse to sell, lease, or rent housing because of race or color. This was met with fierce opposition in the 1966 session, particularly from the Vermont Association of Realtor Boards, whose president argued that Hoff's bill "would discriminate against real estate dealers and property owners." He also argued that "the general fear of a Negro moving into a community is not the actual fear of living near a Negro, but a lowering of the real estate values." The opposition—led in the House by Woodstock Republican John Alden, himself a successful real estate broker—argued that the bill would infringe on property rights and was not needed because discrimination was not a problem in Vermont. The bill failed in the House by a vote of 72–69. When the bill was reintroduced in the 1967 session, Alden proposed a compromise that substituted a Human Rights Commission to investigate complaints and try to resolve them "through conciliation and persuasion" but without any penalties for violations. Hoff and the Vermont Civil Rights Union rejected Alden's plan as lacking enforcement powers, and—after passionate and intense lobbying and debate—the original bill from 1966 passed the House by nine votes, only to be defeated three weeks later by one vote in the Senate. The very next day, the president pro tem of the Senate, George W. F. Cook, who had voted against the bill, introduced an amended version that included Alden's Human Rights Commission. It passed with a unanimous vote and was sent back to the House, where it was approved 95–38 after another version of the "Mrs. Murphy's Boardinghouse" exemption was added to exclude the sale of owner-occupied housing with two or fewer units and the rentals of owner-occupied homes with fewer than four units. When Hoff signed the bill four days later, the Vermont Commission on Human Rights came into being. The vcru disbanded after what it considered a victory, and Hoff appointed three of its leaders—Fitzsimons, Hackel, and the Reverend Roger Albright—to the new Human Rights Commission, along with Margaret Lucenti of Montpelier. While the legislature passed the bill, it made no appropriation for either an office or staffing for the Human

Rights Commission, and in its early years the commission had neither. That of course made it rather weak and ineffective, which some of its Republican backers likely had intended, and much of its work ended up being done out of Lucenti's Montpelier kitchen. Hoff nonetheless said during the bill signing that there had been "few bills during my tenure as governor I have derived greater pleasure from signing."

The 1968 election was the first in that decade in which Hoff wasn't a candidate. He had decided to put his political career on hold until 1970, when he intended to run against incumbent Winston L. Prouty for a U.S. Senate seat. George Aiken was up for reelection in 1968, but the popular incumbent would run unopposed. And although Hoff trailed both Aiken and Prouty in various polls, Prouty was considered a much more vulnerable opponent. But that began changing during the summer and autumn of 1968.

The midwinter 1968 meeting of the National Governors Conference had been held in February in Washington, D.C., and Hoff had attended. Back in July 1967, after the race riots in Newark and Detroit and the release of a highly controversial report by Daniel Moynihan, then an assistant secretary of labor, which said that dysfunctional black families—with a high number of fatherless households and high numbers of out-of-wedlock births—were contributing to racial disorders, President Johnson had appointed a National Advisory Commission on Urban Disorders. There had been more than three hundred racial disturbances—some of them full-fledged riots—in more than two hundred cities in the previous three years, resulting in many deaths and serious property damage. In the 1967 riots in Detroit alone forty-three people died and about 1,400 buildings were burned. Illinois governor Otto Kerner had been named chairman of the commission, and New York City mayor John Lindsay the vice chairman. Their report quickly became a bestseller (more than two million Americans bought copies of it) and is still remembered four decades later for its flatly stated conclusion that the United States was quickly "moving toward two societies, one black and one white—separate and unequal."

During the course of the three-day governor's conference Hoff had obtained an advance copy of the report, and he had read it, along with a summary published in the *Washington Post*, while flying back home on a Vermont National Guard plane. The converted Air Force cargo plane was cold that day, and the engines seemed to be straining to stay aloft. Hoff kept reading the report as the plane droned over the Pennsylvania and New Jersey countryside. It criticized both the federal and state governments for failures large and small when it came to improving the conditions of blacks, particularly in the areas of education, housing, and social services. It concluded that a principal cause of black rioting was white racism and said that dramatic steps should be taken by governments at all levels to try to end it and reverse it. By nature, Hoff was less a reader than a listener, someone who could absorb people's ideas and then make a decision for himself. He also had a good lawyer's ability to absorb the salient points of a brief. About an hour out of Burlington (the trip between Burlington and Andrews Air Force Base near Washington took just about three hours), Hoff called over his secretary of civil and military affairs, Benjamin Collins, and his special assistant, Arthur Ristau. The three talked for about five minutes, and near the end of the conversation Hoff was overheard to say, "Let's see if we can't do something right off Monday." He then contacted the Kerner Commission vice chairman, John Lindsay, and together they agreed to organize what became the Vermont–New York Youth Project, hastily put together and headed by Collins.

Hoff recalled his reading of the Kerner Commission report in an interview for a Williams College oral history project in 1998:

> It was to my mind (and I insist that it's still true), a clarion call for action on the part of the people in this country. It spoke of two worlds, separate and unequal. I read that report on a plane trip from Washington to Burlington. As we got into Burlington I called the two aides I had with me. I said, "I want you to bring together the leaders of every major religious denomination because I think this is a clarion call for action." Out of that meeting we established what was known as the Vermont–New York Youth Program. In that summer we had something like 1,200 youngsters—600 primarily from Harlem (some from the Bronx), and 600 primarily from Vermont. It was an exciting program and it worked. Unfortunately for me, it engendered a lot of latent racism. I lost about a third of my own party.

Hoff overstated the numbers in the Williams College interview, but not the political damage that it did to him. In the end, a total of 1,152 black and white teenagers took part over a two-year period, housed for the most part on a half dozen college and prep school campuses but in a few cases at private camps. Some of the participants were involved in arts programs, and others learned trade skills, but the main emphasis was just on living and working together and learning about their very different cultures. Deane Davis, who was a candidate for governor in 1968, was guarded about the project, saying that the state already was facing so many problems just in funding education for Vermonters he wasn't sure that it should be taking on more responsibilities. He also said that he doubted whether Hoff's rapid timetable for getting the program started would allow for adequate planning and organization. And in fact there were organizational problems (the site at Vermont Academy at Saxtons River, for example, had planned to house between 150 and 175 teenagers and ended up with close to 400) and friction between organizers. Malvine Cole, a sculptor, lobbyist, former legislator, and political activist who headed an arts program in Ripton, criticized Collins for what she claimed was mismanagement and forcing his personal and political agenda on others. But it quickly became clear that the program was going to be controversial no matter how well organized or how smoothly run. By the summer of 1968, the nonviolent approach of the Reverend Martin Luther King Jr. (who had been murdered in April) had been challenged by such "black power" advocates as Malcolm X (who had been murdered in 1965) and Stokely Carmichael, the former head of the Student Non-Violent Coordinating Committee, and their followers, whose strident and often provocative demands had alienated many Vermonters. And many in Hoff's working-class constituency feared that the Vermont–New York Youth Project would result in large numbers of blacks being lured to Vermont as permanent residents, where they would depress blue-collar wages and compete for jobs. "It destroyed me politically," Hoff said in 1989, admitting that he had gotten too far out of touch with his supporters to understand just how strong the opposition and just how deep the anger would be. "There was a tremendous backlash . . . particularly among working people, which was always the bedrock of my support." Earlier, in 1976, Hoff had said that "If I were to do it again, I would make a greater effort to inform the citizens of Vermont just what was involved. We anticipated many of the problems but failed to anticipate that a substantial number of Vermonters would perceive the project as bringing blacks into Vermont on a permanent basis, who would be competing for work in a limited job market." But he also said repeatedly over the years, as he did in 1989 during ceremonies to mark the twentieth anniversary of the project, that he had absolutely no regrets about starting it. "In fact, I'm very proud of it. I would do it again happily," he said.

Shortly after announcing the program in April, Hoff had left Vermont for a month's tour of the Far East and Central America. He had left confident that Vermonters would welcome the project. When he returned in May, he found that he had been badly mistaken, but continued to push ahead with the program and to argue forcefully for it. "No Vermonter can evade responsibility for the indictment of our society included in the [Kerner Commission] report," he said. "As Americans and Vermonters, we have a responsibility for the safety and welfare of all this country's citizens." His statements did nothing to stem hostile reactions. That same month, Hoff received an anonymous eight stanzas of doggerel mailed from Woodstock that was unique only in the degree of its hostility. Two of the stanzas read

> Hoff wants to bring niggers to the North Country
> and wants them to live with you and me.
> But as any casual observer will see,
> No niggers will be living near his family.

> So Hoff claims Vermont responsibility,
> For riots that happen down country.
> But he and Lindsay overlook one trifle,
> Every Vermont farmer owns a 30–30 rifle.

There was more to come. On July 4, 1968, a black Baptist minister, the Reverend David Lee Johnson, moved with his wife, Ophelia, their three teenage children, and a granddaughter from Seaside, California, to a large thirteen-room Victorian house on Route 14 in rural Irasburg, a town of 750 inhabitants in Orleans County that once had been owned entirely by Ira Allen (hence the name) and given by him to his bride (Jerusha Enos) as a wedding present. The Johnsons were accompanied by Barbara Lawrence, a twenty-three-year-old recently divorced white woman and her two small children, who had been neighbors of the Johnson family in California. Although they were welcomed warmly by some Irasburg neighbors at the start, exactly two weeks after they arrived, at around midnight on July 18–19, a car with three people in it raced by, and multiple shotgun blasts were fired at the home. When the night-riders in the maroon sedan with a white top came back to fire two more blasts, Johnson returned fire with a revolver. No one was hurt in the incident, and the car disappeared into the night. By the next day state police had managed to identify as a prime suspect Larry Conley, a white army sergeant home on leave. Conley was the son of a prominent local businessman in nearby Glover who owned a fence factory, a store, two car dealerships, and a sawmill in the area. He had been arrested five days earlier for verbally molesting black participants in the Vermont–New York Youth Project who had been on an outing in Barton State Park. Conley denied being involved in the shooting, but Johnson had managed to get a pretty good description of Conley's car, and a state police investigation quickly discredited Conley's alibi. It could and should have been a quick investigation and speedy prosecution, but Johnson probably got some sense of what was in store when one of the troopers suggested to him that he had used poor judgment in returning fire with a Lugar, since the "birdshot" fired from the shotgun was relatively harmless and showed there had been no intent to kill.

Attorney General James L. Oakes showed the importance he placed on the shooting by visiting the Johnsons the next day and promising a fast and full investigation. But rather than arrest Conley right away— or even tell Oakes that they had a prime suspect—the state police waited fourteen days while conducting an investigation of Johnson himself. Supposedly this was to try to learn if there was something in his past that would have provoked people other than Conley to fire shots at his house. Meanwhile, rumors began circulating through the Northeast Kingdom community that Johnson had staged the whole incident. When Conley was arrested on August 1, the head of the state police, Colonel Erwin Alexander, himself a native of nearby Glover, made a statement in which— all evidence to the contrary—he insisted that "the case has no racial overtones and was not caused by racial prejudice."

Oakes had suggested that Conley could be charged with assault with intent to kill, but in the end he was prosecuted on the relatively minor offense of breach of peace. Conley, who pleaded nolo contendere, or "no contest," to the charge on August 22, received a suspended six-to-eighteen-month jail sentence (serving no time at all) and a $500 fine. Leonard Pearson, the Orleans County state's attorney, was more aggressive when it came to Rev. Johnson. On August 9, five days before Conley's trial had been set to begin, Johnson and Barbara Lawrence were stopped by state troopers and arrested at gunpoint while driving south near Bethel. They apparently had been headed for Fort Devens, Massachusetts, where— since her former husband was still in the army—Lawrence intended to ask the army to help her and the children return to California. Warrants for their arrest had been issued by Pearson, charging them with adultery. This was based on the statement of state trooper Jean Lessard, who had been one of the troopers assigned to protect the Johnson home. The statement said that on July 22, three days after the shooting, Lessard had gone into the Johnson home at 5:30 A.M. for a cup of coffee, as the Johnsons had told him and other troopers they could do, and found Johnson and Lawrence having sex on the living room sofa.

After several hours of questioning by police, Lawrence signed a statement admitting to having sex with Johnson. Eleven days later she gave a signed statement to Johnson's wife denying the confession and saying she had signed it under pressure from the police. On August 12 she pleaded nolo contendere to the charge of adultery (the same plea that Conley had entered), was given a suspended sentence of six to twelve months, fined $125 plus court costs, and then allowed to return to California. That meant that she received almost as stiff a sentence for allegedly having sex on a living room sofa as Conley did for firing shotgun blasts into a house filled with teenagers and small children.

Prosecutions for adultery were rare at the time, and Pearson himself had refused to prosecute them in the past. In this case, he asked Oakes to help him. Oakes refused, saying such prosecutions were unusual—almost unheard of, in fact—when there was no complaint from an aggrieved spouse, which there wasn't in this case. Johnson himself denied having sex with Mrs. Lawrence, pleaded not guilty to the adultery charge, and tried to get a change of venue on the grounds of racial discrimination in Orleans County. The change of venue was denied, but the case collapsed when it turned out that the trooper who was the source admitted that he hadn't actually seen the couple having intercourse. What he had seen, he said, was Mrs. Lawrence on the sofa with her nightgown pulled up above her waist and with Johnson on top of her, causing him to assume that it either had just taken place or was about to take place. Given that version from the trooper, Pearson realized that he wouldn't be able to prosecute the case, particularly when a California judge refused to force Mrs. Lawrence—who was fighting Pearson's efforts to extradite her—to return to Vermont to testify. The charges against Rev. Johnson were dropped, and shortly afterward the Johnsons returned to California.

There was much blaming of the victims and Hoff. Emory Hebard said, "The governor and his people are determined to stir up Vermont, and created problems, and certainly deserved this one." In essence, he said that Hoff had precipitated the Irasburg incident by bringing minority youths to Vermont. Earlier, Deane Davis, campaigning in the GOP primary against Attorney General Oakes, had said in a June press release,

"I hope that Vermonters will understand that when Gov. Hoff uses the term 'racist' to describe anyone who happens to be confused about his NY-VT program, he is acting neither in the best interest of the negro community nor of the people of Vermont."

And some of the press was weighing in on the side of the Irasburg shooters. At the request of Colonel Alexander, the *Burlington Free Press*, the state's largest newspaper, had assigned at least three reporters—including Joe Heaney, Mavis Doyle, and Maggie Maurice—to dig up dirt on Rev. Johnson. This was disclosed when a board of inquiry created by Hoff to investigate the performance of the state police in the case reported that J. Warren McClure, the *Free Press* publisher, had ordered what it described as "a journalistic criminal investigation of David Johnson" that apparently turned up little if anything of import. That same inquiry found that Lloyd Hayes, a reporter and editorial writer for the *Newport Daily Express*, had phoned a state police lieutenant on August 9—the day Rev. Johnson and Mrs. Lawrence were arrested—and told him the pair were about to flee the state. "Aren't you going to arrest them for adultery? Why don't you get about it?" he had said to the trooper. The board's report was critical of those papers for those actions, and also of the *Vermont Sunday News* for having "attempted to malign the character of Reverend Mr. Johnson" with large front-page headlines and stories disclosing "a criminal record of an ancient single misdemeanor conviction taking place in Florida in 1952 (carrying a concealed weapon), which would not even be admissible against him in a Vermont court of law."

Yet the newspapers' dubious actions paled in comparison to what the board of inquiry's report disclosed about the state police investigation. Although it was crafted in a low-key and matter-of-fact way, the report, in its conclusions, was not just critical of the investigation but scathing, making clear that it considered the state police investigation either racist, or grossly incompetent, or designed to protect local whites at the expense of black newcomers—or a combination of all three.

The board of inquiry had been set in motion on September 11—the same day Pearson dropped the adultery charges against Rev. Johnson—when Hoff had announced he would appoint the board to investigate what was being called "the Irasburg affair," saying that "I think the people of Vermont are entitled to know what this is all about." It was a small panel, but perhaps one of the most impressive ever assembled to investigate anything in Vermont. It was chaired by U.S. Judge Ernest W. Gibson Jr., who as governor had played a key role in the creation of the

Vermont State Police back in 1947; Hilton Wick, the president of the Chittenden Savings Bank and a past president of the Vermont Bar Association; and Dorothy Collins, the dean of Vermont College. Former lieutenant governor Ralph Foote served as counsel for the inquiry board. All served without pay.

The report they produced was a modest document in size, just thirty pages, printed as a nine-inch-by-six-inch pamphlet. But even four decades later it remains a stunning and troubling indictment of a painful time in the history of race relations in Vermont and of the performance of the state's premier police agency. Among other things, it found that the state police had found tire tracks at the site of the shooting but had neither photographed them nor made plaster casts of them, and that it had taken no written statements from people who indicated that Conley had been the shooter and that his alibi was bogus. It found that the state police had withheld key information from the attorney general for days and even weeks. It found that although Conley had become the prime suspect right from the start, the state police failed to quickly close out the case but instead spent the next two weeks trying to develop derogatory information about Rev. Johnson. The state police had, the report concluded, "transferred their investigation from securing evidence of the guilt of Larry Conley to securing some kind of evidence against members of the Johnson residence." It concluded that Conley's lawyer probably had obstructed justice by warning potential witnesses not to testify against him. It noted that while aggressive in pursuing charges of adultery against Mrs. Lawrence and Rev. Johnson, State's Attorney Pearson had refused to prosecute an obvious case of adultery against an Irasburg white man who was living with a woman not his wife and had fathered two children by her, telling the minister who urged him to do so that adultery was "hard to prove." It found "unbelievable" the statements by troopers that they were investigating Rev. Johnson to find a motive for the shooting "as they already had their prime target." It found that a tape recording of the state police questioning of Mrs. Lawrence about the alleged adultery showed that it wasn't until "well along in the interview and not on a timely basis" that she had been told she had a right to counsel. It concluded that "Larry Conley might not have been convicted on the shooting episode" had the attorney general's office not stepped in to take control of the case.

As its final word, the board said, "In view of the widespread public speculation as to the character of the Rev. Mr. Johnson, the Board feels constrained to emphasize: the issue here is not the kind of man the Rev. Mr. Johnson is; the issue here rather involved the safety of a man's home in the State of Vermont."

In one of Hoff's last acts as governor he formally censured Alexander for saying there had been no racial prejudice in the case and for not cooperating with the attorney general. He also directed Alexander to discipline the three state troopers most criticized in the report. Alexander, who projected something of a tough-guy image (he sometimes wore a revolver in a holster under his business suit), at first openly defied Hoff. "He came into my office with an attorney to tell me that he wasn't going to do it," Hoff said. "I told him that under the statute I had to hold a hearing before I fired him. I didn't have to actually find anything. I just had to hold a hearing. So I told him that I would hold a hearing and then fire him."

Alexander—obviously playing for time and looking ahead to the imminent change of administrations—later agreed to consider disciplinary action if, after reading the entire transcript of the inquiry, he found sufficient evidence to support the board's findings. One Hoff aide later said that he thought Hoff might have fired him outright except that—as indignant as he was—he felt it was inappropriate given the very few days he had left in office. Hoff himself said in 2010, "In some ways, I probably should have, but it would have created a huge public controversy" and looked as though he was being vindictive during his last week in office. Once Davis was in office, Alexander told the new governor that he found no reason to discipline his men and then went on to attack the press, the clergy, the attorney general, and the Johnson family itself. Davis didn't join Hoff in censuring Alexander, but neither did he disagree publicly with Hoff or the board of inquiry. Instead, he issued a statement saying that police supervisors should be "constantly on the alert to discover the existence of racial prejudice and if any is discovered to treat it as a cause for dismissal." The *Rutland Herald*, in an editorial written by Robert Mitchell, said the directive was evidence that Davis wasn't happy about what had happened at Irasburg, even though he didn't say so in so many words. "One gains the impression that the governor thought the Irasburg Affair amounted to a pretty sorry performance all around," Mitchell wrote, "and perhaps it would have been much better if he had cleared the air by saying so."

Oakes had lost his primary fight to Davis in the middle of the Irasburg controversy, and while he might have lost in any event, Hoff felt that Oakes had doomed his chances by staking out the strong—and in

Hoff's view very principled—position that he did. Hoff himself suffered lasting damage. There were other things in 1968 that caused his popularity to drop among Vermont Democrats, including his turning against the Vietnam War and his endorsing of Robert Kennedy for president against Lyndon Johnson. But both his launching of the Vermont–New York Youth Project and his involvement in Irasburg became very unpopular. The Vermont–New York Youth Project was discontinued as a state program by Davis and then ended completely after it failed to secure private funding. Contrary to Hoff's hopes and expectations, it had not enhanced Vermont's image as progressive on racial matters but in fact had tarnished it. And while Hoff had seen the Kerner Commission report as a "clarion call" for action, Lyndon Johnson, furious at what he considered criticisms of himself and his administration, rejected the conclusions and totally ignored the recommendations.

Whether Hoff would have started the Vermont–New York project if he had been facing reelection was the subject of much speculation at the time. On one occasion, he suggested he might not have, but also volunteered, "I would like to think I would have." After leaving office, his passion for civil rights issues, if anything, grew more intense. In 1987 he received an award from the Vermont Civil Liberties Union in recognition of his "long career in civil liberties affairs going back a decade before he was first elected governor." And in 2007 he reflected, "If you had to name one thing that you could not really dispute it is that in terms of supporting civil rights and liberties, I was the number one person in the state."

That's something many people would be proud to be able to say, but in the Vermont of 1968 it wasn't a popular thing for a politician to be. Pollster John Becker reported that by the end of 1968 Hoff's popularity had fallen further and faster than any politician he had ever tracked. And two years later, during his unsuccessful campaign for the U.S. Senate against Winston Prouty, Hoff was walking out of Barre's Spaulding High School after making a speech when two football players, covered with dirt and sweat, passed him while walking back into the school after a practice. "There goes Hoff, the nigger lover," one of them said in a matter-of-fact way.

CHAPTER 6

NATIONAL POLITICS

On December 15, 1967, Washington was getting ready for the holidays. It was a particularly busy social season for President and Lady Bird Johnson. Their oldest daughter, Lynda Bird Johnson, had been married to Charles Robb, a captain in the marines, in the White House on December 9 with a reception for 650 guests. And now, just six days later, the Johnsons were hosting another large celebration for the lighting of the Christmas tree on the lawn just south of the White House. The tree was a seventy-foot balsam fir from Rochester, Vermont, that had been grown and groomed by Riley Bostwick, who had provided the very first national Christmas tree for the White House back in 1923 when Calvin Coolidge was president. Jim White, the Bennington County forester who helped wrap the tree for the trip south and who would help grow, select, and transport several other Vermont trees for the White House and the U.S. Capitol over the years, later insisted that it was "the prettiest tree there ever was." It was decorated with 4,000 red, white, and blue lights and 250 gold balls. The president arrived for the ceremony with his white mongrel dog, Yuki, trotting behind him, the dog decked out in a red cap and a white beard, like a canine Saint Nicholas. Philip Hoff had come down from Vermont to share the podium with the president.

Despite the festive setting, it was a troubled time. The year had seen race riots in Tampa, Buffalo, Newark, Minneapolis, and Washington itself, as well as in Detroit, where forty-three people had been killed and where—while there remains some confusion and debate about the exact numbers—probably more than 400 others had been injured, some 1,400 buildings burned, and more than 7,200 people arrested. The opposition to the Vietnam War also had been growing, with antiwar protests in San Francisco, New York, Washington, and many other places. Johnson's new son-in-law himself was headed to Vietnam, where he would command a rifle company, acquit himself honorably, and win a Bronze Star. The number of American troops had grown from just 23,300 in 1964 to 489,600 in

1967, and the opposition to the war had become more intense as the draft calls had increased, the death tolls had climbed, and the end seemed nowhere in sight. While the Johnson administration claimed to be seeing the "light at the end of the tunnel" in Vietnam, many others saw the light as the headlight of a freight train that was rushing straight at them. The protests had grown as the children of the suburbs and the middle class had been drawn into the conflict and as many of the draft deferments for graduate students and married men without children—people who had largely escaped the early years of the war—had ended. Richard Cheney, later the vice president, managed to get five college deferments to escape the war ("I had other priorities in the '60s," he told the *Washington Post*), but thousands of others, who may have had other priorities of their own, lost theirs. And the protests grew as more and more of them found themselves heading off to basic training at Fort Polk, Fort Ord, Fort Knox, and Fort Dix. Just two weeks before the tree lighting, Robert McNamara, the secretary of defense and a chief architect of the American buildup, had resigned because of Johnson's rejection of his recommendations to freeze the troop levels, stop the bombing of North Vietnam, and hand over the ground fighting to the South Vietnamese. The day after that, U.S. Senator Eugene McCarthy of Wisconsin had announced his candidacy for the Democratic Party's presidential nomination, running as an antiwar candidate against a sitting president from his own party.

The social and sexual revolutions of the late '60s also were coming into play. The musical *Hair*, with its brief but, at the time, shocking nudity, had opened on Broadway. The Beatles had released their album *Sgt. Pepper's Lonely Hearts Club Band*, and the British Broadcasting Corporation had banned the playing of one of the album's most popular songs, "Lucy in the Sky with Diamonds," because it considered it to be advocating the use of the psychedelic drug LSD. The feminist movement was growing, and so was the use of illegal drugs. The latter had nothing to do with the former, but it was a time of change and protest and revolt against conventions of many kinds, with the children of solidly middle-class parents suddenly referring to police officers as "pigs" and challenging many of their parents' and grandparents' core values. All of these values were being discussed and debated, often ferociously, not just in the Congress and in the state legislatures, but also in churches, bars, schools, workplaces, and around dinner tables all over America. Not since the Civil War had the nation been so divided, and while the result was far less bloody, the anger nonetheless was intense.

The tree was lit at 5:56 P.M., and the 4,000 lights sparkled in the December night. The Festival Singers of Toronto sang holiday carols. The spectators applauded. But the lights and music and the festive setting couldn't mask the reality that Washington, like most of the country, had become a place of anger, fear, dissension, and dismay. Johnson himself brought the war into the ceremony. "Today, a young soldier, in the prime of his life, was killed in the central highlands of Vietnam," he said. "Half a million brave men who love their country and are willing to die for their land will be celebrating Christmas in a strange land, surrounded by weapons of war. A part of every American heart will be with them."

Hoff had become increasingly, if mostly silently, opposed to the war, coming to believe that it was neither essential nor winnable. At a private audience in the Oval Office after the tree-lighting ceremony, he gathered up his courage and asked Johnson if he couldn't give some consideration to a cessation of the bombing, which many thought was needed before peace talks could begin. "He turned on me as only he could and gave me five minutes worth," Hoff later recalled. "And then he stood up and obviously I stood up, and he said: 'Governor, why don't you go back to Vermont and do the things you have to do there, and let us take care of our problem here.'" Hoff thanked him and left.

Hoff would go back to Vermont, but his last year as governor would in many ways be more preoccupied with national than state issues. The year 1968 would be a traumatic one for the nation in many ways, with the murders of Martin Luther King Jr. and Robert F. Kennedy; with racial disturbances and in some cases full-scale riots in more than a hundred cities, one of the most serious of them in Washington, where marines would set up machine guns on the steps of the Capitol and army soldiers from the Third Infantry would be sent to protect the White House; with increasingly angry antiwar demonstrations across the nation and on hundreds of college campuses; with the Tet Offensive by Vietcong and North Vietnamese troops showing that the war was far from over, let alone won; and with what would be described as a "police riot" at the Democratic National Convention in Chicago, in which protestors outside the convention hall would be bludgeoned by helmeted, shield-carrying, tear-gas-spraying, billy-club-swinging police officers. One New York television station captured the scene vividly with slow-motion film of Chicago police officers bashing heads with no sound except for Frank Sinatra singing

> This is my kind of town, Chicago is
> My kind of town, Chicago is
> My kind of people too
> People who, smile at you. . . .

The "smile" in the song was punctuated by a police billy club smashing down and splitting open a young protestor's head.

Johnson would stun the country by announcing on March 31 that he would not run for reelection. But even before that, Hoff would become the first Democratic governor to break with him over the war and would throw his support to Robert Kennedy for president. He then would attempt to help bridge the nation's racial divide by creating the Vermont–New York Youth Project. In the process of doing both he would generate so much anger among Vermonters that it would alienate and erode his core Democratic base and seriously damage his hopes for national office. His growing opposition to the war and his growing advocacy of civil rights can be seen in retrospect as having been both correct and courageous. But he took the right stands at the wrong time and in the process sowed the seeds of his political demise.

Initially, Hoff's hopes for the 1968 legislative session were high. It would be his last as governor, and he wanted to use it to push through a major reorganization of state government. During the summer of 1967 he had reactivated the Committee on Administrative Coordination to refine the reorganization plans. For three months, citizen committees again were called upon to study the problems of state government, focusing on the structure of the government itself. The proposals presented to Hoff were mainly the ones that he wanted, of course. Among other things, they called for a Department of Natural Resources that would combine Fish and Wildlife, Forests and Parks, and three other agencies concerned with conservation and recreation. They also called for similar consolidations of multiple agencies into a Department of Human Resources and a Department of Library and Archives, and called for future governors—not the boards and commissions—to appoint the department heads, subject to confirmation by the Senate. There was nothing innovative or bold about the proposals. The key provisions were similar to those that had been proposed by Deane Davis and the Little Hoover Commission back in the '50s. Almost everyone in government—Republicans and Democrats alike—agreed they were needed. For many ordinary citizens, however, it was an issue that made their eyes glaze over. A poll on Vermont issues taken by the Quayle Organization for the State Democratic Party in December 1967 showed that 34 percent of those interviewed approved of a reorganization of the executive branch, 13 percent disapproved, and 53 percent weren't sure what they thought about it. "The problem here is that not enough voters know anything about the proposal, and even those that do have few solid reasons for supporting it," the Quayle researchers concluded. "We would urge Governor Hoff to undertake . . . an educational program immediately if he hopes to win public support and passage by the legislature."

In January 1968 a pamphlet was published and distributed with an introductory letter to Vermonters from Hoff that tried to make the case for reorganization clearly and simply, showing how there were five different agencies dealing with natural resources and recreation, none of them working in coordinated ways and none of them reporting directly to the governor. "For all practical purposes our natural resources agencies, rather than functioning as a cohesive executive unit, operate individually, separate and apart from the governor," it said. "Vermont's laws specifically deprive the state's chief executive and delegate of the people in the conduct of their business from the direct lines of administrative authority and accountability necessary for effective management." It was clunky wording, but probably made the point.

The report noted that Vermont was undergoing a dramatic transition from a rural, agrarian society into a much more dynamic and multifaceted one and argued that effective government was essential to keep pace with and control the developments. "Our ship of state is not exploring uncharted waters. We seek no change just for the sake of fashion. We seek it because it is necessary," the report concluded. "If order is to prevail, this incredible transition must not go unguided. We have lived with the old machinery for too long and resisted new ideas too easily. The time for change is upon us. The time is now."

The Republican-controlled legislature, however, decided that the time could wait until Republicans regained control of the governor's office, and when the streamlining of government would be seen as a Republican initiative.

Although he had high hopes for the session at the start, Hoff freely admitted that he was tired and not looking forward to another legislative battle. The session would be his sixth in a row, more than any Vermont governor had dealt with since Isaac Tichenor of Bennington—a native of New Jersey and a graduate of Princeton whose smooth-talking ways had caused him to be called "Jersey Slick"—had dealt with ten annual sessions between 1797 and 1807. In many respects it would become, from Hoff's perspective, a frustrating and maddening political disaster, and a waste of time. And while it was happening, his focus would swing back and forth from state to national and international affairs.

On the last day of January the Vietcong and the North Vietnamese Army launched the Tet Offensive. The coordinated attacks on a hundred different targets overran many of their objectives, and Communist troops even managed, briefly, to force their way into the compound of the U.S. Embassy in Saigon. Eventually, the offensive was repelled, but the sheer size and ferocity of it shocked much of the American public. On March 12, Eugene McCarthy managed to get 42 percent of the vote in the New Hampshire Democratic primary, which was a stinging rebuke to a sitting president. Four days later, Robert Kennedy announced that he also would seek the presidency. Many McCarthy supporters felt betrayed by his late entry, and Murray Kempton, the respected liberal columnist, criticized Kennedy for not declaring his candidacy until McCarthy had shown just how vulnerable Johnson was, saying that he had behaved like a man who had stayed out of the fighting when it was at its most dangerous and then had ridden down from the hill after the battle was over to shoot the wounded. Hoff nonetheless felt that Kennedy would be the stronger candidate, and on March 22—one day before the end of the Vermont legislative session—announced that he would not support President Johnson for reelection but would back Kennedy instead. There were twenty-four Democratic governors at the time, and the *New York Times* later noted that all but four or five of them were staunch administration loyalists, many of them southerners "who would prefer almost any Democrat to Mr. Kennedy." The White House, alerted about Hoff's impending defection, arranged for Secretary of State Dean Rusk to phone Hoff and invite him to a special Washington briefing. Hoff declined and instead phoned Senator Aiken, a member of the Senate Foreign Relations Committee, to ask if he was aware of any new developments that might change his mind. Aiken—who himself had spoken against further escalation of the war—apparently said that he didn't, and at 4 P.M. Hoff made his announcement.

Aiken was widely reported to have said back in 1966 that the United States should just "declare victory and bring the troops home." What he actually said was more nuanced than that, suggesting that we declare that we had won in the sense that the North Vietnamese and Vietcong no longer could hope for a military victory without a major escalation of their own, and then redeploy our troops to cities that they had no hope of capturing, in order to try to force them to negotiate a settlement. But he never claimed to have been misquoted by the people who kept repeating the pithier version.

While Aiken had questioned the war publicly long before Hoff did, Hoff nonetheless was the first Democratic governor to break with the president over it, and in many ways it was a painful break. As a dynamic young Democrat who was showing great promise, Hoff had been encouraged and helped both by John Kennedy and Lyndon Johnson. Kennedy had invited him to the White House to celebrate his first election as governor, and had interceded for him in the Addison County drought crisis by telling the person overseeing emergency aid programs that Hoff was "a good friend of ours." Johnson had enhanced Hoff's status by visiting Vermont, by inviting him to several White House meetings as well as to his Texas ranch, and by dispatching him on a number of foreign missions. And even after the tense scene in the Oval Office at Christmastime, Johnson had rushed over to Hoff at the Governors' Conference early in 1968 and greeted him warmly. Hoff in fact liked and admired Johnson and attempted to soften the break by praising him for acting "bravely and resolutely in the face of overwhelming adversity" and saying that "his courage and determination have always been an inspiration to me." Nonetheless, he said, it was "clear that fresh approaches are urgently needed to revise a national sickness of spirit." And he went on to say that "Senator Kennedy's candidacy offers the most realistic possibility for the people of America if we are to achieve the national regeneration of spirit that is so desperately needed."

Nine days later, Johnson himself would tell a national television audience that "with America's sons in the fields far away, with America's future under challenge right here at home, with our hopes and the world's hopes for peace in the balance every day, I do not believe that I should devote an hour or a day of my time to any personal partisan causes or to any duties other than the awesome duties of this office—the Presidency of your country.

"Accordingly, I will not seek, and will not accept, the nomination of my party for another term as your President."

Hoff's criticisms of the war and his endorsement of Kennedy were not welcomed by many traditional Vermont Democrats. Some party leaders totally disagreed with him and thought that his condemnation of the war would hurt the party in the fall elections. And when Johnson announced he would not be a candidate, many of them quickly lined up behind Vice President Hubert Humphrey, who they embraced as the more traditional Democrat and a supporter of the war, which they still supported, rather than Kennedy or McCarthy. By this point, Hoff's plans to reorganize state government had been defeated by the Republicans, and as the winter snows melted and spring came to Vermont, he found himself both frustrated by the Republican legislative leadership and criticized by some of the Democratic leaders, one of whom had written him asking, "How can you be so stupid as to split the Democratic Party?"

Hoff had said back in 1966 that he wouldn't seek reelection, and observers of the 1968 legislative session could sense that his lame-duck status was causing his influence to wane right from the start. The politics of the session became bitter and acrimonious. It became clear that months of work on the reorganization bills was going for naught because the Republicans in control of the legislature had decided that a Democrat shouldn't be given credit for reorganizing state government. They intended to do it themselves when the next Republican governor was elected, which they expected would be in the fall. With Richard Mallary having shown that he could and would discipline Republicans who broke ranks on key issues, the coalition between Democrats and moderate Republicans that had come together so often in the past never developed. It was an alliance that Hoff had counted on for many of his legislative successes in previous years. But this time it never materialized, and none of his major proposals were enacted.

"In some ways, I could be very naive," he said forty years later. "When I first became Governor, the legislature was not nearly as partisan as it later became or as it is today. Issues were resolved on their merit. But I still should have known better. Dick Mallary was a bright guy and an able guy, but he also was pretty much the head of the Republican party at that time, and he decided it wasn't going to happen until the Republicans could do it on their own." Hoff was openly critical of the 1968 legislature in his farewell address, saying, "The people deserve better than this." And he then threatened to call a special session to put his proposals back into play. The criticism and the threat to call a special session were dismissed by Representative Emory Hebard, who said, "I'm not concerned with what a peacenik lame-duck governor has to say. He doesn't have the guts to call a special session." In the end, Hoff didn't call for a special session, knowing that there was serious opposition from Democrats as well as Republicans and that he didn't have the votes he would need in any event.

There were still nearly ten months left in his term as governor, but from April on he seemed more focused on national affairs than state ones, prodded—not that he needed much prodding—by Gerald Witherspoon, his tax commissioner, and Ben Collins, his secretary of civil and military affairs. Both men were idealists and Quakers, and both urged him to speak out more loudly and frequently against the war and for civil rights, not just because they believed passionately about both but also because they felt the mood of the country was becoming more liberal and that it would better position him for 1970, when he intended to run for the U.S. Senate seat held by Winston Prouty. This advice wasn't fully embraced by Bill Kearns, who while he liked Collins a great deal and shared his liberal politics and his combative nature (he disagreed more often with Witherspoon), didn't always approve of his way of approaching things. Kearns later said he felt that during Hoff's last year in office both Collins and Witherspoon were giving him bad tactical advice.

After the legislative session ended, Hoff undertook to organize a Vermont presidential delegation for Kennedy and agreed to campaign for him in other states. The Indiana primary in May was a celebrated Kennedy victory because it was the first he had competed in, and Ted Kennedy returned to Vermont from Indiana with Hoff to participate in a fund-raising dinner. The younger Kennedy used the occasion to laud Hoff for his accomplishments and suggest that he would receive a place in Robert Kennedy's administration if he wanted one. While Hoff served as the honorary chairman of the Vermonters for Kennedy committee, the working chairman was State Senator Leo O'Brien of South Burlington. The committee sent personal notes to Vermonters elected as state convention delegates, along with materials promoting Kennedy's candidacy. But their efforts didn't prove as successful as the Kennedy team had hoped. The antiwar Democrats in Vermont were divided between Kennedy and McCarthy, while a large core of traditional Democrats supported Humphrey, whom they not only more closely identified with but also were thankful to for having, in previous fund-raising efforts, helped reduce the state party's debt.

The Kennedy campaign believed it was important to defeat Humphrey and McCarthy in New England to have any hope of success at the national convention in Chicago. So they sent William Dunfey, a New Hampshire Democratic activist with Vermont connections, to help Hoff and O'Brien with their efforts. When Dunfey and his team arrived they realized quickly that Kennedy was not going to sweep the state convention. Given that reality, Dunfey then set about to broker a "unity delegation" that would simply divide up the delegates rather than repeat the bitterness between McCarthy, Kennedy, and Humphrey forces that had developed during the Maine convention, and avoid anything that would be seen as a Kennedy defeat. His unpublished memoir depicts Hoff as "the steady hand on the scene and in continuous negotiations with the Humphrey and McCarthy people." It goes on to say that "using his excellent contacts into the rival camps, he was able to reach negotiated levels of delegates that each of the three contestants could agree to and then move on into what was a generally harmonious [state] convention."

Dunfey was happy that Vermont had avoided the "savage" intraparty warfare that had shaken Maine. But shortly after midnight on June 5, just after winning the California primary, and as he walked through the kitchen of the Ambassador Hotel in Los Angeles, Kennedy was shot in the head by Sirhan Sirhan. He died at Good Samaritan Hospital twenty-six hours later. Hoff would give a moving eulogy for Kennedy before four hundred people in the Vermont Capitol, and he and Dunfey would attend the funeral together.

Now without a candidate, Hoff flew to Washington with Maine governor Kenneth Curtis to try to convince Humphrey to resign the vice presidency, both to distance himself from Johnson's war policies and because they felt he couldn't be his "own man in the Democratic presidential campaign while serving in the administration." They failed in this, as Hoff told reporters he expected they would, although he also later said that Humphrey had been exceedingly warm and cordial and seemed to take no offense at their suggestion. Hoff also failed in an attempt to secure a plank in the Democratic platform calling for the immediate cessation of all bombing of North Vietnam. Johnson already had ordered a partial bombing halt in March, and would end all bombing of North Vietnam in October in an effort to speed up the peace talks that by then were under way in Paris. But on Tuesday, August 13, Hoff told the Democratic Platform Committee meeting in Boston that "the failure of the U.S. to stop its bombing has damaged the credibility of the government at home and the reputation of the United States abroad." He also said that while we might once have thought that we were protecting one country (South Vietnam) against aggression by another (North Vietnam), it was now clear that "we have intervened against a revolutionary movement operating in both halves of one artificially divided country." In what the Associated Press characterized as "one of his strongest attacks on the administration to date," Hoff also said that "Vietnam has brought on a moral revulsion in America against the use of our armed forces in a situation where the security of the United States in not directly threatened." On August 15, Hoff threw his support to McCarthy, again becoming the first Democratic governor to do so.

There were other frustrations as well. At the National Governors Conference in Cincinnati in July, Hoff's anger boiled over. While he had responded to the Kerner Commission Report by launching the Vermont–New York Youth Project, he was angered by the failure of the president and the other governors to do anything at all to respond to it. He also criticized the governors for refusing to support tougher gun-control laws, telling them that their rejection of a proposal for a rather modest form of gun control was "the most weak-kneed resolution possible." Vermont—where hunting was celebrated as part of the culture—itself was among the states with the weakest gun-control laws in the nation, and while it hadn't been a priority earlier, Hoff now was urging restrictions on handguns. (Two years later, when it threatened to become a major campaign liability in his race for the U.S. Senate, he would reverse himself and say that he no longer believed that gun control was necessary because he no longer believed that it would reduce crime.) Outside the convention, Hoff's daughter Dagny took part in an antiwar protest, and Hoff's public statement that he was proud of her for doing so drew almost as much attention from the national news services as his denouncing of the governors. He also failed to get the New England Governors' Conference to adopt a resolution calling on their citizens to "become fully aware of the contents of the [Kerner] report and to dedicate themselves to action programs necessary to reverse the erosion of our social structure."

There were some who attributed what they considered Hoff's impulsive behavior during this time to a drinking problem that had worsened during his third term, although it still wasn't known to most Vermonters. But Hoff had always had a reputation for speaking frankly, and the fact that he wasn't running for office in 1968 may have allowed him to be even more so, particularly since he felt passionately about the issues. He was becoming contemptuous of more politically cautious colleagues, feeling that the problems facing America needed to be faced aggressively and with courage, not caution. It's not possible to say whether his drinking had caused him to be what some considered politically reckless, but he may have had reason to think he could still persuade Vermonters to follow his lead. A poll taken in April had shown him as still having a 69 percent favorability rating by Vermonters as a whole. While it was a huge drop from the 84 percent he had enjoyed in 1964 and the 81 percent he had enjoyed in 1966, it nonetheless was a rating most politicians would have been delighted to have. Another poll, taken back in December 1967 for Vermont Democrats by the Quayle organization, concluded that "compared to most Governors, Philip Hoff is in excellent shape," but added that he was suffering to some degree from the attrition due to incumbency. "Voters on the whole still feel that he is doing a fine job[,] but as he has patiently prodded Vermont into the second half of the 20th century, it is only natural that he has made an increasing number of enemies." His attacks on the war and his launching of the Vermont–New York Youth Project, however, would cause the erosion to continue. In the end, Hoff estimated that they would cost him the support of about 30 percent of his Democratic base. That may have been a conservative estimate, and his acknowledgment of his drinking problems would later add to the erosion.

There would be one more moment in the national spotlight before the year ended, and it was one that he later recognized as having been a mistake. While Hoff had backed McCarthy, the Vermont delegation at the national convention ultimately voted for Humphrey. Earlier in the week, some in the Vermont delegation had been boosting Hoff as a candidate for vice president. It wasn't a big, organized effort, but a few "Hoff for VP" signs were in evidence. When Humphrey announced his selection of Edmund Muskie of Maine as his choice, most Vermonters gave up on the idea of Hoff's running, knowing that Hoff and Muskie were very much alike in their politics and appeal and that if Humphrey wanted Muskie, the Democrats would nominate Muskie. Ben Collins, however, didn't give up, having promised some of the dovish factions at the convention that Hoff would run as a protest candidate, both protesting the war and also protesting the actions of Chicago mayor Richard Daley's police, who with help from the Illinois National Guard had teargassed and roughed up antiwar protestors, in some cases brutally. There had been 11,900 Chicago police, 7,500 army troops, and 7,500 Illinois National Guard soldiers called in to control demonstrators, and the ferocious clashes between them, particularly the clashes between demonstrators and Chicago police that were shown live on television news, had shocked much of the nation, widened the rift among Democrats, and caused U.S. Senator Abraham Ribicoff of Connecticut, who was making a nominating speech on behalf of U.S. Senator George McGovern of South Dakota (who had announced his candidacy just two weeks before the convention), to say that "with George McGovern we wouldn't have

Gestapo tactics on the streets of Chicago." When he said that, the television cameras switched to a clearly furious Mayor Daley shouting something that the microphones didn't pick up but that *Mayday*, an underground Washington newspaper, claimed that a lip-reader said was "Fuck you, you Jew son of a bitch! You lousy motherfucker! Go home!" Daley later denied this, saying that he had called him a "faker" and nothing more. A local alderman standing near Daley said that he had just told Ribicoff to "go home." But an editor for the *Chicago Daily News* said that she had a clear view of Daley and "his lips definitely formed the word 'fuck.'" Whatever the case, Daley—who had made more than one malaprop in his life—later defended the actions of his police by saying "the policeman isn't there to create disorder; the policeman is there to preserve disorder." Collins was among those who had been roughed up and tear-gassed.

The night that the nominations for vice president were going to be made, Hoff was drinking with some of his Burlington friends at the Stockyards Inn, near the convention hall. The group included Burlington mayor Francis Cain and party regulars Frank Balch and William Wright. When Hoff announced rather casually that he was going to be placed in nomination as a protest candidate for vice president, they hit the roof and argued fiercely that he should remove himself quickly. They said that it not only would hurt him in the future but could damage state Democratic candidates in the fall and rupture the whole Vermont Democratic Party, which was not as opposed to the war as he was. Collins then arrived on the scene, looking for Hoff because the nominations were about to begin. Hoff told him that he had changed his mind and didn't want his name used as a protest candidate, since it might further splinter the party. Shortly thereafter, Paul O'Dwyer of New York came over to Hoff's table and asked him why he was pulling out. O'Dwyer, who had been born in County Mayo, Ireland, had immigrated to America when he was eighteen and had worked his way up from the docks and the garment district to become a lawyer and a passionate advocate for progressive and underdog causes. He was an antiwar Democrat and a McCarthy supporter and had upset many of the party regulars in the state by winning the nomination for the U.S. Senate. He would later lose to the Republican incumbent, Jacob Javits, in November. Hoff told O'Dwyer that his political friends not only thought it was a bad idea but feared it could seriously divide and maybe even destroy the Democratic Party in Vermont, which he had worked so hard to help build. O'Dwyer seemed to accept the decision and left. Collins, however, remained furious.

The Vermonters returned to the convention hall, and Hoff dispatched William Hunter of Burlington to go to the podium and tell the officials to withdraw his name. The officials refused, saying that if Hoff wanted to withdraw his name he would have to come and tell them himself. Hoff then headed for the podium, accompanied by Mayor Cain, whom the others wanted with him to make sure he really did withdraw and that Collins didn't intercept him and cause him to change his mind again. Hoff withdrew his name and then walked back to the Vermont delegation, where Dan Rather of CBS News was asking where Hoff could be found.

Rather was just five feet, ten inches tall, but with the electronic headpiece he was wearing and the antenna rising above it he seemed to tower over the Vermont delegates. "We have heard that Governor Hoff is going to be a protest candidate for vice president," Rather said. "Is that true? Will he?" Hunter murmured that Hoff would have to speak for himself. "What's that?" Rather said briskly, and poked his microphone toward Hunter. "We have decided that the governor will have to announce his decision himself," Hunter said loudly. Just then the deep voice of Leo O'Brien directed Rather down the aisle. Rather spun about, took five steps, and corralled Hoff.

Looking weary, dejected, and emotionally drained, Hoff told Rather that he would not be a candidate. Protests against the war and the violence already had been voiced strongly by Ribicoff, he said, intimating that there was no good purpose in carrying it further. He said that Muskie was a friend and that he didn't want to do anything that would harm his candidacy, but that he did sympathize with the effort to make some form of protest against the "atrocities" by Chicago police. "The people of this country should understand what's going on," he said. "This is the original police city."

Hoff's moment in the 1968 national limelight was over, and when the convention ended he sent Mayor Daley an angry telegram signed by himself and several other Vermont delegates saying he was glad to be out of the "police state" of Chicago. "We and other members of the Vermont delegation are not yet home, but our arrival in New York City signifies that we are free once again," the telegram said. "We do not believe the people of this country will long endure the police state you imposed on freedom-loving Americans who came to your city to demonstrate the democratic process. We are pleased to be liberated from your streets as well as from your amphitheater." Usually Collins or Kearns or someone else drafted such things for him, but this was one that Hoff wrote himself, later saying it was easy to do because it was exactly the way he had felt.

Hoff was not a candidate in 1968, and it was a bad year for Vermont Democrats. A poll taken in the spring had shown that Aiken was "unbeatable" and was projected to draw 90 percent of the solidly Republican voters who had voted for Snelling for governor in 1966, as well as 42 percent of Hoff's 1966 Democratic support. The undecided vote was just 6 percent. Hoff in fact suggested that the state Democratic convention award Aiken the Democratic nomination. When it didn't, Leo O'Brien admonished it for failing to do so; but neither did anyone run against Aiken. Aiken ended up with more than 62,000 Democratic votes as a write-in on the Democratic line. He would later boast that he had spent only $17.09 on his 1968 campaign. That was all he needed to spend, since he was well known, well respected, hugely popular, totally unopposed, and ended up with 99.9 percent of the vote. But Aiken in fact was concerned that the cost of campaigning, even in Vermont, was becoming so great that it would be harder for candidates in the future to refuse money from special-interest groups and out-of-state sources. This would be seen clearly and dramatically in the race for the U.S. Senate just two years later.

The Republicans, with Deane Davis heading the ticket, won every statewide office in 1968, with Thomas Hayes, a former Prouty aide, elected lieutenant governor, Richard Thomas elected secretary of state, James Jeffords elected attorney general, Robert King elected auditor of accounts, and Frank Davis elected state treasurer. Stafford also was reelected to Congress easily. And while Republicans failed to recapture the huge majorities they had enjoyed during the halcyon days of the 1950s and earlier, they managed to enlarge their legislative majorities. So it was something of a Republican victory celebration that Hoff spoke to in the State House on January 9, 1969, in a farewell address that made clear he had no intention of saying good-bye.

"My appearance before you today is in accordance with what has been traditionally referred to as the outgoing Governor's farewell address," he said. "I, however, do not look upon this as a farewell in any sense of the word.

"One thing that we all have come to realize is that no Vermonter can turn his back upon the affairs of this great state. I think of this citizenship involvement—this public participation in government—as a vital feature of the years you and I have worked together in this, the people's house."

The short-term plan was for Hoff to return to his law practice—although it would be without great enthusiasm on his part. "Politics is in my blood," he said years later, "but practicing law can be a bore." Even while he was giving his "farewell" address it was assumed by almost everyone in the chamber that he would be running for the U.S. Senate in 1970 against Winston Prouty, the state's junior senator and a man who—while applauded for his support of greater funding for health care, education (particularly for children with disabilities), and Social Security—was not a vigorous or charismatic figure. He was less popular and less respected than Aiken, and overshadowed by him both in the Senate itself and back home in Vermont. He had been elected to the U.S. House in 1950 and to the U.S. Senate in 1958, and friends and foes alike noted that the longer he stayed in Washington the less eager he seemed to be to return to Vermont, even for short vacations or for necessary campaigning. In fact, he was such a remote and low-key figure that he seemed to have little or no visible political organization in the state, which hadn't stopped him from winning six straight elections to the House or Senate, even during the Goldwater debacle of 1964.

Prouty had been born on September 1, 1906, in Newport. His family owned a good deal of forestland (some of it in Canada) and ran a profitable lumber and building materials company. He was educated at the Bordentown (New Jersey) Military Institute, spent time at Yale, and graduated from Lafayette College in 1930. Somewhere along the way, while learning the lumber business from the ground up, he lost his right thumb and injured his right arm in a sawmill accident, which caused him to use his left hand to shake hands. A newspaper editor who was meeting Prouty for the first time once reached out impulsively to shake his right hand and—when his own hand slid right past the missing thumb—suddenly found himself in the awkward position of shaking Prouty's right elbow. Prouty was elected an alderman in Newport in 1933 and became mayor in 1938, moving up the political ladder in Vermont while Hoff was still in grade school in Massachusetts. He became aligned with the liberal wing of the Republican Party, backing Aiken for governor in 1936 and becoming closely tied to Ernest Gibson when Gibson was the governor and he was Speaker of the House.

While considered a liberal by the standards of Vermont Republicans in the 1940s, he was generally considered a moderate in the Congress, and a rather quiet and uncontroversial one, although in 1968, to the surprise of many, he advocated a guaranteed annual income for all Americans, which even many liberals were not ready to accept. He was a slim man, who used a pomade to slick his hair flat against his head, like Peter Lorre in *Casablanca*. During his years in the Vermont legislature he had worn a thin mustache, but that was long gone by 1970. He was dogged by ill health during much of his adult like, suffering both from stomach ailments and also sinusitis, which may have been aggravated by Washington's saunalike summers. His public speaking sometimes bordered on the laconic (he once said during a Senate debate, "The Social Security program ought to provide security"), and he often seemed to be almost allergic to campaigning. The *Rutland Herald* once noted in an editorial that he had married twice (his first wife, Frances Hearle, had died in 1960, and he had married Jennette Hall, the widow of an Ohio congressman, in 1962) and that he had "showed unusually discriminating judgment" in both cases, with both wives active participants in his political career and giving him "the kind of moral support that he required more than most successful politicians." In the 1960s, columnist Joe Alsop set out to rank members of the Senate and had rated Aiken as "very good" and Prouty as "good." The *Rutland Herald* rated him in an editorial as "above average."

That was the public image. A less favorable one, gossiped about by newspaper reporters and by Senate staffers but not finding its way into print or back to Vermont, was that he not only had become increasingly conservative as the years went by but also increasingly absent, drinking heavily and not showing up for committee work or floor votes. Hoff's view was that Prouty had been "a big zero" as a senator. "I knew Prouty to be an absolute lush," Hoff later said. "He had absolutely no influence in Washington, no respect among his peers." Which may have caused Hoff to be more confident than he should have been, even while his own popularity was dropping. The Quayle poll of December 1967, in fact, had cautioned that just because Prouty didn't have Aiken's status, "Democrats should not underrate the strength of the junior Senator."

In the end, the 1970 campaign wouldn't be as much about Prouty as it would be about Hoff. And before he could focus on Prouty, Hoff had to deal with not one but two opponents in the Democratic primary: former Representative Bill Meyer, who argued that Hoff hadn't done enough to oppose the war, and State Senator Fiore (Babe) Bove, who argued that Hoff had done too much to oppose it. Both would be a problem, Meyer because he would help found the Liberty Union Party that year and would run a third-party campaign that would drain away some of the most liberal voters in the state, and Bove because he represented the erosion of Hoff's core Democratic base. Although a state senator, Bove was known less for his political acumen than for his meatballs and marinara sauce. His parents, Louis and Victoria Bove, had opened a small restaurant called Bove's Cafe at 68 Pearl Street in Burlington on December 7, 1941—the same day the Japanese bombed Pearl Harbor. After graduating from Burlington's Cathedral High School and serving in the Marine Corps, Bove returned from the war to work at the restaurant and never left. Eventually, he became an owner, along with a brother, and became the public face of the restaurant, since he usually worked out in front, at the bar. Bove's was a small restaurant with a tin ceiling, Formica booths, and unpretentious decor, known for its large portions and low prices. It tended to be crowded, smoky, lively, and loud. There were very few Italian restaurants (or ethnic restaurants of any sort) in Vermont in the 1940s, 1950s, and 1960s, and while Bove's would have been just another neighborhood restaurant in lower Manhattan or Boston's North End, many of its Vermont customers approached it with a sense of adventure, since manicotti, basil, oregano, and garlic were not things found in most Vermont kitchens. Bove himself was something of a raconteur and liked to engage customers in chatter about sports of all kinds, particularly about the New York Yankees, his favorite team. He became a well-known and popular figure in Burlington, and in the mid-1960s he was elected to the state Senate even though many considered him more opinionated than thoughtful. He had become angry at Hoff for breaking with Johnson and opposing the war, and he ran a campaign that began and ended with the charge that Hoff was unpatriotic and not supporting the troops.

Bove issued statements from time to time, mainly criticisms of Hoff, but did little active campaigning. "None. Zero. Nada," said one Hoff campaign worker. "I don't think he campaigned for five days." Hoff himself said, "I'm not sure that he ever left the restaurant." Hoff totally ignored the charges of both Bove and Meyer, deciding that the best course was not to give any credence to either. But Bove nonetheless became a rallying point for many of the blue-collar Vermont Democrats who supported the war and in some cases disliked and feared blacks. In the end, Hoff got 23,082 votes in the primary, Bove got 7,941, and Meyer got 2,024. But Bove ran neck and neck with Hoff in the Democratic hotbed of Chittenden County, where more than 10,000 people voted and where Hoff—once the county's favorite son—managed to win by just 1,000 votes, which was a clear warning of the troubles ahead.

Hoff started off the 1970 campaign the same way he had started the 1962 campaign for governor, with himself and Joan getting into their car and driving to towns all over the state to simply get out, walk the streets,

and chat with people. But 1970 would be a much more expensive campaign—more than twenty times the cost of the 1962 race—and in many
ways a nastier one. Hoff also would be campaigning in 1970 without two
of the men who had been his closest advisers and most-trusted aides in
the past. Ben Collins had left the campaign just as it was about to move
into high gear, taking a job at Goddard College, where his friend Ger-
ry Witherspoon had become the president. Collins, who was described
by Richard Snelling as "the tip of Phil Hoff's lance," had helped shape
many of the major social reforms of the Hoff era, including the drafting
of the 1967 law that abolished the local overseers of the poor. The cover
note summarizing the collection of the Benjamin M. Collins Papers at
the University of Vermont says that some of the confidential memoran-
da in them reveal that an "ideological gap" had been developing between
Collins and Hoff, with Collins growing impatient with what he considered Hoff's shift from liberal to moderate ideals. There was no hint of
this in the letter of resignation that he wrote to Hoff on August 6, 1970,
and little evidence of Hoff's having become any less of a liberal. One
Hoff worker said he believed that a chief reason Collins left when he
did—aside from the fact that the Goddard job seemed likely to provide
the income and job security that Collins was anxious for—was that he
knew he had alienated too many of the old-guard Democrats who would
be important to a Hoff victory, some of whom blamed him more than
Hoff himself for Hoff's increasingly liberal stands. "Ben had become tox-
ic to that group, and he knew it," the worker said. And Bill Kearns had
gone off to become commissioner of mental health and corrections in
Maine, where he would stay for six years and receive an honorary degree from St. Francis College for the major reforms he would institute in
the state's mental hospitals and prisons. Instead, the top organizing job
went to Charles (Chuck) Fishman, a young Rhode Island native Collins
had personally recruited as his replacement. Fishman had been a volun-
teer for McCarthy in 1968 and at the time was teaching at the historically black Howard Law School in Washington. He shared Hoff's ide-
ology, his strong commitment to civil rights and opposition to the war,
but he had never run a campaign before and knew little about Vermont
or the situation he was getting into. "He [Hoff] had totally trusted Ben,
but wasn't fully comfortable with me," Fishman said many years later.
"He didn't really want anyone running his campaign. He wanted to run
it himself. And back then I probably didn't have the skills to do it. . . . I
probably should have been the No. 2, not the No. 1. It would have been a
big plus if Ben had been involved."

Included in the Collins papers at UVM is a one-page flyer that Collins apparently created for use in the Senate campaign, stressing Hoff's accomplishments as governor. It noted that 30,000 new jobs had been created; that the minimum wage had been increased by 40 percent; that investment in new industrial plants had tripled; that general-fund revenues had increased by more than 100 percent; that the state had taken over all public assistance programs; that a strong anti-billboard law had been enacted and that many natural areas, including Camel's Hump, had been preserved; and that state aid to education had increased from $5 million to $15 million and that the Vermont Student Assistance program had been established to guarantee college loans. There was, however, no mention at all of Hoff's opposition to the war or his advocacy of civil rights.

The Democrat running for governor in 1970 was Leo O'Brien, and there was one issue that connected the two campaigns. In one of his first acts as governor, Deane Davis had proposed a 4 percent sales tax, saying that it was necessary to eliminate the deficits of the last Hoff years. Davis's son, Tom Davis, who had overseen welfare programs during the later Hoff years, said that the Hoff deficit itself was not a big deal, but that the more than eighty Great Society programs that had been put in place during the Hoff years were going to require greater state funding in the future. "The fundamental question facing Governor Davis when he took office was whether to slash programs and eliminate some entirely, or to enact a sales or some other tax to maintain the current level of government activity," he wrote in *Echoes of Vermont*, published in 2010. Hoff himself had opposed a sales tax while he was governor, saying that the state didn't need one. But he approved the Davis proposal and told him so, saying that raising taxes was preferable to cutting programs, particularly if a sales tax was crafted to minimize some of its most regressive features.

It became an issue in 1970 because when the state ended up with a surplus, O'Brien argued that the tax hadn't been needed at all, and it showed that Davis was more concerned about budget balancing than people. Davis countered that it had been needed to pay for the mismanagement of the last Hoff years. So the campaign began with O'Brien charging Davis with unnecessarily raising taxes and with Davis charging Hoff with executive mismanagement and with having created deficits that made the tax necessary. The Davis proposal had been modified to become a 3 percent tax and amended to exclude food and medicines. It also had been coupled with a rebate program to mitigate its impact on low-income Vermonters. More than forty thousand Vermonters had applied for and received the rebates, which Davis said was evidence it wasn't the sort of "soak the poor" tax that some Democrats charged. But the issue nonetheless seemed to be hurting Davis and helping O'Brien, until a young advertising man from Wellesley, Massachusetts—Sam Miller—came up with an idea for a masterly political ad. Miller did contract work with the Becker Research Company, a polling firm being used by Vermont Republicans at the time. He put Davis in a small and battered-looking rowboat in Lake Champlain that had VERMONT painted in large letters on its stern. It was half full of water, and Davis—wearing old work clothes and boots and standing shin-deep in the water—was shown furiously bailing to keep VERMONT afloat. The voice-over made the point that Davis hadn't wanted to impose a sales tax but had to do it to provide funds for education, welfare, and police, and to keep the state from sinking financially. Davis later wrote that his wife thought the ad lacked dignity, and he himself thought it was "just plain corny." But it proved to be an instant success, and the day after it first ran, while Davis was campaigning in St. Albans, a farmer waved from across the street and shouted, "Atta boy, Governor. Keep bailing!"

In the end, Hoff found himself taking the blame for one of Davis's least popular actions, the sales tax, and getting little of the credit for one of his most important and long-lasting ones, the revolutionary land-use planning legislation known as Act 250. Hoff had taken the lead in opposing unplanned development in Vermont. But it was the Republican businessman Davis and Republican state senator Arthur Gibb of Addison County who steered Act 250 through the minefield of opposition from business groups and developers and from ordinary citizens who felt deeply that people should be able to do whatever they wanted with their land. The opponents included one of the state's most powerful Republican leaders, Roland Q. Seward of Rutland, a supporter of Davis on almost everything else, who complained, "What are we preserving the environment for? The animals?"*

---

*Seward was a large-scale milk and cheese producer, known for his colorful bow ties, his staunchly conservative politics (the publisher of the *Rutland Herald*, Robert Mitchell, once described them as "antediluvian"), and his fierce dislike of the press, which he felt by and large had been an enemy during the nearly sixteen years (1961 to 1977) that he served as the Vermont GOP's state chairman, national committeeman, and chief fund-raiser. Those of course were years during which—to his anger and distress—Democrats had been elected governor, lieutenant governor, treasurer, attorney general, secretary of state, auditor of accounts, and U.S. senator.

The prosperity of the sixties, along with the opening of the two interstate highways and the explosion of the ski industry, had brought with it unprecedented development. When the International Paper Company proposed construction of 1,400 new homes in Stratton, near the new Stratton Mountain ski resort, Davis intervened to persuade the company to halt development until and unless it received state approval. Davis later wrote that with the agreement of company officials to put the project on hold, "I drew a long breath of relief." But it also made him realize that major legislation was needed to control such projects, and that speed was essential if Vermont was going to be able to "prevent large-scale, improper, poorly planned development." He also knew that any proposal to limit development would run squarely up against one of the most strongly held traditional "rights" of Vermonters, which was "the right to use one's own land as one saw fit." And he realized that it would take broad public support to get such legislation enacted. So he borrowed what he admitted was a technique Hoff had used in the past and set up a statewide citizens meeting at the State House, which he called the "Vermont Conference on Natural Resources." The conference, as Davis had intended, urged him to set up a Commission of Environmental Control and to draft legislation for a statewide land-use plan. The legislation, which was skillfully stage-managed by Gibb, set up nine District Environmental Commissions to review large-scale development projects in their regions, using ten criteria intended to safeguard the environment, aesthetics, community life, and wildlife. While the act itself passed, a companion measure calling for statewide planning failed. Hoff took considerable pride in Act 250, feeling that he had helped pave the way for it, even though he received little credit for its enactment. During the 1970 race he called for even greater environmental regulation, but it never developed into a major focus of the campaign.

Two issues that did develop during the campaign concerned the war in Vietnam and President Nixon's nomination of Florida judge G. Harrold Carswell to the U.S. Supreme Court.

In May 1970 the Ohio National Guard had fired on a large crowd at Kent State University protesting Nixon's expansion of the war to Cambodia and killed four students. Cambodia was a neutral country, but the "Ho Chi Minh Trail" used to funnel supplies to North Vietnamese and Vietcong troops in South Vietnam ran through part of it, and American field commanders wanted the trail bombed to cut the supply lines. Governor Davis was away from Vermont, and Lieutenant Governor Thomas

Hayes ordered the State House flag to be flown at half-mast to mourn the dead students. Davis hurried back to Montpelier and ordered the flag restored to full mast. The *New York Times* described the incident as a State House struggle reflecting the "increasing conservatism" of the Vermont Republican Party. Roland Seward used the opportunity to issue a press release saying that a recent national poll showed that the public supported the expansion of the war into Cambodia. Vermont's congressional delegation had no involvement in the flag controversy, but the presumption was that since both Aiken and Stafford had voiced opposition to the expansion, Seward's press release was intended as a censure of Aiken and Stafford while promoting the upcoming candidacies of Davis and Prouty, both of whom supported the war.

The Carswell nomination involved Prouty more directly. Nixon had nominated Carswell for the Supreme Court after his first nominee, Clement Haynesworth, had been rejected by the Senate. Carswell's nomination also produced a groundswell of opposition, not only from bar association leaders who noted his high reversal rate (58 percent of his decisions had been overturned by higher courts), but also from civil rights advocates who criticized his support for segregation when he had run for a state senate seat in Georgia in 1948, and from feminists who testified that he had demonstrated in words and actions that he was, if not a "male chauvinist pig"—a tag commonly used at the time to describe opponents of equal rights for women—no backer of feminist goals. Prouty had voted against Haynesworth and was vacillating about whether to support Carswell, fearing that to do so would reinforce Hoff's efforts to brand him as a "rubber stamp" for the president, but also concerned that voting against a second presidential nominee would anger his conservative Republican base.

Carswell's opponents published a letter in newspapers throughout the nation, signed by more than 350 jurists, law school deans, professors, and attorneys, alleging that Carswell lacked the legal or mental qualifications to serve on the high court. And they urged Hoff to make it an issue in his campaign, as a way of putting pressure on Prouty to vote no. Hoff did, and in the end Prouty first voted for a move to send the nomination back to the Senate Judiciary Committee in hopes that it would just die there, and then—when that effort failed—voted against him. Aiken, who earlier had voted to confirm Haynesworth, voted for Carswell. Aiken's main goal at the time was to secure a federal judgeship for James Oakes, which Deane Davis had opposed in hopes of instead having John Dinse, himself a respected attorney who had chaired the Davis primary campaign against Oakes in 1968, given the job. But federal judicial nominations were usually considered Senate prerogatives, and Aiken was insistent that he wanted Oakes nominated. In the end, the White House agreed, even though Oakes was more liberal than Nixon or Attorney General John Mitchell would have preferred. On the same day that Carswell was defeated, both Aiken and Prouty voted for Oakes, who was approved for a seat on the Second Circuit and who would go on to a long and distinguished career as a federal judge.

Prouty stayed in Washington until late in the race, not returning to Vermont for any sustained campaigning until early October. Hoff had been campaigning for more than a year, and his campaign took two tacks. He countered Deane Davis's condemnation of his administration by extolling his own record as governor. His campaign literature stressed that he had been "in the forefront of the fight to preserve Vermont's environment" long before other Vermont politicians had embraced it, and long before it had become a national concern. He also denied that it was his financial mismanagement that had created the deficit that had led to the sales tax. The deficit, he said, had come about because the Republican-controlled legislature had exceeded his budget requests and then refused the tax increases needed to fund them.

The heart of the campaign, however, was a mutual vilification contest between the candidates, with Hoff charging that Prouty had been missing in action for the past twenty years, citing his high absenteeism in the Senate and his rare appearances in Vermont. At one point, Hoff charged that during the three prior years Prouty had missed 83 percent of the meetings of the three most important committees he was a member of. At another, while trying to deflect criticisms from a Mrs. Carl Davis during a campaign stop in Manchester, Hoff told her that she obviously was a Prouty supporter.

"No," she protested. "Why if he came up and kissed me, I wouldn't even know who he was."

"Neither would a lot of other people," Hoff replied.

At the same time, Prouty and his supporters were engaging in what the *New York Times* called a "whisper campaign" about the source of some of Hoff's campaign money and about his "personal conduct." The Prouty camp also set out to portray Hoff as a "left wing radical liberal," and the deputy chairman of the Republican National Committee, speaking at a fund-raising dinner, denounced Hoff as a "radiclib," a shorthand term for "radical liberal" that was said to have been coined by Vice President Agnew. Hoff charged often during the campaign that Prouty was just a "rubber stamp" for Nixon, not just in connection with the war but with almost everything else, while doing little or nothing for Vermont. But Chuck Fishman, the Hoff campaign chairman, said, "Prouty wasn't a real factor in my mind. The whole thing was a referendum on Hoff."

Both sides spent what at the time was a huge amount of money for a Vermont campaign, probably well in excess of $250,000, with about half of it going for television ads. In September, Roland Seward reported to his county leaders that Hoff had received $250,000 from California alone (which Hoff later said was nonsense), and that much of his money had come from out-of-state backers who had been known to say that Vermont was the cheapest state in the union in which to buy a Senate seat. In fact, a $5,000 contribution to a Vermont campaign could have much more impact than a $5,000 contribution to a campaign in New York or California, and that probably led to some of the contributions to Hoff by out-of-state groups, labor unions in particular. Seward also insisted some of this was coming from radicals, although his definition of "radical" tended to be very broad—U.S. Senator James Jeffords once noted that Seward was so conservative he had "nary a moderate bone in his body." Prouty himself told the *New York Times* that some of the contributions to Hoff were coming from people who most Vermonters would "consider radical," although he didn't say just who they were. Hoff countered that Prouty was taking a good deal of out-of-state money from oil companies, railroads, coal interests, drug companies, and other business groups, much of it funneled through the Republican Senatorial Campaign Committee. Fishman later agreed that Hoff got money from unions and leftist groups, but insisted that it had been nothing more than the sort of backing that any progressive Democratic could expect. "There was nothing nefarious about it. It was the cleanest kind of money you could hope for," he said. "Most of it came from people who just wanted to elect a social progressive who would help end the war."

The source of Prouty's money was never made public during the campaign because it was funneled through various campaign committees that the campaign laws at the time didn't require to make public reports. In short, Prouty took advantage of a well-known and often-used loophole to hide the sources. Hoff, however, made an extensive disclosure, and it suggested that Fishman was right: most of the money came from somewhat left-of-center but hardly radical groups, like the Council for a Livable World ($2,500), the United Steelworkers Political Action Fund ($4,000), the United Auto Workers ($2,000), the International Garment Workers Campaign Committee ($2,000), and the National Committee for an Effective Congress, which had been founded by Eleanor Roosevelt ($10,000). The NCEC was a particularly important contributor because it also funneled at least another $10,000 to Hoff through paper organizations called "Professionals for Hoff" and "Conservationists for Hoff."

The reporter who wrote the October 3 story for the *New York Times* about the "whisper campaign" was Bill Kovach, who at the time was the paper's Boston bureau chief. He later recalled that several Prouty supporters and at least one Prouty campaign official had told him that Hoff had a "drinking problem" and urged him to write about it. While he noted in his story that there were whispers about Hoff's "personal conduct," he didn't specify what the alleged conduct was. That was standard for the time, when newspapers seldom wrote about the personal behavior of politicians unless there was something that caused it to become too public to ignore, such as allegations filed in a divorce case, or an intoxicated senator being stopped in a traffic incident and having a stripper jump out of his car and into Washington's Tidal Basin. But the whisper campaign came into the open later that same day, at a $50-a-plate GOP fund-raising dinner in Barre that attracted nearly a thousand Republicans.

The featured speaker at the dinner was Al Capp, the creator of the cartoon strip *Li'l Abner*, which was still quite popular at the time. Capp in fact had played a leading role in the transformation of comic strips from mainly entertainment for children into political and social commentary for adults, paving the way for such later political strips as *Pogo* and *Doonesbury*. The toastmaster was the Vermont House majority leader, Walter (Peanut) Kennedy of Chelsea, a conservative politician well liked by many of his colleagues (he would be elected House Speaker in 1971) but also known to play hardball when it came to enforcing Republican party discipline. Kennedy was a small-town car dealer who tended to make decisions based more on his judgment of people's character than their bank accounts. He gave car loans to many people who might not have gotten them elsewhere, and they became grateful customers and political backers as well. He had a rural wit that often involved rather crude language and barnyard humor. "Nothing stinks as bad as a stirred turd" was a favorite saying. Another was "as nervous as a whore in church." His humor also could be self-effacing, and he was known to have said more than once that "Peanut," a childhood nickname he used all his adult life, referred to the size of his brain. He opened the fundraiser dinner by warning the crowd that Hoff was a very popular man. He then added, "You have seen him plastered—all over the landscape." The long pause after "plastered" brought laughter and applause (and a few gasps) from the audience, which understood that Kennedy wasn't talking about Hoff's face on the billboards. He then went on to raise the race issue, which had been a very real but largely unstated issue in the campaign, saying, "We don't want someone who will import trouble into Vermont." The *Rutland Herald* account of the dinner said that this line also won applause from the audience, but that "quite a few Republicans sat on their hands and looked a little bit uncomfortable."

There was more. An empty chair at the head table had a sign on it saying "Reserved for Leo." It later was filled by a chimpanzee munching on a banana, whose owner, Carl Kelton of White River Junction, later said was intended as "good, clean fun" and that he doubted Leo O'Brien would take offense at it. O'Brien did take offense and a few days later demanded an apology from Davis, who was appearing on the same platform with him at a campaign event at Mount St. Joseph Academy in Rutland. Davis apologized, and said that he thought some of the rhetoric and activities at the Barre dinner had been "indefensible," including some of the comments by Capp. The cartoonist, who had been a liberal in the '40s and '50s and who had become increasingly conservative in the '60s, had followed Kennedy's remarks about Hoff importing trouble by saying that the Vermont–New York Youth Project had been Mayor John Lindsay's way of sending "all the rapists and criminals from New York up here to Vermont." By the end of the evening, both the race issue and Hoff's drinking had been put on the table, and both would remain there for the rest of the campaign.

In public, Hoff professed to be more angry about Capp's remarks about the youth project than about Kennedy's remark about his drinking, saying that Capp's statements had marked "a new low in Vermont politics." But he also said that even before Kennedy's remarks at Barre, rumors about his drinking had been part of a "smear campaign" launched by Prouty's campaign manager, Frank Dione of Montpelier. Dione denied it, but Hoff said, "There is no question about the fact that Frank Dione in particular has been spreading this far and wide. . . . There are the most lurid tales. They had me drunk in Colchester, when I wasn't within 50 miles of Colchester. They've said I was drunk in a store in Shelburne, and I wasn't within 100 miles of Shelburne." But he felt the need to address the drinking issue in a formal way, not just to deny that it was a current problem, and four days after the Barre dinner he held a news conference at which he said that he had in fact had a drinking problem in the past but no longer did, and now was limiting himself to an occasional beer at the end of the day.

Robert Mitchell, in an editorial in the *Rutland Herald*, called Hoff's admission "an act of courage" but questioned whether he should have done it at all, saying that it "may not have been well advised." Mitchell's view was that there had been a strong public reaction building against the innuendo and heavy-handed attacks by Kennedy and Capp and that Hoff might have benefited from it if he had kept silent. Some Hoff staffers, whose advice hadn't been sought, felt even more strongly that it was a mistake. Art Ristau said long afterward that Hoff's admission of drinking problems had been "unnecessary and, ultimately, catastrophic." Ristau believed that it would have remained a nonissue if Hoff had ignored it. Fishman said that "it destroyed the campaign." Subsequent polls showed Hoff's support sinking quickly and dramatically, suggesting that many people doubted that someone could admit to a drinking problem and then claim to have licked it while still drinking beer. And once that happened, Fishman said, "raising any money was just impossible."

Also, Hoff wasn't being entirely candid. He was still doing serious drinking at the time, although there was little evidence of it in his public appearances, where he usually seemed to be vigorous, articulate, and very much in control. He in fact would continue his heavy drinking for several more years and in 1972 would be arrested in Burlington and prosecuted by Patrick Leahy, then the state's attorney, on a charge of driving while intoxicated. He pleaded no contest and was fined $100. And then, on the morning of July 4, 1973, he woke up with another hangover and decided to stop. He quit drinking cold turkey that day, all on his own and without medical treatment or any participation in Alcoholics Anonymous or any other structured program. Thirty-seven years later, in July 2010, he said that he had not had a drink since then.

"It was a very serious mistake," Hoff said of his decision to admit to his drinking problem. Politically, a wiser course would have been to ignore it, he said, or to challenge Republicans to show a day of work missed, a speech not given, legislation jumbled, or any public business compromised. And he said that the decision to admit to it had been his alone. "If I had been wise enough to discuss it with Ben Collins or Bill Kearns or people involved with the campaign, they probably would have talked me out of it and I wouldn't have done it," he said. He also said that he never harbored any resentment of Kennedy for his crack, although it had annoyed him that he had been singled out for his drinking while Prouty—who himself was known by Republican insiders to be a serious drinker—was given a pass, particularly since Hoff believed that Prouty's drinking had affected his work, while his own drinking hadn't. But at bottom, he said, it was his own fault. "He [Kennedy] knew that I had a drinking problem, and he was right. I did. He did what he did to try to help the Republican Party, and I understood that. I never had any resentment about that."

Kennedy's remarks nonetheless were unusually nasty and mean-spirited for a Vermont campaign, as was the portrayal of Leo O'Brien as a monkey. And something even nastier reportedly took place during Kennedy's campaign for governor against incumbent governor Thomas Salmon in 1974, although it never became public at the time. According to Alex Ray, a young political operative imported from Maine to manage the Kennedy campaign, there was a plan to try to entrap Salmon with a prostitute at the Holiday Inn at White River Junction, where he sometimes stopped for drinks on Friday nights en route from Montpelier back home to Bellows Falls. Ray doesn't say specifically just what, if anything, Kennedy himself knew about it. But according to the account in his 2008 memoir, *Hired Gun: A Political Odyssey*, Ray and an official from the Republican National Committee worked out a plan to hire a prostitute to try to entrap Salmon in the Holiday Inn bar and have him drive her to an apartment just across the river in New Hampshire. "Once they crossed the state line," he wrote, "New Hampshire State Police, under the orders of Governor Mel Thompson [the conservative New Hampshire governor] would stop them on a speeding charge. The prostitute would then cause enough trouble so the police would make out a full report. Of course, we would make sure that the report made it into the newspapers."

That plan, however, didn't work. "For two Friday nights, the prostitute sat in the Holiday Inn cocktail lounge waiting," Ray wrote, "but Governor Salmon never showed and we gave up on the project."

There was, in fact, another whisper campaign going on in 1970, but it was much more limited and low-key, and both Hoff and Fishman later said they knew nothing about it. That concerned rumors about Prouty's health, and speculation that he was suffering from cancer. The rumors reached the point where it was said that Walter Paine, the publisher of the *Valley News*, had written an editorial either saying or suggesting strongly that Prouty had cancer, only to have it yanked at the last minute—chiseled off the lead plates already on the presses, in fact, so that it could be removed without having the paper miss deadline. That supposedly happened after Henry Black, a prominent attorney and a friend of Prouty's, had gone to Paine and strongly urged him not to print it. Paine says flatly that it never happened—that he never wrote any such editorial and never ordered it removed at the last minute. But less than a year later Prouty, in fact, would be dead of stomach cancer.

Democratic polls had never shown Hoff in the lead in 1970, although they did suggest that—before the drinking issue became public—he was closing the gap. They also concluded that "over the past four years Vermonters have been consistently less liberal and more conservative than have the voters of the nation as a whole." The poll takers recommended that "in light of this we reiterate that it is essential that in the closing days of the campaign Mr. Hoff present himself as a moderate." But Hoff long ago had established himself as a quintessential liberal, and there was no way he could have changed that image on short notice, even if he had wanted to, which he didn't.

Then, much to Hoff's surprise and disappointment, Aiken—who had been obvious in his lack of public support for Prouty—suddenly endorsed Prouty late in the campaign, in a statement that was published in newspaper ads. Aiken had said earlier that he didn't intend to endorse anyone because he didn't think Vermonters liked to be told whom to vote for, adding that he had endorsed Barry Goldwater in 1964 and probably hadn't changed six votes. But Aiken had found himself in a difficult spot, not only because his failure to endorse Prouty had been widely noted in the press and was being grumbled about by national Republican leaders, but also because some of the Prouty workers had begun complaining that Aiken was employing a Hoff supporter on his staff. Specifically, they were saying that Stephen Terry, Aiken's legislative aide (and one of the authors of this book), had been feeding information to Hoff's campaign that Prouty was a drunk and not showing up for work. Terry in fact felt that was true and in the past had talked about it with reporter friends he had worked with during his newspaper days. But he hadn't been involved in any way with the Hoff campaign and hadn't been passing along information about Prouty's absentee record. Aiken never asked Terry if he had been bad-mouthing Prouty, but the complaints by Prouty people may have caused Aiken to feel the need to help his fellow Republican. The GOP National Committee had planned a major newspaper advertising campaign for the last days of the race that would accuse many Democrats, including Hoff, of being "radical liberals." Space for such ads had been reserved in the *Rutland Herald* and the *Burlington Free Press* and some other Vermont newspapers. Instead of running that planned ad attacking Hoff, Prouty—at the suggestion of Aiken—used the space to run the statement from Aiken endorsing his candidacy.

It wasn't exactly a thumping endorsement. It began by saying that

"Ordinarily I take little part in political campaigns, even my own." It then went on to say that Prouty was being charged with being negligent in his duties by failing to attend committee meetings, and that while Aiken didn't try to keep track of Prouty's whereabouts at all times, "I do know that Senator Prouty's attendance record at meetings that count is excellent." The five-paragraph statement ended, "Winston Prouty has been a good Senator and should be re-elected."

The Aiken endorsement hurt the Hoff effort. The admission of his drinking problems probably hurt it much more. The charges that he was getting much of his money from out-of-state radical groups also may have hurt to some degree. But the campaign in fact may have been lost before any of those factors came into play. The *Rutland Herald*, which always had endorsed Prouty in the past, this time endorsed Hoff, saying that "if Hoff isn't elected this year, the chances are he will be lost to the public life of the state and he is too good a man to lose." But lose he did, and the results were even more devastating than Vermont Democrats had anticipated. Hoff lost by almost 30,000 votes (91,198 to 62,416), losing much of his conservative Democratic base and not pulling in the liberal Republican votes that he had in the past. Although the entire state Democratic ticket went down to defeat, Hoff trailed many other losing Democrats, with only 40.2 percent of the vote. Hoff later said that it was clear from Babe Bove's success in the primary that he was in trouble, mainly because he had moved too far away from his constituents in his support of civil rights, his opposition to the war, and his identification with such strong liberals as Robert Kennedy, Eugene McCarthy, and George McGovern. The primary vote had shown that, long before his drinking became an issue, he already had lost a third or more of his base, and he never got it back. By the last weeks of the campaign, even Samuel Fishman of Vergennes, a prominent and respected middle-of-the-road Democrat who had been a state senator, Addison County Democratic chairman, and Democratic candidate for state treasurer, had joined the Prouty campaign as it toured central Vermont. "Once you get beyond your constituents, you're going to get out of there," Hoff said. "And that's what happened to me."

EPILOGUE

No individual deserves more credit (or in the view of political rivals more blame) for the transformation of Vermont than Philip Hoff. Many of the changes would have occurred eventually, but they wouldn't have been as rapid and thus not as dramatic. In the years before Hoff, Vermont had been seen as a small and sleepy rural state where change came about only slowly and grudgingly. In the years during and after Hoff's time as governor, Vermont became known for social ferment and rapid change, and for cutting-edge initiatives in the areas of social policy and the environment. Far more than most of his predecessors, Hoff was an activist governor, pushing new ideas, concepts, and programs and challenging the idea that Vermont governors should be caretakers in the way that Arthur, Emerson, Johnson, Stafford, and Keyser had been. As Bill Kearns put it, "He wasn't afraid of the past."

Hoff very much believed that government was and should be the primary force in bringing about social change, saying, "Every significant decision of our time is going to be made in the governmental arena." He was quick to support efforts to modernize government operations that he considered obsolete and inefficient. At times he was incautious, as was seen when he raced in to support the Kerner Commission report while President Johnson was trying to bury it and many other governors were trying to ignore it. And even his wife, Joan, reprimanded him for his hectic pace, once complaining that "we hardly get used to one idea when you throw another at us. It's more than we can take."

But his influence on the state was profound and long-lasting. At the time he left office in January 1969, the *Rutland Herald* predicted that "it will be impossible to turn back the clock to the political era of caretaker governors." And in the four decades after Hoff left office, Vermont in fact had governors who were considered liberal, centrist, and conservative, but none of whom tried to retreat into a caretaker role. Even the most conservative of them, Deane Davis, oversaw aggressive state involvement in restricting developments that threatened the water quality, soil erosion, aesthetics, or scenic beauty of an area, or that threatened to impose an undue burden on its schools. Hoff himself left office believing that his six years as an activist governor had finally "got Vermont off the dime." Bill Kearns put it more bluntly, saying that Hoff had "picked up the state by the back of the neck and gave it a damned good, much needed shaking."

One of the key factors that allowed Hoff to do what he did was unprecedented population growth. The state grew by 54,000 residents during the '60s, and those newcomers tended not to be locked into traditional Republican ways. As early as 1952, well before this influx of newcomers, Democrats were gaining voters, as the success of the Robert Larrow and Bernard Leddy campaigns had shown. Hoff's victory in 1962 had come about with the help of the Vermont Independent Party, which allowed Republicans to vote for Hoff without having to do it on the Democratic line, since there still were many Vermonters who simply couldn't bring themselves to vote Democratic. Keyser, as was noted earlier, in fact received more votes on the Republican line than Hoff did on the Democratic line, and it was the Vermont Independent Party votes that pushed Hoff over the top. But by 1964, Vermonters not only were electing a Democrat as governor but supporting a Democratic presidential candidate for the first time since the Republican Party had been founded in 1854. They also were electing an entire state Democratic ticket of lieutenant governor, treasurer, auditor, attorney general, and secretary of state. Hoff had been Vermont's first Democratic governor in 109 years, but in the 40 years that followed him, three other Democratic governors would serve for a total of 22 years.

Hoff never had a Democratic majority in the legislature and never had a totally free hand in running state agencies. The Senate and House remained safely Republican all through the Hoff years. But the newcomers helped make the state much more culturally and politically diverse and helped elect people of both parties who were less resistant to change. They didn't transform Vermont into a Democratic stronghold (voters gave majorities to Republican presidential candidates from 1968 through 1988), but they did help turn it into a two-party state and into a place that suddenly became willing—eager, even—to try new ways of doing things.

It also helped that the Hoff years, in the main, were prosperous ones, with the interstate highways opening up Vermont to skiers, tourists, second-home owners, and many kinds of development. Vermont added 40,000 jobs during the Hoff years, and the average weekly wage and total personal income increased substantially. It helped that the excitement and enthusiasms of John Kennedy's "New Frontier" presidency had carried into Vermont as well as the rest of the country, generating more political involvement by a younger and larger cross-section of people. The various planning groups, tasks forces, and study commissions that Hoff set up in his first year as governor pulled more than five hundred people, many of them new to political activism, into the governmental process. And it helped that legislative reapportionment had removed many of the most resolute and reactionary opponents of change. All these changes didn't result in the sort of large, immediate Democratic gains in the legislature that Hoff had hoped for, but he said often that they resulted in a much more progressive legislature, and one he could work with in a bipartisan way. As Emory Hebard had noted ruefully back in November 1966, when much of the Hoff agenda was being pushed through the reapportioned legislature, "All those farm boys who used to vote 'no,' they aren't here any more."

But while all those were factors, the important reality was that Hoff himself—young, handsome, vigorous, and dynamic—had created a sense of excitement that helped Vermonters change their attitudes about government and about themselves. While many politicians are wary of change because it threatens their ability to control events, Hoff thrived on change and became a catalyst for it, not just a beneficiary of it. Looking back on the changes more than forty years later, Hoff said, "Of course it would have happened eventually, but it would have been somewhere further down the road. I *do* think I started it. We had an administration that was liberal and very activist. It was an exciting time. . . . A new liberal tradition took hold in Vermont, and I played a major role in starting it. I don't think there's any question about that."

Hoff's initial victories had been welcomed by some liberal Republicans. Federal judge Ernest Gibson Jr. thought the 1962 victory would bring "a breath of fresh air into the musty tombs" of state government. Gibson, along with his friend and mentor George Aiken, had been a leader of the liberal wing of the Republican Party in the '40s. After defeating incumbent governor Mortimer Proctor in the 1946 Republican primary, Gibson had presided over a short but unabashedly liberal administration. But Gibson, like Aiken himself, had quickly been succeeded by less-activist governors, and by the late '60s, as Hoff himself came to be seen as too liberal by some elements of his own party, there was concern that this pattern would repeat itself. Hoff had announced in 1966 that he wouldn't run for a fourth term, and 1968 in fact saw a Republican victory in which Deane Davis was elected governor and Richard Nixon won Vermont's presidential votes. As the head of the so-called Little Hoover Commission appointed to study the organization of state government in the late 1950s, Davis had urged some of the same kinds of streamlining and consolidation of agencies that Hoff later proposed. As governor, Davis managed to install a Cabinet system of government in which government agencies reported directly to him, which was something that Hoff himself—surrounded by and outnumbered by Republicans—had never been able to do. And Davis ran state government for four years with balanced budgets, while managing to eliminate the deficits of the last Hoff years. But while personally popular, his conservative politics no longer had the wide appeal they would have had in Vermont's past. When Republicans selected Davis's choice of the conservative Luther (Fred) Hackett over the more liberal James Jeffords in the 1972 primary, Democrat Thomas Salmon—with the help of former Jeffords supporters who either crossed party lines or stayed home and didn't vote—defeated Hackett by close to 20,000 votes, despite Nixon's defeating George McGovern in a landslide in Vermont that same day. Salmon wasn't as liberal as Hoff, and because he didn't have the benefit of the sort of economic boom years that Hoff did, he operated under greater fiscal restraints. But his election showed that Hoff had been a transitional figure, not an aberration, and that Vermont had moved away from its rigidly Republican past.

Contributing to the growing Democratic demography, along with the influx of new residents and the economic expansions helped by the completion of the interstate highways, was the decline of the rural farm population, which had been overwhelmingly Republican. Dairy farming had long been the most important component of the Vermont economy, but it had become increasingly capital intensive. During and after World War II, dairy farmers invested in labor-saving equipment, initially to compensate for labor shortages brought on by the war and subsequently to attain greater efficiency and achieve a more sanitary product. These efforts culminated in 1952 with mandates from the Massachusetts Heath Department (which could impose mandates in Vermont because much Vermont milk was sold through the Boston milk market) requiring the adoption of bulk tanks and the phasing out of the heavy forty-quart milk cans that had long been used to distribute milk. By 1960 about 72 percent of Vermont dairy farms had refrigerated bulk tanks where milk was stored and cooled before being transferred into large tankers to be transported to bottlers and other bulk customers.

The shift to bulk tanks cut down on labor costs and also on back injuries to the farmers who had been hefting the forty-quart cans. But it also necessitated a greater capital investment that made it more difficult—sometimes impossible—for small farms to compete. At the same time, dairy farmers had begun shifting from Jersey to Holstein cows. Holsteins were larger animals and produced a larger quantity of milk with a lower butterfat content. But they also required larger barns, and this also required more capital and accelerated the shift toward fewer and larger farms. In 1947 there had been 11,206 dairy farms in Vermont. By the time Hoff was elected to his second term, the number had dropped to 6,687. By the time Salmon was elected in 1972, there were only 3,982. In fact, milk production had increased by more than a third during that same period because of these changes, but in a very real way the disappearance of milk cans and small dairy farms had brought about a parallel decline in the traditional Republican constituency.

All the changes did not always work to Hoff's advantage, as the 1970 campaign for the U.S. Senate showed. His defeat can be attributed in part to his admission that he had had a drinking problem, which he later said was one of the worst political miscalculations he ever made. But it also was due to the fact that—at a time when the nation and the state were not just in a period of change but also of great turmoil, with angry and seemingly endless debates over the Vietnam War, civil rights, feminism, sexual liberation, and alternate lifestyles—Hoff's political and social philosophy had become more liberal than that of most Vermonters. While Vermont had moved away from its agricultural roots and Republican orthodoxy, it hadn't moved as far to the left as Hoff had. He had, as he later put it, gotten "too far beyond the electorate."

In 1984, John McClaughry, a former aide to President Reagan and a staunch Vermont conservative, described Hoff as having been "one of the savviest and most experienced politicians in modern Vermont history," adding that his administrations had brought "freewheeling exuberant change to replace the cautious, prudent, unimaginative rural dominated Vermont governments of the past." This may have been one of the few things that McClaughry ever said about Vermont politics that Hoff and his supporters agreed with. There were suggestions from time to time that he make another run for higher office, but Hoff's standard response was that he had no further political ambitions. He said repeatedly that "timing is everything in politics . . . and if your time goes by you have to recognize it and get into other things." At the same time, in the aftermath of his loss to Prouty in the 1970 race for the U.S. Senate, he found the lack of political office a letdown and that practicing law, while lucrative, was sometimes boring. So he plunged into "other things" with a vengeance, while never straying far from politics and with little concern about stirring controversy. In 1971 he admonished the University of Vermont for requiring a loyalty oath for its faculty, and then more forcefully criticized the state for lacking a serious energy plan. In response to what was billed as a "draft" by Esther Sorrell, a state senator and a fiery Democratic activist, Hoff ousted Salmon's hand-picked state party chairman, Leonard Wilson, to help prepare Vermont Democrats for the 1974 elections. Watergate had thrown the state's Republicans into disarray, and George Aiken, the most successful Republican vote-getter, was retiring. But some key Democrats felt that Wilson wouldn't be able to sufficiently inspire voters, while Hoff was someone who could get momentum going. With Hoff as chairman, and with Republicans everywhere reeling from the public anger about Nixon and Watergate, the 1974 elections were just about all that Vermont Democrats could have hoped for. Salmon beat Walter (Peanut) Kennedy, who back in 1970 had ridiculed Hoff as having been "plastered all over the landscape," by more than 50,000 votes, with Kennedy getting just 32 percent of the vote, a stunning and humiliating defeat for a Republican. Patrick Leahy became Vermont's first popularly elected Democratic U.S. senator by beating Congressman Richard Mallary, who later said that he had been hurt not just by Nixon and Watergate but also having the very conservative Kennedy (who was more conservative and less committed to civil liberties than Mallary was) running for governor. And the Democratic candidates for lieutenant governor, attorney general, and treasurer also were elected, along with gains in the state Senate and the election of a Democratic House Speaker, despite the Republicans' still holding a razor-thin majority there.

The triumphs were not achieved without discord between Hoff and Salmon. Both men possessed large egos, as governors generally do, and both felt strongly that their views on party direction should prevail. Initially, Hoff had moderated his tone, focusing mainly on just a "return to traditional values," cleaner campaign financing, and a slate of strong candidates. He seemed to have learned from his disastrous 1970 campaign that there could be electoral advantage in being less outspoken and also in telling your constituency what it wanted to hear. The conversion, however, neither lasted nor kept him and Salmon from sparring over party leadership. Salmon believed that as governor he was entitled to the last word and wanted to direct the state campaign. But Hoff felt that this was the state chairman's role, and given that Wilson had been Salmon's personal choice, Hoff's election as chairman was seen by many as a rebuke to the sitting governor.

Some of this friction may have been inevitable. Despite his public statements to the contrary, many thought that Hoff took the job in hopes of resurrecting his political career, which could have made him a potential rival for Salmon. Even after the stunning victories in 1974, Salmon was critical of the party's organizational efforts, saying that it had been "simply not well organized in many parts of the state." Some of the fault, he suggested, lay with Hoff, who was "too much concerned with philosophical ideals and too little concerned with fund-raising, party organizing, and winning elections." Hoff retorted that philosophy was important because a party shouldn't endorse candidates unless it agreed with and embraced their views. It had been philosophical ideals, not just an anti-Nixon sentiment, that had helped Leahy beat Mallary, he said, adding that Salmon's "emphasis on just winning shows a narrow view of how change takes place in society." Finally, after a flurry of charges and countercharges, Salmon called time out and made a bid for peace, saying, "How the hell can we be fighting among ourselves on the strength of what happened Nov. 5 . . . especially with that donnybrook that's going on the other side?" That calmed the rhetoric, but within a month Hoff would announce that he was leaving the job as state chairman because of a "lack of time."

But he nonetheless had the time for many other things. In 1975 he went to Washington for a time to coordinate the short-lived presidential campaign of former North Carolina governor Terry Sanford, whom he admired. He headed a Burlington citizens' group called Friends of Health Care, which pressured the Vermont Medical Center to cut the cost of its proposed hospital expansion from $64 million to less than $50 million in order to hold down medical costs for the public. He worked aggressively against expansion of nuclear power in Vermont. And he was harshly critical of suggestions that the Vermont State Colleges and the University of Vermont be centralized under the University of Vermont umbrella, calling the proposal "absurd."

The transformation of the state colleges was something Hoff was particularly proud of, and he had launched it because he believed that UVM itself—despite its state charter and its land grant status—had never been a real state university and never would be. UVM in fact had more out-of-state students than Vermont students when Hoff first became governor, and its tuition for in-state students was the highest of any state university in the country. The school operated very much like a private university, placing so much emphasis on recruiting out-of-state students, who were charged tuition as high as some of the best and costliest private schools in the Northeast, that many qualified Vermonters couldn't get accepted, and many who could get accepted couldn't afford to go there. So Hoff had made it a priority to transform the state colleges at Lyndon, Johnson, and Castleton, which had been focused mainly on the training of teachers, into larger and more broad-based liberal arts colleges, providing quality education at affordable cost. His chief architect in the transformation was former UVM professor and Vermont lieutenant governor Robert Babcock, who was named "provost" (a title more common in England than in this country, but one that the former Rhodes Scholar Babcock was fond of and insisted on) and put in charge of all three schools, as well as the Vermont Technical College. Babcock's goal was to transform Castleton (which had 626 students in 1965), Johnson (378 students), and Lyndon (305 students) into 900-student campuses that could develop into what he suggested could become "little Swarthmores," modeled after the small Quaker school in Pennsylvania known for its academic excellence and commitment to social activism. Hoff had felt it was important to develop the schools, not just for students but to create cultural centers and beehives of economic activity in the regions where they were located. When the legislature called for a study of merging everything in hopes of cutting costs overall (a suggestion that UVM was quick to embrace, since it would be the big dog in the pack and likely to set the agenda, while the others opposed it), Hoff lobbied to help prevent it from happening.

The last years of the 1970s were not strong ones for the Democratic Party, in part because of the emergence of third parties to the left of the Democratic base from which they had split. Although third-party primaries attracted few participants, Democratic primary participation declined sharply. On occasion, the Liberty Union and Citizens parties nominated candidates to oppose incumbent Republicans when the Democrats failed to do so. And throughout the period, Hoff complained about the Democratic Party's failure to embrace policies he approved of, and voiced pessimism about its direction. At the same time, although not entirely happy practicing law, he increasingly focused himself on improving bar standards. He took on assignments as chairman of the Supreme Court's Standing Advisory Committee on Admissions and as chairman of the Committee for Continuing Legal Education, which imposed and regulated the requirements for continuing legal education.

Once freed from the restraints of the party chairmanship, Hoff increasingly advocated political philosophy over party loyalty, openly criticizing what he felt was the state party's move toward the center. After first endorsing losing gubernatorial candidate Brian Burns in 1976, he then refused to support the Democratic candidate, Stella Hackell of Rutland, even though she was running against (and would be defeated by) his old political nemesis, Richard Snelling of Shelburne. He became an early and strong supporter of Burlington's self-styled "socialist" mayor and later Independent congressman and U.S. senator Bernie Sanders. In fact, he went so far as to endorse Sanders in his campaign for Congress as an Independent in 1988 instead of the Democratic candidate, Paul Poirier, the House Democratic leader. Poirier and Sanders split the Democrats and progressives, allowing former Republican lieutenant governor Peter P. Smith to be elected with just 41.2 percent of the vote. Hoff complained often that the Democrats were abandoning the have-nots of the country just as the Republicans had. "There is a frightening redistribution of wealth going on in this country," he commented at one point, saying that by becoming less progressive and more centrist, the Democrats had "turned their backs on the welfare of the people."

Although he approved of all three in general ways, he considered Salmon too conservative, the liberal Republican Jeffords too centrist (when the Democrats failed to nominate a candidate to oppose Jeffords in 1980, Hoff backed the Citizens Party candidate, Robin Lloyd), and he infuriated Governor Madeleine Kunin by saying that her agenda made her seem more like a Republican than a Democrat.

By January 1982 it had become apparent that Hoff's sabbatical from elective politics was coming to an end as he began making plans to run for the state Senate. For a former governor to seek a seat in the state legislature raised questions about why he was taking what many regarded as a step down. His response was that he didn't look at it as a step up or a step down. "It's just something I can do and make a contribution and I'm going to do it," he said. "The alternative is to sit on the outside." He also said that he thought he might be able to be a more effective legislator than he had been as a young House member because he had developed more patience over the years and also had "licked the drinking problem nine years ago." Running from the combined Chittenden and Grand Isle district, Hoff received the most votes both in the primary and in the general election of all the six senators (three Republicans and three Democrats) who were elected. It quickly became clear that Hoff had retained his liberal vision. During one of the regular lunches that

Governor Snelling had with small groups of state senators, he asked Hoff what his goal as a senator was. "My goal is to make your life as miserable as possible," Hoff told him. But it also became clear that he hadn't in fact become more patient, and after serving three two-year terms he announced that he wouldn't seek reelection because of "frustration with the legislative process."

Hoff's approach during this time no longer emphasized the bipartisanship he had advocated as a Young Turk and as governor. It wasn't necessary, and might not have been possible in any event. In 1984 the Democratic Party had elected Madeleine Kunin as governor and also had elected a majority in the Senate. In addition to Democrat Peter Welch of Hartland serving as the Senate's president pro tem, Democrat Ralph Wright of Bennington had been elected House Speaker, even though the Republicans maintained a slim majority there. "It was a much more partisan place than it had been in the '6os," Hoff said in 2010. "And it's probably even more partisan today." But the Democratic strength didn't always translate into the objectives Hoff sought. He was critical of Welch for failing to set a clear and strong legislative agenda, and cited the length of the 1985 session (five months) as evidence of the legislature's lack of organization and discipline. It was during this period when he also began, in moments of exasperation, to refer disparagingly to Kunin as a Republican, and said later that the combination of his unhappiness with Kunin's agenda and the inability of legislative Democrats to set a more liberal one of their own "drove me right up a tree."

For his part, Peter Welch felt that "at times I think he [Hoff] was clearly frustrated that being a legislator wasn't the same thing as being the governor. Phil was very much one to take a position and charge ahead." Hoff himself said that he was never entirely comfortable in the Senate and that—although a recovering alcoholic—he nonetheless lacked the energy he had had during his earlier years in Montpelier, when he was drinking heavily late into the night. And he was still fighting some of the same losing battles, including consolidation of school districts. Way back in 1892 the legislature had forced consolidation of the multiple tiny school districts—neighborhood schools, for the most part—within most towns into a single town district. That had reduced Vermont's 2,214 school districts by almost 90 percent. For years afterward, the law was referred to by advocates of local schools as "the Vicious Act of '92," and all through Hoff's years as governor the resistance to further consolidation was widespread and often fierce.

In January 1975, Governor Salmon had appointed Joan Hoff as chair of the Vermont Board of Education, and in June of that year she had registered the only school board vote in favor of greater school district consolidation. Sentiment hadn't altered much by 1987, when Governor Kunin withdrew her own plan for further consolidation. Hoff, both as chairman of the Senate Education Committee and as the former chairman of the state commission to explore consolidation, never abandoned his efforts to achieve a more regional school system. His proposals stirred much debate, and while he conceded that he was "sympathetic" with the people who wanted to retain local control, he felt that small and fragmented districts simply were too "Balkanized" to provide the quality of education that Vermont students deserved. "Education today is a matter of national concern," he liked to say, adding that "the educational needs of our children are the same whether they be born and raised in Springfield, Vermont; Springfield, Massachusetts; or Springfield, Illinois."

Despite his frustrations with the process, he nonetheless felt that the legislature he served in during the 1980s was a better one than he had served in and worked with in the 1960s. "The caliber of people is better," he said. And there were many who thought that it was Hoff's own impact on Vermont politics that had helped pull a higher caliber of people into the process.

The common wisdom that liberalism in one's youth is as natural as conservatism in old age did not hold true for Hoff. For his eightieth birthday celebration he chose to sponsor a dinner for the Vermont Teacher Diversity Program, for which he had established a foundation to train minority students to teach in Vermont schools. Richard W. Mallary was among the attendees who offered a testimonial to Hoff. Mallary began by noting his own Republican roots and confessed that "there have been lots of times when I would never have been invited to a celebration for Phil Hoff. And lots of times I would not have wanted to come." He concluded by saying that although he had come "as one who differed with him on his approach and speed," he had "always embraced his ultimate goals and have had enormous admiration for the passion with which he pursued" them.

Hoff had started out as fundamentally pro-business and had ended up a strong environmentalist, believing that protecting Vermont's beauty and natural resources was essential to the state's economic well-being. That won him many supporters, but it also generated opposition from developers and entrepreneurs. His crusade for black rights in a state that was almost whiter than Sweden angered many, in part because it highlighted a latent racism that many didn't want to acknowledge. And some opponents criticized his six years as having been "hyperactive," suggesting that hyperactivity was a sin or at least something to be wary of. The Richard Mallary of the 1960s had attributed much of his opposition to Hoff's proposals to the speed with which Hoff attempted to change things, rather than to the ultimate goals. But Vermont governors are elected to just two-year terms, and none since 1835 had ever served more than four years. So if a governor was to make a mark, it was necessary to do it quickly. It was the hyperactivity of Hoff and the people around him—their insistence on rapid and dramatic change—that converted Vermont into a state that came to be seen nationally as not just responsive but innovative and sometimes daring. And Bill Kearns believed at the time that Mallary's opposition to Hoff's attempts to reorganize government (Mallary had said in 1967 that "we need it, but this isn't the time for it") had less to do with speed or timing than simple party politics. "It isn't time for it yet because if it goes through the Democrats will get credit for the God-damned thing," Kearns said. "That's about the size of it." It went through quickly in the Deane Davis years, and with Mallary in the Kearns job as commissioner of administration.

In contrast to the immediately preceding administrations, Hoff did indeed appear hyperactive, roaring through the state like an express train in ways that sometimes left people breathless. He presided over reapportionment, and his years as governor saw judicial reform; a quadrupling of school aid; the banning of billboards on state highways; the virtual elimination of the death penalty; the elimination of the poll tax as a voting requirement; a welfare reform that included elimination of the town overseers of the poor; the transformation of the three small and independent teachers colleges into a unified, stronger, and much more vibrant state college system; and a civil rights commission. And as William Doyle noted in *The Vermont Political Tradition*, he "brought Vermont into the age of federal largess" by attracting eighty federally funded programs for development, manpower training, education, welfare, and other things. His greatest disappointments were the response of Vermonters to his efforts to mend the nation's racial divide and the refusal of the legislature to adopt his Canadian power plan. Many years later, Hoff still fumed about the success of the utility lobbyists in killing the bill in the House after it had sped through the Senate, and remained angry about—and somewhat bewildered by—the last-minute criticisms of the plan by George Aiken, who had long been an advocate of public power. "It would have given Vermont the cheapest power in New England by far" and lured many kinds of new businesses, Hoff said more than four decades later, admitting that he still "bridled" at the heavy lobbying by the utilities and the last-minute involvement by Aiken. And he noted that the promises utility executives had made at the time of much cheaper rates from nuclear energy may have been bogus from the start and had never materialized in all the years since.

At the start of his political career, with the Democratic Party a woefully weak legislative minority, Hoff had worked closely with like-minded Republicans in a bipartisan alliance (the Young Turks). Robert V. Daniels of Burlington, a UVM professor who as chairman of the Democratic Policy and Planning Committee was responsible for the Democratic platforms, said that Hoff at first wasn't enthusiastic about party platforms because he wanted to work in bipartisan ways. But as reapportionment created more legislative opportunities for Democrats, and as Vermont GOP leaders became more conservative, Hoff became increasingly insistent that Democrats reflect his social commitment and do so as a party. His view was that the Republican drift to the right had attracted liberal Republicans and independents to the Democratic Party, and that this appeal would be lost if the Democrats became a party of the center. As time went by, and as the '70s moved into the '80s, he acknowledged that the move toward the center had helped make Democratic majorities possible in those years. But he felt that it had come with great cost, because the party was paying less attention to the have-nots that it traditionally had represented. In protest, Hoff occasionally would abandon Democratic candidates for those who more closely reflected his personal views. It was in this spirit that he supported the candidacy of Bernie Sanders rather than Paul Poirier in the 1988 race for Congress, which gave Sanders a statewide credibility that he hadn't earlier had but also helped Republican Peter Smith of Middlesex be elected with a 41.2 percent plurality.

And while Hoff never lost his impatience with prolonged deliberation, and was critical of the 1987 legislative session for what he saw as missed opportunities and endless haggling, Deborah Sline, then the chief of the Vermont Press Bureau, insisted he had been the "unsung hero" of that session, saying that he had "injected much needed doses of sanity and sage advice during critical House-Senate negotiations" on important bills. She commended Hoff for "filling a void" left by Senate president pro tem Peter Welch, whose "poor personal relationship with Speaker [Ralph] Wright seemed to prevent him from filling that role."

After leaving the Senate in 1988, at age sixty-four, Hoff did not disassociate himself from politics. He continued to endorse, and otherwise support, candidates, not always with success. He never again ran for office, but he remained active in political debate, increasingly emphasizing the need for Democratic liberalism and party loyalty.

In looking back, there is no one scene or moment that can capture the Hoff years, but a photo album of his political career would include pictures of memorable moments large and small.

It would include the jubilant night in Winooski when Hoff stood in an open convertible, surrounded by a shouting, shoving, arm-waving crowd, wearing a tinfoil crown that said "King of Winooski" on it and shouting repeatedly to the crowd and to the television cameras and radio microphones all around him, "A hundred years of bondage broken!"

It would include the March afternoon in 1966 when Hoff, at the peak of his popularity, ended the legislative session in bizarre fashion by moving a chair to the front of the Capitol, taking Republican representative Kenalene Collins of Readsboro, whom he considered not only an opponent but a scold, bending her over his knees and, using a large wooden paddle, spanking her bottom on the State House steps while scores of her colleagues laughed and applauded, and in a few cases cringed.

It would include the late afternoon in March 1968 when he announced he was breaking with the Johnson administration and supporting Senator Robert Kennedy's campaign for president because of his own growing opposition to the Vietnam War. And it would include the hot June night just three months later when he stood before more than four hundred people in the U.S. House of Representatives and agonizingly eulogized the murdered senator.

It would include the late September day in 1966 when he was campaigning in the Pownal area. He was tired and feeling low. He spotted a two-room elementary school housing Grades 1 through 6, the very kind of school he had tried to eliminate in Vermont. The school day was over, and the boys and girls were playing a last game of kickball. Hoff's state trooper drove the big black Lincoln into the schoolyard. The students recognized the tall sandy-haired governor and flocked to him. Hoff stayed and chatted with them for twenty minutes. When he left, he was feeling upbeat again, energized by the session with the children who symbolized for him the future he had been talking about all during the campaign.

It would include the autumn day in 1970, during his U.S. Senate campaign, when he was leaving Spaulding High School in Barre after a speech. Two football players passed him, returning from practice, one of them saying to the other in a matter-of-fact way, "There goes Hoff, the nigger lover."

And it would include the late December afternoon in Rochester, after the ceremonies had ended for a tree that had been cut in the Vermont woods to be sent to Washington as a Christmas tree, when he lingered behind, helping a youngster look for a mitten he had lost.

Reid Lefevre, who considered Hoff clumsy in some of his dealings with the legislature, nonetheless said that his impact on Vermont was much like John Kennedy's impact on the nation. "This state had been stagnant and he got it moving," he said during Hoff's last year as governor. "He stimulated the interest of young people in government and made them realize how important good government was to their future."

Hoff set out to bring about reapportionment, reorganization of government, and regionalization of public services. Not everything was completed on his watch, but he set the course that ultimately resulted in all three. He was the first governor to leave behind a comprehensive state planning program and planning goals. And he left behind a culture of activism and innovation that caused Vermont to enact pioneering legislation after he left. In 1970 the state adopted Act 250, which would have been unthinkable in the years before Hoff became governor. And in 1999 Vermont became the first state to allow civil unions for gay couples.

In 2007, when state Democratic legislators took another step to test Vermonters' opinion on whether to extend full marriage status—not just civil union status—to gay couples, Hoff was among those tapped to join the study commission. Full marriage status eventually was extended.

By then the Hoffs had begun escaping Vermont's winters and legislative sessions by heading southwest for three months of relaxing in New Mexico, where he played golf with more enthusiasm than skill. For Joan Hoff it was just a game she enjoyed, but Phil Hoff came to see it as something very much like the politics he had loved. "Golf is not a sport. It's a disease that tends to dominate those who play it," he said, adding that golfers had much in common with politicians because both could find themselves afflicted with "night sweats, loss of all reason, obsession, cheating, hostility to opponents, irrationally [and] despair."

The 1931 Country Life Commission's *Rural Vermont: A Program for the Future* had strongly advised against developing more golf courses in Vermont. The authors never regarded the game as a metaphor for politics, but felt that it was insufficiently divorced from daily chores to "bring a person out of his work-a-day personality"; golf was "too much like going after the cows to be a compensating recreation in the routine of the farmer." But as the twentieth century ended, there were many fewer Vermont farmers going after the cows, and the twenty-first-century Vermont that Hoff had helped prepare the way for had one of the highest number of golf courses per capita of any state in the union.

It also had become one of the bluest of the so-called blue states, regarded by much of the rest of the nation as a bastion of liberalism and social activism. Much of that was due to fifty years of changing demographics and lifestyles, and not the influence of any one person. But much of it in fact flowed from the legacy of Philip Hoff, which showed that government could solve problems and be a positive force in society, and that bipartisan problem-solving could bring much worthwhile change. Fifty years after he first went to Montpelier as a freshman legislator, there still were no physical monuments to the eighty-six-year-old Hoff. Although there was a state office building in Newport named for his longtime conservative nemesis Emory Hebard; a child development center in Brattleboro named for Winston Prouty; buildings at Castleton State College named for Robert Stafford and James Jeffords; buildings at the University of Vermont named for Stafford, Jeffords, and George Aiken; a Gibson-Aiken Center in Brattleboro; a Lake Champlain Center on the Burlington waterfront named for Patrick and Marcelle Leahy; and an entire town named for the Proctors, who had owned most of it, there were no Philip H. Hoff schools, libraries, office buildings, highways, or bridges. But as the first decade of the twenty-first century came to an end, with more politicians seeming to be campaigning *against* government than for it, and with partisan gridlock stalling and crushing initiatives in state capitals and in Washington, the Hoff legacy and the lessons that flowed from it—that government in fact could be a force for positive change—continued to shape and give character to the state that he did so much to transform.

INDEX